APPROACHES TO LITERATURE THROUGH GENRE

APPROACHES TO LITERATURE THROUGH GENRE

THE ORYX READING MOTIVATION SERIES

BY LUCILLE W. VAN VLIET

ORYX PRESS
1992

The rare Arabian Oryx is believed to have inspired the myth of the unicorn. This desert antelope became virtually extinct in the early 1960s. At that time several groups of international conservationists arranged to have 9 animals sent to the Phoenix Zoo to be the nucleus of a captive breeding herd. Today the Oryx population is nearly 800, and over 400 have been returned to reserves in the Middle East.

Copyright © 1992 by Lucille W. Van Vliet
Published by The Oryx Press
4041 North Central at Indian School Road
Phoenix, Arizona 85012-3397

Published simultaneously in Canada

All rights reserved
No part of this publication may be reproduced or transmitted in any form or by any means, electronic or mechanical, including photocopying, recording, or by any information storage and retrieval system, without permission in writing from The Oryx Press.

Printed and Bound in the United States of America

∞ The paper used in this publication meets the minimum requirements of American National Standard for Information Science—Permanence of Paper for Printed Library Materials, ANSI Z39.48, 1984.

Library of Congress Cataloging-in-Publication Data

Van Vliet, Lucille W., 1926-
  Approaches to literature through genre / by Lucille W. Van Vliet.
    p. cm.—(The Oryx reading motivation series)
  Includes bibliographical references and index.
  ISBN 0-89774-773-9
  1. Children—Books and reading. 2. Children's literature—Study and teaching. 3. Children's literature—Bibliography. 4. Literary form. I. Van Vliet, Lucille W., 1926- Genre approaches to literature. II Title. III. Series.
Z1037.A1V33   1992
372.64—dc20   92-13073
                                                              CIP

To Victoria, Alexandra, and Taz
May you have a lifetime of reading pleasure!

Contents

Series Statement, xi

Foreword, xiii

Preface, xvii

Acknowledgments, xxiii

Introduction: Gateways and Gauntlets, 3

1 *Gateways to Teaching Literature,* 7
   Planning, 7
   Mapping the Way, 9
   Making the Curriculum Connection, 10
   Emphasizing the Literary Elements and
      Communication Skills, 11
   Scheduling, 12
   Gathering Resources, 13

2 *Humor,* 19
   Introduction, 19
   Element of Literature: Focus on Tone, 21
   Recommended Lists, 25
   Teaching Tips: The Humor Genre and Tone, 37
   Focus on Critical-Thinking and Communication Skills:
      Listening Skills, 38

Activities, 40
Nonprint Resources, 43

3   **Mystery, 45**
    Introduction, 45
    Element of Literature: Focus on Plot, 48
    Recommended Lists, 49
    Teaching Tips: The Mystery Genre and Plot, 60
    Focus on Critical-Thinking and Communication Skills:
        Reading Critically, 61
    Activities, 62
    Nonprint Resources, 65

4   **Fantasy, 67**
    Introduction, 67
    Element of Literature: Focus on Design/Illustration, 69
    Recommended Lists, 74
    Teaching Tips: The Fantasy Genre and Design/Illustration, 85
    Focus on Critical-Thinking and Communication Skills:
        Visual Communications, 87
    Activities, 88
    Nonprint Resources, 90

5   **Science Fiction, 93**
    Introduction, 93
    Element of Literature: Focus on Theme, 96
    Recommended Lists, 99
    Teaching Tips: The Science Fiction Genre and Theme, 109
    Focus on Critical-Thinking and Communication Skills:
        Reading for Detail and Analysis, 110
    Activities, 111
    Nonprint Resources, 114

6   **Realistic Fiction, 117**
    Introduction, 117
    Element of Literature: Focus on Characterization, 119
    Recommended Lists, 125
    Teaching Tips: The Realistic Fiction Genre and
        Characterization, 140

Focus on Critical-Thinking and Communication Skills:
   Oral Communications, 143
Activities, 144
Nonprint Resources, 150

7 Historical Fiction, 153

Introduction, 153
Element of Literature: Focus on Setting, 154
Recommended Lists, 160
Teaching Tips: The Historical Fiction Genre and Setting, 169
Focus on Critical-Thinking and Communication Skills:
   Writing Skills, 172
Activities, 172
Nonprint Resources, 180

8 Animal, 183

Introduction, 183
Element of Literature: Focus on Point of View, 186
Recommended Lists, 188
Teaching Tips: The Animal Genre and Point of View, 199
Focus on Critical-Thinking and Communication Skills:
   Research and Organizational Skills, 200
Activities, 201
Nonprint Resources, 207

9 Adventure, 209

Introduction, 209
Element of Literature: Focus on Style, 211
Recommended Lists, 217
Teaching Tips: The Adventure Genre and Style, 225
Focus on Critical-Thinking and Communication Skills:
   Vocabulary Development, 227
Activities, 228
Nonprint Resources, 234

Appendix, 237

Index, 243

Series Statement

What makes an individual want to turn the page and read more? That question has puzzled many in the field of education. The answer is not always forthcoming. And, the answer is not the same for every individual. However, that is the question that prompted this series of books about getting students to read. The Oryx Reading Motivation Series focuses on the materials and approaches that seem to be prominent for grouping literature. The prime purpose for the investigation is to identify promising methods, techniques, and strategies that might motivate students or get students in grades five through nine to "turn the page."

Each book in the series examines a particular approach to grouping literature: thematic, subject, genre, literary form, chronological, author, and comprehension skills. In each case, the literature is grouped for presentation in a different way to meet a specific purpose. For example, the comprehension-skills approach groups literature useful for teaching the same skill. That skill might be comparison: literature of all types that might be grouped together to exemplify the pattern of comparison. Literary form examines the structure of the literary work, such as the diary, novel, short story, and so forth, with an emphasis on the elements of those structures, including plot, characterization, etc. An author approach provides a study of the works of one author that might allow students to examine style, growth, and changes a writer has undergone. Works written over a given period of time or at the same time might be grouped for a chronological approach. Such an approach allows the reader to examine interrelationships between writers and their society. The interest of students in a particular subject makes the subject approach useful for grouping different literary formats and forms about the same subject. The genre approach capitalizes on particular student interests or skills, such as problem solving or history, and combines this with works of similar literary form and subject patterns. And, finally, the thematic approach groups materials around a common theme that may be investigated in depth by students.

Each book in the series is written for the classroom teacher and library media specialist. This partnership offers rich possibilities for combining the knowledge of teaching and literary content with the multiple resources of two professions that have long addressed literature and have searched for ways to make students want to turn the pages. Although the approaches, methods, strategies, and techniques may be used at any level, the materials have been selected for use by students in grades five through nine and are so noted in interest and reading levels. The titles may, in fact, be appropriate for older readers as well. Grades five through nine represent a period of development during which many students become lost and begin to lose faith in reading as a way of finding answers and gaining satisfaction.

Each book in the series is meant to provide one method for beginning an exploration with students. One would not expect every approach to work with every individual. Nor would one expect every teacher and library media specialist to enjoy or feel comfortable with every approach. Each approach is an option.

Finally, the sources and materials suggested in the series were selected given a number of criteria:

- General literary quality and accuracy;
- Availability;
- Readability and interest levels;
- Ethnic, racial, and sex-role representation;
- Availability of media support materials; and
- Recommendations in selected journals and guides.

It is the hope of the author that the suggested books and materials will serve as stimuli for grouping literature in attractive packages. Perhaps each package will tempt some reader to open the book and turn the page.

Paula Kay Montgomery

Foreword

"I want a book just like. . . ."

That's what catches the reader. Lucille Van Vliet examines a number of genres that have proven popular with young readers over time. These genres are popular not just with the instructional personnel, but with the readers themselves. It is fun to pretend to go back in time and feel what a boy or girl might have been subjected to within the context of his or her existence. Many individuals can't get enough of imagining what goes on when one enters another kingdom totally fabricated by the author. It is exciting to scare oneself with strange monsters or creatures and know that when the book closes, the monsters will be gone. "Who did it, anyway?" asks the young reader who reads the clues buried in a mysterious setting.

Why would a genre approach appeal to adolescents? Betty Rosenberg explains that "genre is patterned fiction" in *Genreflecting: A Guide to Reading Interests in Genre Fiction* (page xix). Such patterned fiction follows certain rules for the plot, characters, settings, tone, mood, and theme. These patterns manipulate the subject, theme, and structural elements of a novel's or novelette's literary form. Individual genres have developed from patterns set by a few successful authors who have written books that became read and cherished by a segment of the general population. The success and popularity of the novels encouraged publishers and other authors to copy the patterns.

Traditional literary forms such as folktales, myths, and others are reflected in many of the genres. However, the newer patterns may be distinguished from traditional literary formats because of the manipulation of certain literary forms with given subjects developed by known or more current authors. The most common adolescent fiction genres include adventure, animal fiction, fantasy, historical fiction, horror, humor, mystery, realistic fiction, romance, science fiction, sports, and westerns. These patterns of fiction are usually developed for pleasure and escape reading. Although some genre fiction for children teaches, the better-written works are less didactic with logical plots, fully developed characters, meaningful themes, appropriate settings, and suitable mood and tone. Better-written novels follow characteristic patterns rather than a formula. In other words, a genre is not a formula followed with precision; rather, it is a general pattern proven to be successful.

The genre approach differs from the thematic and subject approaches in that the emphasis is on the pattern or structure of the fiction work. For example, when collecting materials on the topic of "animal" for a subject approach, one would expect to see poetry, folk tales, animal novels, and other literary forms. In a genre approach to animals, one would find only the novel with given plot and character patterns. When books are collected for a genre as opposed to a subject approach, it is assumed that the reader is interested and finds comfort in the patterns or internal structure presented within that work. A similar comparison may be made between the thematic and the genre approach. In this case, the difference is in the focus between a generalized theme or idea as opposed to the manipulated patterns of elements and subjects.

This emphasis on the pattern means that one can motivate readers based on patterns which the readers find reassuring, comforting, or stimulating. The fact that young adults and adults enjoy reading certain genres is evidenced by those readers who sample one and request a book "where the owner of the horse wins . . ."; "the girl finally gets the guy to pay attention to her like . . ."; or "where the detective solves the problem just like . . . ." One might expect genres to correspond to basic needs for love and acceptance, self-esteem, curiosity, and the need to know more about the world around us.

Lucille Van Vliet suggests ways to introduce these genres and to make them seem like gold to the early adolescent. She offers the teacher and the library media specialist sample resources that she has come to love during her experience with these people. She offers valuable suggestions on methods and strategies for presenting these resources, using them, and evaluating their effect on the reader.

Each offering has been tested and used with students and teachers during Mrs. Van Vliet's career as a library media specialist, most recently at Hammond Middle School in Howard County Public Schools, Howard County, Maryland. While at this school, she was awarded the Mae I. Graham Award for School Library Media Program of the Year for the program that she managed. Her skill and devotion to the students were demonstrated by the many film festival winners, the success of her students in senior high school, and the continued desire of faculty to work with her in the library media center. Now retired, Mrs. Van Vliet has taught at Western Maryland College in the Instructional Media program. She has also served as a consultant to other schools and school systems.

Mrs. Van Vliet's first book, entitled *Media Skills for Middle Schools,* was published by Libraries Unlimited, Inc. It is still used by library media specialists for the practical ideas suggested on integrating the use of the library media center into the school curriculum.

This book will provide teachers and library media specialists with a practical approach to motivating students to read in the many genres prevalent in juvenile fiction.

Paula Kay Montgomery

Preface

Why is a library media specialist writing a literature teaching guide for use by reading specialists, language arts teachers, and classroom teachers? It is because of the desire to share the innovative ideas and teaching techniques that I learned by working with outstanding reading and language arts teachers at Hammond Middle School in Howard County, Maryland, over the past 20 years. It is also because I want to express my deep commitment to teaching library media skills and communication skills as an integral part of the curriculum. It is my hope that the teachers using *Approaches to Literature through Genre* will work very closely with the library media specialist to fully implement the suggestions.

DEFINITIONS

Students can be encouraged and enticed to turn the page through literary units using the genre approach to literature. Most students in the intermediate classes of elementary, middle, or junior high schools are already familiar with a variety of genres. Even the students who do not or cannot read have been made aware of the many types of literature from their reading texts, book talks, anthologies, displays, class discussions, school library media centers, and public libraries. Students who are readers may be dedicated science fiction fans, amateur mystery sleuths, enchanted fantasy believers, courageous adventure seekers, loyal animal friends, fun-loving humor addicts, eager historical fiction buffs, practical every-day realists, staunch sports supporters, or incurable romanticists. These types of literature are called genres.

The term *genre* comes from a French word meaning a kind or

type. *Webster's Seventh New Collegiate Dictionary* defines genre as "a distinctive type or category of literary composition." Genre denotes the major literary classification, division, category, variety, type, style, kind, or class of literature. It is a type of literature in which the components share a common set of characteristics. It provides a sense of order and systematic arrangement according to established criteria and framework of reference to use in evaluating books based on literary criteria. The genre approach is now a widespread method of literature study. The genres or types of books included in this book are adventure, animal stories, fantasy, historical fiction, humor, mystery, realistic fiction, and science fiction. Realistic fiction includes friendship, romance, and sports stories as subgenres.

The grouping of literature by genres provides form and structure for teaching the literary units in this book. Bernice Cullinan, in *Literature and the Child,* Second Edition, gives some distinguishing features that provide assistance in categorizing the genres:

Realistic fiction—Focus on events that could happen today
Historical fiction—Stories that are set in the past
Fantasy—Events that could not happen in the real world
Science fiction—Events that might happen in the future

Literature is a writing in prose or verse, especially "writings having excellence of form or expression and expressing ideas of permanent or universal interest," as defined in *Webster's Seventh New Collegiate Dictionary.* Literature is the art of telling a story using well-chosen language. Carefully selected words are presented in the unique style of an author who uses the literary elements with realistic or imaginative events. Literature can entertain, enrich, and expand the boundaries of students and guide them into a lifelong pursuit of reading pleasure.

AUDIENCE

This book is designed to be used primarily by classroom teachers such as reading teachers, reading specialists, language arts teachers, and generalists, with cooperative teaching and assistance by the library media specialist. Suggested teaching tips and activities reflect this cooperative effort. This book is intended for use with students who read at grade-levels five through eight and who have reading-interest levels at grades five through nine. This flexible approach allows for the wide range of reading and interest levels within a given grade or class. Thus the teaching units may be adapted for different grades based upon the abilities, developmental stages, and interests of students.

PURPOSE

The purpose of this book is to share books, ideas, and activities with teachers and library media specialists from my experiences of working with reading and language-arts teachers and student teachers over the last 25 years. It reflects my deep feelings for instilling in students the joy and pleasure of reading, and opening to them the treasurehouse of knowledge in books and related media. My purpose is also to provide practical and useful units for the study of literary genres that include stimulating, enjoyable, and meaningful activities.

ORGANIZATION

The focus and organization of this book affords many opportunities for reading specialists, classroom teachers, and library media specialists to work creatively with students to assist them in experiencing, observing, and relating to various genres of literature.

This book is organized into eight teaching units with each unit centered upon one genre, one literary element, and one critical-thinking and communication skill. The organization is summarized as follows:

GENRE	LITERARY ELEMENT FOCUS	CRITICAL-THINKING AND COMMUNICATION SKILLS
Humor	Tone	Listening Skills
Mystery	Plot	Reading Critically
Fantasy	Design/Illustration	Visual Communication Skills
Science Fiction	Theme	Reading for Detail
Realistic Fiction	Characterization	Oral Communication Skills
Historical Fiction	Setting	Writing Skills
Animal	Point of View	Organizational and Research Skills
Adventure	Style	Vocabulary Development

Guidelines are presented to facilitate the teaching of the these skills. By focusing on only *one* literary element and *one* communication skill in correlation with *one* genre, students will have a better opportunity for greater comprehension and for an in-depth application of the skills.

Each teaching unit is organized under the following headings:

1. Genre Introduction

    The introduction includes a definition and examples of the genre. It includes a detailed discussion of the genre assimilated from a variety of sources, including many authorities in the field of children's literature.

2. Focus on Elements of Literature

    The definition of the literary element is accompanied by evaluative criteria and examples. Details for an in-depth examination of the literary element are provided. Examples that exhibit effective methods for teaching the literary element are highlighted.

3. Recommended Titles for Genre Teaching Units

    An annotated list of titles appropriate for classroom reading, instruction, and discussion is provided. These books represent carefully chosen titles with a mixture of reading levels and interest levels. The reading levels are based on a combination of Fry's Readability Scale, professional sources, and personal experience from working with students and books. They are provided as a guideline only. If the books are available in paperback editions, the notation PB with the name of the publisher is provided. If the books are available in large print editions, the notation of Cornerstone or Windrush is given.

4. Recommended Titles for Individual or Group Study

    Additional suggestions for reading guidance are given in this annotated list. The purpose is to provide titles especially suited to individual or group reading rather than class study.

5. Picture Storybooks for Teaching Literary Elements

    Picture storybooks are annotated and discussed to provide an interesting teaching tool with students. The appeal of picture storybooks and their clear, direct narration make them suitable for the purpose of teaching the literary elements of plot, theme, style, characterization, tone, point of view, setting, and design/illustration. They serve as excellent samples of the genres and literary elements.

6. Teaching Tips

    Introductory activities are provided along with ideas for grouping, sharing, reading, and discussing the genre, the literary element, and the critical-thinking and communication skill. The importance of planning, preparing objectives, and evaluation are stressed. Strategies are suggested for teaching, preparing displays, planning field trips, and obtaining resources.

7. Focus on Critical-Thinking and Communication Skills

    A definition of the critical-thinking and communication skill is presented with examples and teaching methods. Suggestions for teaching this skill are incorporated or integrated with the reading discussions and related activities in each genre.

8. Activities Related to Teaching the Genre

    Oral and written activities, computer activities, drama, art, music, games, and media productions are suggested as methods for integrating skills with the study of each genre.

9. Activities Related to Teaching the Critical-Thinking and Communication Skills or the Literary Elements

    Specific activities that relate to the communication skills or literary elements are emphasized to provide students with reinforcement of the skills and with enjoyable activities. Sometimes the activities focus on communication skills and sometimes they focus on the literary elements. In some instances the two are combined.

10. Additional Activities

    Additional activities are suggested to be used for independent study, enrichment, or extended scheduling.

11. Nonprint Resources

    A list of suggested nonprint media is included to use with the teaching units. These include audiocassettes, computer programs, films, sound filmstrips, and videotapes. The list contains the names of the producers or

distributors. Videotapes are listed as follows:
    Animated Videos: Contain animated sequences
    Enhanced Videos: Transferred from filmstrips and enchanced to give the illusion of movement
    Iconographic Videos: Filmed from the original art with continuous motion
    Live Action Videos: Live action footage
    Transferred Videos: Transferred from filmstrips

12. References

An alphabetical list of professional sources and works cited accompanies each genre unit. These may be used for further study and as resources for the teacher and library media specialist.

In addition, there is an appendix that provides addresses of distributors of nonprint materials, and there is a subject, title, and author index.

Acknowledgments

Grateful acknowledgment and thanks to the following people and organizations:

For assistance, guidance, and professional services: Dr. Paula Montgomery, Ron Martin, Celeste Smalkin, Dr. Margaret Denman West, Dr. H. Thomas Walker, Joseph Duckworth, Peter Wilcox, Alfreda Martino, Phyllis Weller, Sylvia Hazzard, Hope Chase, and Steven Wilson.

For ideas and inspiration by reading and language arts teachers with whom I worked: Shirley Ashcraft, Cindy Bridner, Albertha Caldwell, Wayne Danley, Patricia Lavin, Debra Miller, Patricia Rees, Nancy Rhead, Dorothy Sensabaugh, Sue Deemer Witty, and Kathy Yerep.

For providing facilities and resources: Professional Library and Processing Center of the Howard County School System, Howard County Public Library: Children's Services Division, Lewes Public Library in Delaware, Hoover Library of Western Maryland College, Hammond Middle School Staff and Library Media Center, and Patuxent Valley Middle School Staff and Library Media Center.

For providing interest and moral support: Alpha Gamma Chapter, Alpha Beta State, Delta Kappa Gamma, and Rolling Hills Baptist Church staff and members.

For understanding, patience, and encouragement by members of my family and friends: my husband, Robert, and our children and their spouses, Alan and Elaine Van Vliet and Jo Ann Van Vliet and Hans Juergen Guth.

Family members: Doris Wright, Phyllis Nanney, Virginia Harrell, and Taz Painter.

Friends: Marge and John Gibbens, Becky and Bob Hudson, Elizabeth and Curtis Ewing, Kathy and Charles Prince, Evelyn Wilson, Annice Rhue, and Ella Mae Earp.

APPROACHES TO LITERATURE THROUGH GENRE

Introduction

Gateways and Gauntlets

"I say to you, you elegant fowls, keep singing. Sing about books for children, sing about reading, sing about poetry.... And may the singing never be done."
Frances Clarke Sayers
"You Elegant Fowls"

Sing about books for children and young people through open gateways and gauntlets. Open gates to reading as a lifetime happening and give students challenges to inspire, combat, and conquer. This theme is expressed in the illustrations by Leo and Diane Dillon in Zena Sutherland's and May Hill Arbuthnot's *Children and Books,* Seventh Edition. The illustrations present three characters in search of knowledge: a teacher, a librarian, and an editor. They plan their journey in the front-cover illustration, begin their travels in the frontispiece, find books in Part I, read the books in Part II, and pass books on to children in Part III. Their quest ends in the back-cover illustration as they leave the children reading by themselves. Katherine Paterson sings about books and children and quests in *Gates of Excellence: On Reading and Writing Books for Children,* and *The Spying Heart: More Thoughts on Reading and Writing Books for Children.* She encourages the sharing of works of the imagination to invite children to go within themselves to listen to the sounds of their own hearts.

Strategies that teachers, reading specialists, and library media specialists may use toward developing lifelong readers who travel to imaginative worlds, face and conquer human experiences, discover adventures, expand interests, find meaning in their lives, and know the enchantment of books include:

Establishing a purpose for reading
Providing an environment that encourages reading
Displaying books, pictures, and other resources
Reading aloud to students
Reading books while students are reading silently
Providing class time for reading
Stimulating reading through meaningful activities
Integrating reading skills into the literature program
Diagnosing differences in learning styles
Allowing students time to talk about books
Teaching all students based on their abilities
Using cooperative group-learning techniques
Training students in group work
Personalizing learning
Providing meaningful feedback
Allowing time for thinking in discussion periods
Being flexible

New technologies and new patterns of school organization offer challenges to the literature program. Commonly used acronyms are invading the teaching and learning scene. Some of these terms are:

CAI	Computer-Assisted Instruction
CBI	Computer-Based Instruction
IVD	Interactive Video Disc
TOM	Technology on Microfiche
CD-ROM	Compact Disc–Read Only Memory
LCID	Liquid-Crystal Imaging Device

These technologies are supplemented by computerized card catalogs, multimedia encyclopedias, online searching, and networking. The electronic age, with television, videocassettes, and computer programs, impacts students, teachers, and literature and reading programs. Arthea Reed, in *Comics to Classics: A Parent's Guide to Books for Teens and Preteens,* states that when used effectively, television and electronic media can be marvelous educational and entertainment tools. Students need to be taught the advantages and disadvantages of television, movies, and computers. She concludes that "we have a responsibility to teach young people to use electronic media to their benefit" (p. 93). Resource-based, literature-based, and whole language teaching strategies are widely being used. Site-based and school-based management are spreading throughout the national school systems. Being aware of these trends and capitalizing on their benefits will greatly enhance the literature program.

No matter what the present and future technologies, reading skills of locating, selecting, interpreting, and analyzing will be necessary. Students must be taught a process approach to effectively utilize information. They must question, doubt, reason, create, judge, and become independent learners.

Accepting the ideas of change and promoting new programs involves risk taking. Rosabeth Kanter states in *The Change Masters* that the power tools of change masters are an information system based on open communication, support from all kinds of networks, and resources that are decentralized. Change requires a departure from tradition, strategic decisions, and action.

The literary teaching units in *Approaches to Literature through Genre* involve new programs, ideas, and techniques. Putting the program into use involves hard work, dedication, and risk taking. To accomplish this, the following challenges are presented:

1. Accept new methods of teaching
2. Learn to use new technology
3. Reach all students on their own level
4. Be a collector of resource material
5. Set up attractive displays in an inviting environment
6. Provide activities that stimulate and nurture development
7. Incorporate computer programs in the learning activities
8. Use television and movie tie-ins to books
9. Nurture partnerships with the library media specialist and other teachers
10. Know the reader *and* the literature and keep them in contact with each other

The use of knowledge is the heart of learning. Making lifelong readers is the heart of the literature program. The gateways are open; accept the challenge!

References

Kanter, Rosabeth. *The Change Masters.* New York: Simon & Schuster, 1983.

Paterson, Katherine. *Gates of Excellence: On Reading and Writing Books for Children.* New York: E. P. Dutton, 1981.

———. *The Spying Heart: More Thoughts on Reading and Writing Books for Children.* New York: E. P. Dutton, 1989.

Reed, Arthea. *Comics to Classics: A Parent's Guide to Books for Teens and Preteens.* Newark, DE: International Reading Association, 1988.

Sayers, Frances Clarke. "You Elegant Fowls." *Horn Book Magazine* 65 (November/December 1989): 749.

Sutherland, Zena, and May Hill Arbuthnot. *Children and Books.* 7th ed. Glenview, IL: Scott, Foresman and Company, 1986.

Gateways to Teaching Literature

"It is not enough merely to suggest good books to students; they have to be guided in strategies that will give them the knowledge and skills to explore books on their own."
  M. Jean Greenlaw and Margaret McIntosh
  "Science Fiction and Fantasy Worth Teaching to Teens"

Gateways that are open allow the uninterrupted flow of traffic that may stretch to the horizon. *Approaches to Literature through Genre* is based on the premise of opening the flow of good literature, ideas, and activities to teachers and library media specialists who in turn guide and direct their students and expand their horizons.

PLANNING

Planning is an essential ingredient for implementing these literary genre units. This planning should take place as soon as possible at the beginning of a new school year. This will ensure time for scheduling and obtaining the necessary resources.

Begin planning by reading the introductory chapter of this book and skimming through the genre units. Look closely at the recommended titles with their designated reading levels and interest levels. Browse through the teaching tips, skills sections, and suggested activities. Select the genre units to be used during this school year and carefully read the entire genre chapter.

Plan objectives and goals based on the overall philosophy of the school system and the specific objectives designated by the curriculum in the local school. The organizational pattern of the school will determine the type of classroom organization, scheduling of class time, planning of activities, availability of resources, cooperative teaching efforts, and grouping of students. A flexible schedule and interdisciplinary organization greatly facilitate the implementation of the recommended and suggested activities, but with careful planning a successful program can be attained in schools with fixed schedules adhering to self-contained classrooms, departmental, or disciplinary organizations.

Classroom teachers, reading specialists, and language arts teachers should jointly plan these genre teaching units with the library media specialist. The library media specialist has the training and background to serve as the "NUMBER ONE" resource person for the units. Services include:

> Giving book talks
> Teaching skills lessons
> Directing reference sessions
> Preparing bibliographies
> Reserving books
> Providing reading guidance
> Obtaining resources
> Ordering books and materials
> Evaluating nonprint media
> Reading aloud to students
> Planning and setting up displays
> Working with students in small or large groups
> Guiding students in the process of locating and utilizing information in all formats
> Teaching and implementing production skills
> Assisting with media-related activities
> Accompanying groups on field trips

If the library media specialist has a heavy teaching assignment of scheduled classes or is a part-time member of the faculty, many of these services may still be provided by cooperative planning and scheduling.

Plan the overall design of the program for teaching the genre units. Decide the order in which to teach the units and the types of activities to include. When these decisions are made, discuss them with the appropriate team leaders, supervisors, and administrative staff. It may be necessary to obtain permission to include the units in the curriculum. Enlist the support of other staff members with whom cooperative teaching is envisioned.

MAPPING THE WAY

Use the recommended list of books for teaching the genre units provided in each genre chapter to select the book or books for the unit. Be sure to read unfamiliar books before making the selection. Additions to the list may include personal choices and children's choices as promoted by reading associations. From the final list, select the books for specific classes based on the reading levels, interest levels, maturity levels, learning styles, and abilities of the students in each class. Consider the developmental and formal operational stages of the students in making the selection. An excellent source to assist in the selection is Donna Norton's *Through the Eyes of a Child*, in which she discusses the characteristics and implications of language, cognitive, personality, and social development and gives suggested literature titles for students aged 8 to 10 and 10 to 12. Arthea Reed's *Comics to Classics: A Parent's Guide to Books for Teens and Preteens* provides additional helpful information. Remember to include books for students with special needs when making selections. Use the school system's curriculum guides, selection policies, and input from the library media specialist, team leaders, department heads, and administrative staff to select books and materials in accordance with local policies.

Assigning reading levels and interest levels to books is not an exact science. There are many factors that influence reading levels. These factors include the type size, page margins, illustrations, vocabulary, syntax, syllables in words, length of sentences, number of sentences, and style of writing. Reading-interest levels depend upon the stages of development, characteristics, cultural background, peer influences, personal interests, fads, and motivation of the students.

A number of tools assist in determining reading levels. *The Graph for Estimating Readability—Extended*, by Edward Fry, is a widely used formula. Additional formulas are the *Gunning Fog Readability Index* and *The SMOG Readability Formula*. Computer software formulas include *Readability Calculations*, from

Micro Power & Light, and *Fry Readability Program* by Jamestown Publishers. Marianne Pilla, in *Resources for Middle-Grade Reluctant Readers*, states the pros and cons of using readability formulas and concludes that formulas have their place and are useful tools when used with professional expertise.

The graded reading levels (RL) and interest levels (IL) given for the recommended and suggested titles in this book are guidelines only. They are based on a combination of Fry's readability formula, stated levels in professional sources, and personal experience gained in working with students and books. When checking reading levels in professional sources that use the Fry formula, it was found that the reading levels differ by approximately one grade level. This is true also of professional reviewing sources, paperback books, and publishers' designated reading levels. According to Edward Fry, the readability scales are accurate to within one grade level if correctly applied. The recommended and suggested titles are for reading–grade levels (RL), with the exception of a few that do not fall within this range.

MAKING THE CURRICULUM CONNECTION

The curriculum in language arts and reading is often revised and expanded in individual schools as well as in entire school systems. With the nationwide interest in promoting reading and basic skills, various methods and approaches are being used. Many of the ideas promoted by resource-based or literature-based teaching, whole language learning, and school-based management are an important part of the genre teaching units and activities in this book. These include reading aloud, sustained silent reading, and use of natural text as promoted by literature-based instruction. The whole language approach is reflected throughout the suggested activities. This approach arises out of the needs and interests of students and is fostered by the use of a wide variety of print and nonprint materials of interest to students. Cooperation is nurtured through group activities, discussions, sharing, and production of related media projects. Goals include helping students to learn the *process* of locating and utilizing information and to develop the necessary skills to become independent and lifelong learners. The whole language approach is discussed in a special supplement to the December 1989 issue of *School Library Media Activities Monthly* in an article by Agnes Stahlschmidt, "Support for the Whole Language Program—What the Library Media Specialist Can Do," and in the May 1990 issue of the magazine in an article by Daniel Barron, "Whole Language and Literature-Based Reading: May Day!" The latter provides an extensive annotated bibliography of source material. The school-based management approach is brought out in the suggested activities of the genre units delineating tactics of teacher involvement in decision making, flexible scheduling, teacher evaluation of programs, cooperative teaching, administrative support for innovative school-based programs, implementing measures of encouraging reading for pleasure, sponsoring local reading contests, inviting parents to participate in school activities, and sharing activities with community groups. Another recommended resource is Eleanor Kulleseid's and Dorothy Strickland's *Literature, Literacy and Learning: Classroom Teachers, Library Media Specialists, and the Literature-Based Curriculum*, available from the American Library Association. Cooperative teaching involves the integration of art, music, drama, and media production into the language arts and reading programs. It includes suggestions for relating historical fiction to social studies, science fiction to science, and adventure and survival to physical education. It suggests cooperative ventures across disciplines to include field trips, museum visits, guest speakers, performers, and special programs at school.

If the curriculum of the school specifies the use of basal readers, the genre teaching units in this book may be used to extend and expand the readers. Teaching tips, strategies, skills lessons, and activities may also be incorporated into the basal reader units.

EMPHASIZING THE LITERARY ELEMENTS AND COMMUNICATION SKILLS

The inclusion of literary terms and concepts within each genre teaching unit serves to acquaint students with the literary elements of plot, characterization, theme, tone, point of view, style, setting, and design/illustration. Knowing the literary devices provides students with a frame of reference for discussing literature, sharpens insights into the author's purpose and methods, increases reader appreciation, instills perception of techniques of style, evokes critical judgment, and promotes appreciation and pleasure. By focusing on one literary element in the study of one genre, the students have an opportunity to concentrate on that literary element with many reinforcements throughout the genre unit. Picture storybooks are suggested for use as springboards to teach the literary elements. Susan Hall's *Using Picture Storybooks to Teach Literary Devices: Recommended Books for Children and Young Adults* is an excellent additional resource. After several weeks of directed focus on style or theme or the other literary elements, students should understand the meaning of the literary device and be able to use it effectively.

The focus on critical-thinking and communication skills provides students with instructional activities and experiences related to reading critically, reading for detail, vocabulary development, and the skills of listening, oral communication, writing, organization, and research. One skill is integrated into one genre unit to allow repetition and practice of the skill. For example, listening skills are emphasized throughout the humor genre unit, and writing skills are emphasized throughout the historical fiction genre unit. Students should show improvement in these basic skills as they are given many opportunities to practice the skills while enjoying the literature and the activities.

SCHEDULING

Use a yearly plan-book to map out the schedule for teaching the genre units. Include as many genre units as practical within the requirements and guidelines of other teaching responsibilities. A genre unit may be scheduled from two or three weeks up to six weeks depending on the activities selected. Refer to the teaching tips and activity sections included in each genre unit to assist in determining the amount of time to schedule for each unit. As soon as the schedule for genre teaching units has been established, meet with the library media specialist to plan and jointly schedule cooperative teaching sessions, research activities, and production functions. Include requests for ordering multiple copies of paperback books, requests for placing books on reserve, and requests for bibliographies of the school library media center's holdings of books in different genres. Remember to schedule time for field trips, activity periods, cooperative teaching times with other teachers and disciplines, and guest speakers.

GATHERING RESOURCES

Numerous resources are suggested in the genre teaching units. They range from print and nonprint sources to people and associations. To utilize these resources requires planning, effort, and scheduling. Taking the time to acquire additional resources should be rewarded with student interest, excitement, motivation, and learning.

Professional books and curriculum guides are available to assist in teaching about the genres and individual titles within some of the genres. Many of these sources are cited throughout the genre unit. Some of these professional books of special merit are presented in the following citations. *Children's Literature in the Reading Program,* edited by Bernice Cullinan, has sections on children's literature in the intermediate and upper grades, with enrichment activities, teaching higher order skills with literature, enriching the basal reader with literature, and resources to identify children's books for the reading program. *Those Blooming Books: A Handbook for Extending Thinking Skills,* by Carol Sue Kruise, applies Bloom's Taxonomy to children's literature. While many of the books are for younger children, several books for older children are included: *One-Eyed Cat* by Paula Fox; *The Sign of the Beaver* by Elizabeth George Speare; and *My Brother Sam Is Dead* by Sam and Christopher Collier. It also includes a list of read-aloud books for grades 3–6. Joni Bodart's series of *Booktalk!* provides practical, step-by-step guides for planning, presenting, and follow-up activities with books for students in a wide reading range. Some paperback book companies such as Dell, Viking, Penguin, and Avon have teaching guides available for some titles. *Bookwise Literature Curriculum Guides* (written by Sonia Landes and Molly Flender for such books as *Tuck Everlasting* by Natalie Babbitt, *Julie of the Wolves* by Jean George, and *Sarah, Plain and Tall* by Patricia MacLachlan) are available from Christopher-Gordon Publishers, Inc. Carolyn Bauer, in *This Way to Books,* provides interesting and creative activities to use with books, from quilt patterns, log cabins, greeting cards, and puzzles to creative writing projects. Marsha Rudman's *Children's Literature: An Issues Approach,* Second Edition, presents a reference and selection guide to children's books based on the societal and developmental nature of students, and has a long list of suggested activities for personalizing and extending reading. *Best*

Books for Children, by John Gillespie and Christine Gilbert, provides highly recommended books for recreational reading and typical school curricula from preschool to advanced readers in grade 6. Betsy Hearne, in *Choosing Books for Children: A Commonsense Guide,* discusses children's literature and its uses and includes some of her favorite books and authors. Michele Landsberg's *Reading for the Love of It: Best Books for Young Readers* presents criteria for choos-ing children's literature arranged by genres. As a well-known critic of children's literature, her frank discussions of the likes and dislikes of many children's books are very informative and enlightening.

Resources that can provide special assistance to teaching the literary elements and terms are Rebecca Lukens's *A Critical Handbook of Children's Literature,* Third Edition, and *The Elements of English* by Stan Malless and Jeff McQuain. They are invaluable aids and are suggested for purchase for use in the classroom, department, and the library media center.

Nonprint material such as audiocassettes, computer programs, films, sound filmstrips, and videotapes are excellent resources for teaching literature. Many titles are listed in each genre teaching unit and in the nonprint resources at the end of each unit. Some of these resources may be purchased or they may be obtained through the school library media center, departmental resource centers, professional libraries, professional associations, or the public library. Selected addresses of vendors and distributors are included in the Appendix. Additional addresses and telephone numbers of producers and distributors are listed in the *Audio Video Review Digest, 1989 Cumulation,* edited by Susan Stetler and published by Gale Research Inc. This digest is an excellent guide to 10,000 reviews of audio and video materials appearing in general and specialized periodicals. Each entry includes the title, format, rating, subject, run time, digest of the review, and audience. Another very useful guide is *A-V Online,* available on Compact Disc Sp-007-005 produced by Silver Platter International. This resource describes the contents and identifies sources of videotapes, 16mm films, filmstrips, and audiotapes.

A very useful source book filled with ideas and resources for using computer programs and media productions is *Media Production & Computer Activities,* edited by H. Thomas Walker and Paula Montgomery (ABC-CLIO, 1990).

When using print and nonprint resources be sure to observe school and/or district guidelines and copyright laws as well as previewing and evaluating these resources.

Professional organizations such as the International Reading Association, National Council of Teachers of English, American Association of School Librarians, and the Children's Book Council publish valuable and useful information on children's literature. Their publications are probably available through the school library media center's journal subscriptions, the professional library, or the public library. Other professional organizations and associations publish journals, pamphlets, guides, and photographs of value to the genre literature units. Ask the library media specialist for assistance with these.

Community resource lists of guest speakers, local business and professional organizations, local colleges and universities, museums, libraries, historic and unusual places of interest, and local and state organizations may be obtained from the informational or vertical files of the library media center, public libraries, P.T.A., societies and organizations, and the telephone directory.

Resources are a part of the rich heritage of children's literature. They extend the teaching ideas and student activities. Generate student interest and encourage their involvement by utilizing many resources.

References

Barnet, Sylvan, Morton Berman, and William Burto. *A Dictionary of Literary, Dramatic, and Cinematic Terms.* 2d ed. Boston: Little, Brown & Company, 1971.

Barron, Daniel. "Whole Language and Literature-Based Reading: May Day!" *School Library Media Activities Monthly* 6 (May 1990): 51–54.

Bauer, Carolyn. *This Way to Books.* New York: H. W. Wilson Company, 1983.

Bodart, Joni. *Booktalk! Two: Booktalk for All Ages and Audiences.* 2d ed. New York: H. W. Wilson Company, 1985.

Cochrane, Orin, Donna Cochrane, Sharen Scalena, and Ethel Buchanan. *Reading, Writing, and Caring.* New York: Richard C. Owen Publishers, 1984.

Cullinan, Bernice. *Literature and the Child.* 2d ed. New York: Harcourt Brace Jovanovich, 1989.

———, ed. *Children's Literature in the Reading Program.* Newark, DE: International Reading Association, 1987.

Gillespie, John, and Christine Gilbert. *Best Books for Children.* 3d ed. New York: R. R. Bowker, 1985.

Greenlaw, M. Jean, and Margaret McIntosh. "Science Fiction and Fantasy Worth Teaching to Teens." In *Children's Literature in the Reading Program,* edited by Bernice Cullinan. Newark, DE: International Reading Association, 1987.

Hall, Susan. *Using Picture Storybooks To Teach Literary Devices: Recommended Books for Children and Young Adults.* Phoenix, AZ: Oryx Press, 1990.

Hearne, Betsy. *Choosing Books for Children: A Commonsense Guide.* Rev. ed. New York: Delacorte Press, 1990.

Kruise, Carol Sue. *Those Blooming Books: A Handbook for Extending Thinking Skills.* Littleton, CO: Libraries Unlimited, 1987.

Kulleseid, Eleanor, and Dorothy Strickland. *Literature, Literacy and Learning: Classroom Teachers, Library Media Specialists, and the Literature-Based Curriculum.* Chicago: American Library Association, 1989.

Landes, Sonia, and Molly Flender. *Bookwise Literature Curriculum Guides.* Needham Heights, MA: Christopher-Gordon Publishers.

Landsberg, Michele. *Reading for the Love of It: Best Books for Young Readers.* Englewood Cliffs, NJ: Prentice-Hall, 1988.

Lukens, Rebecca. *A Critical Handbook of Children's Literature.* 3d ed. Glenview, IL: Scott, Foresman and Company, 1986.

Malless, Stan, and Jeff McQuain. *The Elements of English.* New York: Madison Books, 1988.

Norton, Donna. *Through the Eyes of a Child: An Introduction to Children's Literature.* 2d ed. Columbus, OH: Merrill Publishing Company, 1987.

Pilla, Marianne. *Resources for Middle-Grade Reluctant Readers.* Littleton, CO: Libraries Unlimited, 1987.

Purves, Alan, and Dianne Monson. *Experiencing Children's Literature.* Glenview, IL: Scott, Foresman and Company, 1984.

Reed, Arthea. *Comics to Classics: A Parent's Guide to Books for Teens and Preteens.* Newark, DE: International Reading Association, 1988.

Rudman, Marsha. *Children's Literature: An Issues Approach.* 2d ed. New York: Longman, Inc., 1984.

Stahlschmidt, Agnes. "Support the Whole Language Program—What the Library Media Specialist Can Do." *School Library Media Activities Monthly* 6 (December 1989): 31.

Sutherland, Zena, and May Hill Arbuthnot. *Children and Books.* 7th ed. Glenview, IL: Scott, Foresman and Company, 1986.

Trelease, Jim. *The New Read-Aloud Handbook.* New York: Viking, 1989.

Walker, H. Thomas, and Paula Montgomery, eds. *Media Production & Computer Activities.* Santa Barbara, CA: ABC-CLIO, 1990.

2

Humor

"Have fun with humorous books. Laughter is the best of the serious business of life."
Caroline Feller Bauer
"What's So Funny? Humor in Children's Books"

INTRODUCTION

The humor genre is composed of a wide variety of types of literature, including fantasies, adventures, realistic fiction, animals, tall tales, and folktales. Although humor often is not considered a genre or class by itself, the great appeal and popularity of humorous stories among children and young people warrant that it be included as a separate category. The focus in this chapter is humorous fiction as a genre and how it relates to other literary forms such as tall tales, jokes, riddles, and comedy sketches. According to Betsy Hearne in *Choosing Books for Children,* two of the important elements of fiction for young children are plot and humor. "Children will read to find out what happens and to laugh" (p. 66).

Humor can be classed under the broad category of comedy: anything amusing or laughable. Comedy is defined in *Webster's Seventh New Collegiate Dictionary* as "the genre of dramatic literature dealing with the comic or the serious in a light or satirical manner." Comedy typically has a happy ending. Humorous literature includes burlesque, satire, slapstick, vaudeville, and farce.

Humor is comical, amusing, and sometimes absurd. In *Nonsense Literature for Children,* by Celia Anderson and Marilyn

Apseloff, nonsense literature is described as the world turned upside down, figurative language taken literally, overexaggeration, and absurd connections. Edward Lear wrote and illustrated absurd limericks in the mid-1800s. His *Book of Nonsense,* published in 1846, still brings gales of laughter and entertainment to children of all ages. Carl Sandburg's *Rootabaga Stories* combines his gift of storytelling with imagination and humor. He created and told stories to his own children about simple, amusing people. His unusual characters, such as Gimme the Ax and White Horse Girl, who live in Rootabaga Country, get into many ridiculous situations. The stories are included in *The Sandburg Treasury.* Exaggeration and humor abound in Astrid Lindgren's popular *Pippi Longstocking* books and in Roald Dahl's *James and the Giant Peach.* Theodor Geisel, better known as Dr. Seuss, uses rhyme, rhythm, and nonsense humor in his 40-plus books for children including the classic *Cat in the Hat.* Peggy Parish's amusing *Amelia-Bedelia* uses figurative language taken literally, to the delight of children.

Jokes, riddles, puns, and funny poems are a part of humorous literature. Corny jokes like those found in collections by Charles Keller, such as *It's Raining Cats and Dogs* and *Driving Me Crazy,* are rollicking good humor. Riddles and puns bring out the groans and laughter from such books as *What's Gnu? Riddles from the Zoo* by Thomas Mase. Tongue-twister books are especially read-aloud fun, such as *Twist These on Your Tongue* by Joseph Rosenbloom.

Folk literature contains a great deal of humor in folktales, fables, tall tales, and cumulative tales. The stories allow people to laugh at themselves and others. Talking beasts, sillies, numbskulls, giants, ordinary and extraordinary people provide humorous situations and incidents to appeal to a wide audience.

Many realistic stories about families, school, growing up, and friendship contain humorous elements. Authors of humorous fiction often use situations that could happen to real people. Beverly Cleary's Ramona, Henry Huggins, and Ellen Tibbets are favorite humorous characters of the younger set. Peter and Fudge of Judy Blume's *Tales of a Fourth Grade Nothing* and *Superfudge* bring laughter with their humorous conflicts. Authors such as Paula Danziger, Lois Lowry, Betsy Byars, Helen Cresswell, Jamie Gilson, Shelia Greenwald, Thomas Rockwell, Bette Greene, Jerry Spinelli, Robert Peck, and Marjorie Sharmat write humorous stories that appeal to children from fourth grade up.

The popularity of humor and comedy is evident in the large number of television programs and movies currently being shown, as well as reruns from the sixties and seventies. These include situation comedies, cartoons, and shows featuring comedians. Bob Hope, Lucille Ball, Steve Martin, Bill Cosby, and Arsenio Hall are comedians familiar to many children.

There is a therapeutic value to including humorous books in a literature program for children and young people. Humor is a major ingredient in a healthy childhood. Humor helps children to see the light and entertaining side of life. It encourages them to laugh at themselves and at human shortcomings and behaviors. It helps define human emotions. Humor often highlights real problems through the powers of humorous observation and gives children a better understanding of the adult world. Humor is enlightening and fulfilling. Laughter is "good medicine" and contagious.

ELEMENT OF LITERATURE: FOCUS ON TONE

Tone is the attitude of the author to a work of literature. It indicates how the author *feels* toward the subject of the literary work, toward the characters, and toward the readers. The author's attitude toward a work can be described in part as formal or informal, playful or serious, happy or angry, confident or sarcastic, delightful or scornful, accepting or rejecting. In spoken communication, tone is conveyed through the speaker's lilt or voice intonation, modulation and pitch, choice of words, and facial expressions. In written literature, tone is conveyed solely through the author's choice of words and is therefore more difficult to communicate. Readers must understand by the author's selection and sequence of words the way in which the words are meant to be heard. Tone has been described as being very close to how the author speaks silently to himself or herself when alone.

Many kinds of tone can be found in all genres of children's literature, according to Rebecca Lukens in *A Critical Handbook of Children's Literature*. Authors often vary tone to show their change in attitude toward different characters and situations. In realistic fiction like Katherine Paterson's *The Great Gilly Hopkins,* the tone is one of empathy, concern, and acceptance of reality. In historical fiction such as Rosemary Sutcliff's *Knight's Fee,* the tone is one of fulfillment of purpose in a specific historical period of time. In mystery stories like Roderic Jeffries's, *Against Time,* the tone is one of suspense, drama, and trust.

Mood and tone are sometimes difficult to distinguish. Mood is the atmosphere created by the author to permeate the literary work, such as an atmosphere that is calm, sinister, mysterious, or melancholy. The setting or locale of a story often reinforces the mood or atmosphere. The tone for Jamie Gilson's *Do Bananas Chew Gum?* is humorous, light, and entertaining on the surface, but it also has a serious tone. The serious tone depicting the plight and joy of Sam Mott's learning to read and spell is couched in humorous incidents. The author's attitude toward Sam Mott is handled skillfully and unobtrusively to convey his message of hope for nonreaders.

There are many different reactions by readers to the author's tone in a story. Rebecca Lukens observes that a reader's personal taste and experience result in these differences. She also states that children often express their reactions to the tone in words such as "silly, funny, and boring."

Some of the elements that contribute to tone are humor, values, and language. The author's attitude toward suspense, humor, and descriptive language is cleverly presented in Ellen Raskin's *The Westing Game* through amusing and suspenseful situations, absurd happenings, and zany characters. Jerry Spinelli's tone of acceptance of an adolescent boy's sexual maturing, growing pains, and problems at home and school reflect the attitude of changing values in some contemporary fiction. Tastes in tone change, but not everyone fully accepts the changes. Language and the writer's style convey tone in literature. The use of exaggeration or hyperbole, euphemism, connotations of different words, patterns and arrangements of words, and figurative language are devices used by authors to influence the tone and meaning of the story.

Negative elements reflected by the author's tone are condescension and didacticism. Kenneth Donelson and Alleen Nilsen state, in *Literature for Today's Young Adults,* that one of the most distinctive things about young adult literature is its tone. They give an example of condescension by reading a few pages from two similar books and telling which one is written for adults and which one is written for teenagers. Condescension, or "writing down," is demeaning and insulting. Children and young adults deserve to be treated as intelligent people worthy of the best writing an author can produce. Didacticism occurs when an author fails to establish an acceptable tone. When the message appears to be the reason for writing the book, it is overly preachy and didactic. Preaching and teaching are not the functions of literature. Worthwhile goals and values can be conveyed without didacticism. Cynthia Rylant's *A Fine White Dust* is an excellent example of a novel that could be preachy but instead is a well-written, memorable story of a boy who is torn between his strong religious beliefs and friendship with the "preacher man" and his feelings toward his family and his best friend. The author uses various tones to comment on family ties, religious beliefs, loyalty, and friendship.

Tone is an important part of every story. The author's attitude toward the story, the characters, and the readers can promote pleasure, understanding, acceptance, sympathy, and meaning.

Tone is especially important in humorous books. An informal, playful, happy, delightful, hilarious, or funny tone is often found in humorous literature.

Rebecca Lukens discusses the sources of humor in children's books and classifies them as:

1. Situations
2. Actions
3. Style
4. Unexpected phrasing or situation
5. Dialogue
6. Description
7. Verbal humor
8. Irony
9. Exaggeration
10. Figurative language and imagery

Authors develop humor by using these sources and combinations of these sources. Situations play a role in Beverly Cleary's *Ramona and Her Father,* as Ramona reacts to her father's loss of a job and her mother's finding one. Actions are very important in Jamie Gilson's *Do Bananas Chew Gum?* when Sam Mott takes a babysitting job and when he becomes interested in archeology after his discovery of relics in the aftermath of a tornado. Style and word usage are special features of Lois Lowry's *Anastasia Krupnik,* as Anastasia is very conscious of words and keeps a secret green notebook where she lists favorite words, things she loves or hates, a name for her baby brother-to-be, private information, and important things that happened the year that she was ten. Unexpected situations develop in Eve Bunting's *Sixth-Grade Sleepover* when Pebbles, the rabbit, has baby rabbits in the cafeteria at the sixth-grade sleepover, and Janey and Rosie share secrets. Dialogue is used to develop humor in Avi's *Romeo and Juliet—Together (and Alive) at Last*. Pete Saltz and Ed Sitrow have lively discussions concerning love and Anabell Stackpoole. The dialogue from the scenes of the play *Romeo and Juliet* is used to enhance the story. Descriptions of the little people and their way of life are used by Mary Norton in her book *The Borrowers* as a source of humor. She describes in great detail the food, furnishings, and everyday happenings of the little people. Verbal humor abounds in Helen Cresswell's *Bagthropes Abroad*, as Mr. Bagthrope and his extended family and cook banter continuously in their "vacation home." Irony prevails in Peggy Parish's *Amelia-Bedelia* when Mrs. Rogers hires Amelia-Bedelia as a maid and expects her to follow written instructions about cleaning. Amelia-Bedelia does the opposite by interpreting the instructions literally. Exaggeration is used by Astrid Lindgren in *Pippi Longstocking*, as Pippi is portrayed as the strongest girl in the world and the most unconventional one as well. Figurative language and imagery are used in amusing ways by Carl Sandburg in his *Rootabaga Stories*. He uses alliteration such as "wrinkly, wriggly, wraggly faces," an analogy of the little railroad trains and skyscrapers, and hyperbole when he describes a book falling out of the mouth of a spider in his "One Story about Big People Now and Little People Long Ago."

Since tone tells how the author feels about the subject, characters, and readers, it is imperative for the reader to discern these feelings. A careful reading using comprehension skills, inference, and evaluation is necessary. Recalling information about the attitudes and traits of characters can assist in this search. There can be clues given by the author through narration, dialogue, or undertones that relate directly to the author's attitudes. The author can editorialize or give opinions through the characters. The author's choice of material can reveal feelings. It may be necessary to ask questions to discern the author's attitude toward the literary work. Is the tone serious or lighthearted? Is it positive and enlightening? Is it gentle or harsh? Is it full of anger and hatred? Is it kind and gentle? Does it convey acceptance or rejection? Does the tone vary toward different characters and situations? Does it provoke sympathy and understanding? Is the tone critical or judgmental? Is it humorous and entertaining? Is it optimistic? Does the author promote or reject the expressed values of the characters? Is the author's attitude toward the reader condescending, sentimental, or nostalgic? Is it didactic?

Another way of finding the author's attitudes is to learn something about the author. There are many good reference books, magazine articles, and nonprint materials about authors readily available in library media centers. Often, learning details about family life, background, and interests of an author can provide helpful insights to the author's attitudes. Locating additional books written by the author can reveal patterns, themes, and causes of importance to the author.

Tone in humorous books is often light and amusing. It is entertaining and filled with figurative language and imagery. It is an adventure into the absurd and unexpected. It ranges from simple to sophisticated humor. The author's tone permeates the story and can bring laughter and happiness.

RECOMMENDED LISTS

Recommended Titles for Teaching the Humor Genre Unit

There are great numbers of humorous books for children and young adults. Many of these books are available in paperback and large-print editions. Reading levels in many humorous books tend to be lower than for books in other genres. Popular authors whose books are in great demand by students in grades 5–9 often have reading levels of grades 4–6. Books with lower reading levels are quick, easy, and satisfying for many students. For this reason the following suggested titles for teaching units include extra suggestions so that students may read more than one book during this unit.

Avi. *Romeo and Juliet—Together (and Alive) at Last.* New York: Franklin Watts, 1987. RL: Grade 5. IL: Grades 7–10. PB: Avon.

Ed Sitrow and Pete Saltz are best friends. They say that they are as "close as a pair of eyes." Pete Saltz falls in love with Anabell Stackpoole even though he does not really know her, look at her, or ever talk to her. He writes poems about her all the time. Sitrow decides to help his lovelorn friend by proposing that they put on a play. This play is not just any play but it is, according to the teacher, the greatest love story ever written, *Romeo and Juliet.* Saltz is Romeo and Stackpoole is Juliet. In the play they have to look at each other and even kiss a couple of times. At their rehearsals they read the parts as if they were "checking the telephone book for spelling mistakes." They never do practice kissing. With many mishaps and hilarious scenes, the play is performed for the school. Ed Sitrow is assisted in producing the play by lovely Lucy. The two of them think about playing the leads in *Antony and Cleopatra.* Ed begins to think of the dictionary definition of love. After the play is over, Saltz and Stackpoole sit side by side in class. She reads and he writes a poem.

The tone of *Romeo and Juliet—Together (and Alive) at Last* is one of humor and gently poking fun at young love. Avi's attitude toward the characters is one of acceptance and understanding. He shows insight concerning the characteristics of young people. His attitude toward the adult characters, the teachers, and the principal is one of letting them stay in the background and not involving themselves in the student production much to the delight of the students. The author's attitude toward the readers is one of invitation to the joy, humor, and pleasure of reading.

Bunting, Eve. *Sixth-Grade Sleepover.* New York: Scholastic, 1986. RL: Grade 5. IL: Grades 4–7. PB: Apple.

Janey loves books and reading. She joins a special reading club at school called R.A.B.B.I.T.S. (Read-A-Book: Bring-It-To-School). The class mascot is a rabbit named Pebbles. The club is sponsored by the sixth-grade teacher, nicknamed Putt-Putt, and the reading specialist, nicknamed Goldie. A marathon reading sleepover is planned for a Friday night in the school cafeteria. Janey and her best friend are very excited about spending the night with the other Rabbits, both boys and girls, until Janey realizes that it will be dark and scary. She has a phobia of the dark. With the help of her parents and her friend, Janey works out a plan that will allow her to go to the reading marathon sleepover. After the games, food, and reading time, it is time for lights-out. Janey discovers that Rosie has a problem as great as her phobia and is determined to overcome her problem and help her new friend with hers.

The tone of the book toward the subject of reading and students is one of joy and affection for books and young people. Reading is presented as a fun activity. The titles of books being read and discussed are popular ones with sixth-grade students. The author's attitude toward the characters is one of understanding and concern. The tone toward readers is expressed through the light and humorous situations that invite everyone to spread the news of books around the world.

Sixth-Grade Sleepover received the Mark Twain Award at the Spring Conference of the Missouri Association of School Librarians in 1990. The award is chosen by the Missouri school children in grades 4–8 who read and vote for their favorite book.

Cleary, Beverly. *Dear Mr. Henshaw*. New York: William Morrow, 1983. RL: Grade 5. IL: Grades 4–7. PB: Dell. Cornerstone.

Leigh Botts is a sixth-grade boy with a problem: the divorce of his parents. When his teacher asks students to write to their favorite author, Leigh writes to author Boyd Henshaw. Leigh includes ten questions in the letter. The author replies with answers to the questions but asks Leigh to answer ten questions also. Leigh at first refuses to answer the questions until his mother convinces him that he should answer them. Leigh's answers prompt him to face his feelings about his parents' divorce and his feelings about himself. Mr. Henshaw suggests that Leigh keep a diary. The entries in the diary help Leigh to further understand and come to terms with his feelings. Leigh relates everyday experiences that are both humorous and sad.

The tone of *Dear Mr. Henshaw* is one of empathy and caring for the characters. The attitude of the author is reflected in the positive change in Leigh's attitude toward his father and himself.

As mentioned earlier, Beverly Cleary describes her own view of life as funny and sad in "The Laughter of Children." She has chosen "reality twisted to the right into humor." The tone of this book reflects this attitude.

Other books by Beverly Cleary, such as *Ramona and Her Father* and *Ramona Quimby, Age 8,* are very funny and very popular with children. The reading levels are below the levels selected for this book, but they could be used as read-alouds or for students with special needs.

Cresswell, Helen. *Bagthorpes Abroad.* New York: Macmillan, 1984. RL: Grade 6. IL: Grades 4–8.

The eccentric Bagthorpes go "abroad" on vacation in Wales after Mr. Bagthorpe places an advertisement for a haunted house so that he can write a ghost story. The family includes mother and father, four children, and grandma and grandpa. The extended family includes an aunt, uncle, niece, and housekeeper. A pet dog, cat, and goat accompany the family on vacation. The dilapidated house without a proper kitchen prompts the uncle to state that it is "rather short on creature comforts" and that it resembles a Victorian doghouse. Mr. Bagthorpe declares that he is a great believer in living rough because it builds character. The family becomes involved in power struggles to establish their own territory, channel their considerable energies, pursue their own theories, and follow their own individual interests. The niece, Daisy, is five years old and a terror. It is declared that by the time she is seven she will have tried everything and live the rest of her life in boredom. Her pet goat charges and challenges Mr. Bagthorpe, and the telepathic dog, Zero, sees a ghost. The family goes on a ghost watch. Daisy gets involved with the police, and mayhem and chaos abound.

The tone of *Bagthorpes Abroad* is one of exaggerated humor overflowing with picturesque language, irony, and metaphors. The author pokes fun at human foibles through the eccentric characters. The author's attitude toward the reader is one of providing laughter, pleasure, and glimpses of themselves.

Danziger, Paula. *The Cat Ate My Gymsuit.* New York: Doubleday, 1974. RL: Grade 6. IL: Grades 5–9. PB: Dell. Cornerstone.

Marcy is tired of being fat, hearing her parents quarrel, and being bored in school. At age 13, she is unhappy at home and school until an English teacher shows special interest and concern. Marcy even learns to laugh at herself. Life begins to have more meaning;

then the teacher is dismissed. Marcy takes on the task of supporting the teacher's reinstatement. Her involvement and actions have a humorous flavor.

The tone of the book is one of humor and truth with a real feeling for the characters and their problems. The author's attitude toward being fat and unpopular and toward feelings of hatred for one's father is hidden under the humorous aspects of the story, but these are nonetheless heartfelt problems. The author's attitude toward the readers is one of fun and laughter and encouraging empathy for the characters.

Gilson, Jamie. *Do Bananas Chew Gum?* New York: Lothrop, Lee & Shepard, 1980. RL: Grade 5. IL: Grades 5–8. PB: Archway.

Sam Mott is a sixth-grade student who reads on a second-grade level. He considers himself dumb because he cannot read. His family keeps moving because his father has the "Greener Job Syndrome." Sam was diagnosed as having a learning disability and was getting special help until the family moved again. Sam tries to cover up his reading disability with humorous and clever antics. He spends a lot of time at the orthodonist. He memorizes the doctor's explanation of his teeth problems and loves to tell people that he has a "severe malocclusion of the upper mandibular palate." He gets to know Alicia when she starts going to the same orthodontist. Alicia is very bright and is in Sam's class in school. She has also just moved to town and is trying to make friends. Sam gets a job after school babysitting two lively, rambunctious boys. Sam wants the money from babysitting to buy a tape recorder to help him with his reading problem. Problems develop on the job because Sam cannot read the notes and messages. A tornado uproots a tree and discoveries are made that are important enough to bring an archeologist to see them. Sam gets excited about becoming an archeologist until he realizes that it will take a lot of reading. Problems at school develop during a spelling contest in which Sam is embarrassed because he cannot spell "cute." However, Sam has good math skills, can memorize, and can analyze situations. He is given special tests at school. Some of the tests are weird, with strange questions like "Do bananas chew gum?" He finds that he can learn best by what he hears. He is told that many people learn by listening to other people, to movies, and to television. He tells his friend Alicia about the tests and about his resolve to work with the teacher several times a week. He carries a piece of paper with him with the written word, "Arc-he-ol-o-gy."

The tone of *Do Bananas Chew Gum?* is one of concern and empathy for the main character told in a humorous and light vein. The funny episodes and incidents highlight the real problem. Jamie Gilson understands the problems facing nonreaders and, in a humorous way, presents a message of hope. Her attitude toward readers is one of using humor to make her message more palatable. She imparts knowledge and provides information about obtaining help to solve a reading problem without being didactic or condescending.

Greene, Bette. *Philip Hall Likes Me, I Reckon Maybe.* New York: Dial Press, 1974. RL: Grade 5. IL: Grades 4–6. PB: Dell. Cornerstone.

Beth Lambert, an intelligent, humorous, lively eleven-year-old, has a "crush" on Philip Hall, who is friendly when boys are not around. It is a different story when he is surrounded by his friends, much to Beth's anguish. Beth is constantly trying to involve Philip in joint activities. These develop into some very amusing situations. Beth even lets Philip believe that he is the smartest person in class. Together they catch some turkey thieves and attend a county fair where they compete against one another. Beth pickets a store where she and her friends are cheated, finds lost Philip who injures his foot at a picnic, and develops an allergy to dogs.

The tone of *Philip Hall Likes Me, I Reckon Maybe* is one of light humor and pleasure. Bette Greene's attitude toward the realistic characters is one of acceptance and appeal. She portrays a picture of a loving, caring black family in rural Arkansas and a delightful protagonist in Beth Lambert. Her attitude toward the readers is one of universal appeal for a young girl and boy just discovering that they like each other. She speaks to readers of any ethnic heritage.

Lindgren, Astrid. *Pippi Longstocking.* New York: Viking, 1950. RL: Grade 5. IL: Grades 4–7. PB: Puffin. Cornerstone.

Pippi is an unusual, lovable brat whose unconventional behavior makes her a favorite with readers. With her red hair, pigtails, freckles, and stockings of different colors, her looks match her outrageous antics. Pippi lives by herself in a rundown house, Villa Villekulla, with her monkey, horse, and gold pieces. She does not go to school, eats whatever she likes, and does whatever she likes. She is always in charge of the situation and always puts adults in their place.

The tone of the book is comical and tongue-in-cheek. The whimsical exaggerations are told in straightforward language. The author's attitude toward Pippi is one of joy and pride in a young girl who refuses to grow up and who lives out her fantasies. Her attitude toward her readers is one of poking fun at conventional behavior and inviting readers to enjoy the hilarious fun with Pippi. Astrid Lindgren has stated that she does not write books for children but for the child she is. She writes to please herself but in so doing she pleases children all over the world.

Lowry, Lois. *Anastasia Krupnik*. Boston: Houghton Mifflin, 1979. RL: Grade 6. IL: Grades 5–7. PB: Bantam. Cornerstone.

Anastasia is a bright ten-year-old who experiences the roller-coaster ups and downs of growing up. She is mature and cooperative one minute and babyish and insensitive the next. Her inquisitive mind and delight in words are seen through the notes she makes in her secret green notebook. Her parents are caring and involved in Anastasia's life; they let her explore and experiment with different styles and concepts of dress, behavior, and even religion. Anastasia's father is a poet and professor and her mother is an artist. Anastasia becomes very angry when she learns that her parents are going to have a baby "at their age!" She is given the opportunity to name the baby and writes down in her notebook the most terrible name she can imagine. Coming to terms with her elderly grandmother's death, Anastasia develops an "inward eye" that helps her to begin to accept the other changes in her life.

The tone of Anastasia Krupnik is delightful, amusing, and entertaining. The author's attitude toward the characters is one of belief in the joys and trials of parenthood and family life. Patience, love, anger, humor, happiness, and sadness are realistically portrayed. The author's attitude toward the reader is one of invitation to partake of the delight of Anastasia's world.

Additional titles about Anastasia are *Anastasia Again!* (1981), *Anastasia at Your Service* (1982), *Anastasia on Her Own* (1985), and *Anastasia Has the Answers* (1986). Some titles are available in large-print editions from Cornerstone.

Rockwell, Thomas. *How To Eat Fried Worms.* New York: Watts, 1973. RL: Grade 6. IL: Grades 5–8. PB: Dell. Cornerstone.

Billy has a bet with one of his friends that he can eat 15 worms in 15 days. Since the bet is for $50, Billy is determined to win even though he does not know how he will be able to swallow the worms. He is allowed to cook them and eat them accompanied by various condiments or "dressings." Billy tries a lot of ingenious recipes including horseradish sauce and peanut butter. Billy's friend tries to prevent Billy from winning the bet, but Billy prevails and even begins to like the taste of worms.

The tone of the book is light, zany, gross, and adventuresome. Thomas Rockwell sees his characters as fun-loving daredevils who love a challenge. The tone of the book toward readers is one of fun-and-games, with a dash of tongue-in-cheek. Rockwell's *How To Fight a Girl* (Watts, 1987) follows the same pattern. It is an excellent choice for a read-aloud or class study.

Recommended Titles for Individual or Group Study

Blume, Judy. *Starring Sally J. Freedman as Herself.* New York: Bradbury Press, 1977. RL: Grade 6. IL: Grades 5–7. PB: Dell.

Sally and her family move to Florida for the winter. Sally has problems adjusting to school, the environment, and classmates. She lives partially in her own dreamworld. Meeting Peter and Harriet adds variety and spice to her life. As she comes to terms with herself, she makes some decisions that have a far-reaching effect.

The tone of *Starring Sally J. Freedman as Herself* is light-hearted and humorous in spite of the problems. Judy Blume's attitude toward her characters is bright and cheerful even when they have problems. Her attitude toward her readers is one of gratitude for acceptance and pleasure in sharing her stories with them.

Conford, Ellen. *Dear Lovey Hart, I Am Desperate*. Boston: Little, Brown & Company, 1975. RL: Grade 5. IL: Grades 7–9. PB: Scholastic.

Carrie writes an advice column for a school newspaper. The column is received well, sometimes with gales of laughter, until her advice is taken seriously.

Conford, Ellen. *We Interrupt This Semester for a Very Important Bulletin*. Boston: Little, Brown & Company, 1979. RL: Grade 5. IL: Grades 7–9. PB: Scholastic.

Carrie is recruited to work on the school newspaper by the editor, whom she finds very interesting. She gets into trouble when she tries to expose a school scandal in the newspaper. After many funny incidents, her interest in the editor finally turns to thoughts of love.

Cresswell, Helen. *Ordinary Jack*. New York: Macmillan, 1977. RL: Grade 6. IL: Grades 6–9. PB: Avon. Cornerstone.

Jack is worried about not having any special talents until his uncle helps him become the family prophet to the eccentric, talented, funny Bagthropes. This is the first book in the Bagthropes series and is a rollicking introduction to this adventurous, comic, and entertaining family.

Danziger, Paula. *It's an Aardvark-Eat-Turtle-World*. New York: Delacorte Press, 1985. RL: Grade 5. IL: Grades 7–10. PB: Dell.

Rosie Wilson just wants to be a part of a real family. When her mother falls in love with Phoebe's father, Rosie's family is increased by Jim and his daughter who come to live with them. Phoebe is a friend of Rosie. There are many amusing incidents as everyone adjusts to the new living patterns. Rosie is part white and part black. Her biracial background becomes a problem when she and Phoebe travel to Canada and Rosie meets and dates Jason. In this amusing and perceptive story, everyone learns that making a real family takes a lot of hard work.

Foley, June. *It's No Crush, I'm in Love.* New York: Delacorte Press, 1982. RL: Grade 6. IL: Grades 7–9.

Annie Cassidy declares that she loves her ninth-grade English teacher. She can imagine marrying a good-looking, scholarly man just like him. Her friend, Susanna, encourages her to do something about her feelings. She volunteers for special English projects to be close to her English teacher. When he needs a research assistant to help with his book, Annie is delighted to be accepted. She follows him around and spies on him in the library. Her favorite book is *Pride and Prejudice,* and she tries to be like the heroine. When her English teacher mentions that he has a surprise to tell her, Annie imagines that he will declare his love for her. What he tells her really is a surprise!

Rodgers, Mary. *Freaky Friday.* New York: Harper & Row, 1973. RL: Grade 4. IL: Grades 5–8. PB: Harper. Cornerstone.

Annabel gets into some hilarious situations when she wakes up one morning to find that she and her mother have switched places. She comes to a better understanding of her mother after trying to cope in the adult world.

Spinelli, Jerry. *Space Station Seventh Grade.* Boston: Little, Brown & Company, 1982. RL: Grade 6. IL: Grades 6–8. PB: Dell.

Jason Herkimer finds that being in the seventh grade has many problems since he is a nobody to the ninth graders. He has to deal with a maturing body, frustrations at home and school, and girls. Humor abounds in this frank, irreverent, and earthy story.

Travers, P. L. *Mary Poppins.* San Diego: Harcourt Brace Jovanovich, 1934, 1962. RL: Grade 7. IL: Grades 6–8.

The Banks family engages an unusual nanny who blows in with the east wind. Mary Poppins has magical powers that she uses to discipline and entice the children. Her empty bag produces many surprises. Mary is a little stuffy and stern but wins over her charges and some readers.

Picture Storybooks for Teaching Tone

Using picture storybooks to teach the literary element of tone is an efficient way to help students understand the author's attitude toward the story and the readers. There are many humorous picture storybooks that can be used for this purpose. The following are a few of these choices:

de Paola, Tomie. *Strega Nona.* Retold and illustrated. Englewood Cliffs, NJ: Prentice-Hall, 1975.

Strega Nona has an apprentice who is greedy and lazy. One day when Strega Nona is away, Big Anthony uses the magic words used by Strega Nona to start spaghetti making. All is well until Big Anthony tries to turn off the magic when the spaghetti starts filling the house, the street, and the town. Strega Nona returns to restore order and to see that a fitting punishment be given to Big Anthony.

Tomie de Paola's retelling in pictures and words of this noodle-head folktale shows his attitude to be one of hilarious exaggeration and robust humor. His tone is one of involving himself and the readers in robust humor and poetic justice. In the *New York Times Book Review* (November 13, 1977), Tomie de Paola states that he writes for children to "instill in them the great love I personally have always had for books."

Gerstein, Mordicai. *Roll Over!* New York: Crown Publishers, 1984.

The little boy gets in his huge bed that already has an assortment of nine unusual animals under the covers. The little one says "Roll over!" So they all roll over and, after opening the fold-out flap, Papa Pig falls out. The little one says "Roll over!" So they all roll over and Mama Mouse falls out. And Brother Beaver, Sister Seal, Aunt Alligator, Uncle Unicorn, Grandpa Goat, Grandma Goose, and Cousin Camel fall out in turn, after opening the fold-out flap of course. Then there is only one little boy left in the bed, and he says "Good night" and goes to sleep. All of the animals crawl back in bed and say "Good night."

The tone of this counting book is one of delight, humor, and surprise. The author's attitude toward the readers (or very young listeners) is one of caring and attention with a dash of bedtime fun.

Mase, Thomas. *What's Gnu? Riddles from the Zoo.* Pictures by Susan Burke. Minneapolis: Lerner Publications, 1990.

Two examples in this collection of zany animal riddles are:

"Q: Which insects are whizzes at math?"
"A: The arithmetick and the inchworm."

"Q: Have crocodiles learned to cook in microwave ovens?"
"A: No. They're still using croc pots."

The tone of the book is one of witty word play and funny situations. The author's statement at the beginning of the book that there are "no bad puns, only people who don't appreciate good word play" sums up his attitude. He obviously enjoys creating and solving puzzles and word games and wants the same thing for his readers.

Parish, Peggy. *Amelia-Bedelia.* Illustrated by Fritz Siebel. New York: Harper & Row, 1963. PB: Scholastic.

Amelia-Bedelia is hired by Mrs. Rogers to clean house. Mrs. Rogers leaves written instructions and Amelia-Bedelia carries out the instructions to the letter—cutting the towels to change them, dusting the furniture with dusting powder, drawing a picture of the drapes, putting the light bulbs outside, and measuring the rice with a measuring tape. Her performance of these absurdities is forgiven when she serves the delicious lemon meringue pie that she baked.

The tone of *Amelia-Bedelia* is one of tongue-in-cheek, exaggerated humor provided through the multiple meaning of words. Taken literally, words are used by the author to create humorous situations. The author's attitude toward the readers is one of fun and games with words.

Viorst, Judith. *Alexander and the Terrible, Horrible, No Good, Very Bad Day.* Illustrated by Ray Cruz. New York: Atheneum, 1972. PB: Aladdin.

Alexander has a very bad day from the time he steps out of bed; he eats his breakfast, rides in the car pool, draws a picture and eats his lunch at school, goes to the dentist, goes shopping for new sneakers, visits his dad's office, gets caught for fighting, watches television, and finally goes to bed at night. He has one terrible misfortune after the other and keeps thinking about going away to Australia. His mother tells him at the end of the day that everyone has this kind of day sometimes, even in Australia.

The tone of this book is one of lighthearted amusement and of reconciliation to the fact that bad days do happen to everyone, but there is always hope for a better day tomorrow. It is a good book for sharing with teachers or other adults as well as children.

TEACHING TIPS: THE HUMOR GENRE AND TONE

The humor genre lends itself to a fun unit with many opportunities for shared laughter and good times. Even the teaching of the literary element, tone, is not difficult and affords a relaxed and light treatment. This is especially true since there is no right or wrong answer to what a person feels or thinks about the attitude of the author to the subject, characters, and readers. Brainstorming and sharing ideas gain significance and greater participation when all ideas are accepted in a positive way.

For a change of pace, begin the unit with riddles, puns, and humorous poetry. Charles Keller's *Driving Me Crazy: Fun on Wheels Jokes* is sure to grab the attention of all students. It contains jokes and riddles about cars, buses, trucks, bicycles, and other vehicles on wheels. They are flip, wacky, and contagious. Examples are: "What happened to the boy who thought he was a muffler? He woke up exhausted."; "What was the turtle doing on the highway? About a half-mile an hour." Let students give thumbs up or thumbs down to show their reactions. There will be plenty of groans and laughs also. For tongue twisters, use Joseph Rosenbloom's *Twist These on Your Tongue*. Copy some of the best of these and ask students to volunteer to read them aloud to the class. Include twisters like "Should Shirley share her shortcake with sharp Sherman, or should Shirley share her shaped sherbet with shy Herman?" and "The zany zoo's zesty zebra zigzags with zeal." For humorous poetry use Shel Silverstein's *Where the Sidewalk Ends,* Lewis Carroll's "Jabberwocky" from *Through the Looking Glass,* or Laura Richard's "Eletelephony." These "teasers" should alert students to the fact that the new genre study unit is humor.

Give the students an overview of humorous literature using notes and ideas from the genre introduction. Let students briefly discuss humorous books that they have read.

Tell the students that the literary element they will study will be tone. Give examples from those provided and add ones of special significance from other sources. Use picture storybooks to illustrate the elements. Remind students to ask themselves questions like "What is the author's tone or attitude in this book?"

Decide if all students will read the same humorous title, if small groups of students will read the same title, or if students will read separate titles. The grade level and reading level of the students will play a big part in determining the teaching strategies. The availability of books should not be a big problem since there are so many humorous paperback books in school library media centers and public libraries. Of course, if all students read the same title, books will have to be ordered ahead of time.

If Avi's book *Romeo and Juliet—Together (and Alive) at Last* is selected for class study, it is suggested that students know the story of Romeo and Juliet. This can be accomplished by letting students listen to a recorded version or summary of the story without detailed study of the play.

Suggestions for activities to use with students during this unit will not only focus on humorous books and tone but will also focus on listening skills. Examples will be given following the introduction to listening skills.

FOCUS ON CRITICAL-THINKING AND COMMUNICATION SKILLS: LISTENING SKILLS

In this information age, people are informed and entertained through listening and viewing as well as reading. Listening is becoming a very important skill because of television, radio, and cassette players. People are seen with headphones and their portable cassettes when they are jogging, walking, and riding bicycles. Car stereos and personal televisions are the order of the day. While children and young people often listen to music, they are still bombarded with advertising. Listening intelligently to these messages can help prepare them to be better consumers.

Listening is an active process that requires attention and mental participation. Candy Carter and Zora Rashkis emphasize this fact in *Ideas for Teaching English in the Junior High and Middle School*. They cite studies done by Ralph Nichols and Leonard Stevens about the discrepancy between speaking and listening rates. Since thinking is five or six times faster than speaking, what does the listener do with the spare thinking time? All too often that time is consumed by daydreaming or thoughts outside of the subject under discussion. Students especially need to be made aware of critical-listening skills to improve their listening ability.

Critical-listening skills include the ability to follow directions, to draw conclusions, to obtain information, to become involved in what the speaker is saying, to be inspired, to be motivated, and to be entertained. Students can be encouraged to review what has been said, to apply what is being said to what they already know, to weigh the pros and cons of what is being said, and to search for meaning.

The following listening skills from Language Arts and Reading Curriculum Guides are desirable goals, competencies, and learner outcomes for promoting good listening skills:

1. Identify the speaker's purpose
2. Demonstrate attention and courtesy to the speaker
3. Identify the speaker's tone or attitude toward the subject and the listeners
4. Identify the speaker's method of appeal (humor, exaggeration, emotions)
5. Demonstrate attention by asking questions either orally or silently to self
6. Evaluate content of message or information by determining fact from opinion and realism from fantasy
7. Adjust listening strategies according to purpose and content
8. Identify and appreciate ethnic or regional speech patterns
9. Identify descriptive language, imagery, and figures of speech
10. Respond to oral performances of literature, music, and drama
11. Identify verbal and nonverbal communication techniques of the speaker
12. Suspend judgment until the speaker concludes the talk

Many of these skills will be emphasized in the suggested learning activities for humor and tone.

ACTIVITIES

Activities Related to Teaching the Humor Genre

To stimulate students to read humorous materials, plan a number of sharing sessions using riddles, puns, jokes, poetry, tall tales, and short stories. Before students share their versions, discuss and give examples of appropriate material for sharing with a class. Explain what types of language and materials are inappropriate and unacceptable.

Read nonsense literature aloud to the class from Carl Sandburg's *Rootabaga Stories* and Edward Lear's *Book of Nonsense*. Discuss listening skills and the need to adjust listening techniques to the purpose and content of the message.

Invite a local author of humorous books, comedian, drama group, or clown to perform at a school assembly. Before the performance, discuss proper etiquette and response to oral performances.

Ask students to write a letter to a favorite author of humorous books. Use Beverly Cleary's *Dear Mr. Henshaw* as a guide.

Show a videotape or movie of one of the classic comedies such as Charlie Chaplin movies, Laurel and Hardy movies, or *I Love Lucy* TV programs.

Ask students to write about their funniest experience. Let them submit their article anonymously. Publish a class newspaper of "Humorous Happenings." If available, let students use a computer desktop publishing program.

With their parents' permission, ask students to share home videos showing humorous episodes.

Activities Related to Teaching Listening Skills

To encourage students to listen carefully and to retain details of oral instructions, tell them that during this unit all assignments and instructions will be given orally. Remind them to listen carefully, ask questions, clarify instructions, and take notes.

Tell the students that during the introductory period, they

will learn about the humor genre and the literary element, tone. Review with them listening strategies for identifying your purpose and your attitude toward the subject and listeners.

Divide the class into small groups. Ask students to tell the funniest incident in the book they read. Let them choose one person from the group to share their funny incident with the rest of the class. Remind students to demonstrate attention and courtesy to the speaker.

Play "Pass It On" with the students. Let them make a large circle. Whisper a message in the ear of the first student in the circle. Let students whisper the message to the person sitting next to them. Take the message from one of the humor books that was read during this unit. Write the message on a slip of paper to keep for comparison after the message has made the rounds. An example of the message is: "From the book *Do Bananas Chew Gum?* Alicia and Sam help Wally find his retainer in the lunch trash." Write down one or two more messages to use if the game is successful and fun for the students.

For an assignment, ask students to write a paragraph describing in exact sequence how to perform some very simple task that they read about in their humor book. Tell them that they will read the directions one at a time, and another student will *listen* and follow the directions. Videotape each group and show the results to the class and perhaps to parents. Following are a few examples:

> *How To Eat Fried Worms:* Recipe for tasty worms (using spaghetti noodles)
> *Bagthorpes Abroad:* How to fight a goat
> *Romeo and Juliet—Together (and Alive) at Last.* How to kiss (using a doll for practice)
> *Anastasia Krupnik:* How to curl your hair

Ask students to record their favorite jokes, riddles, or humorous poetry. Play the tape for the class and donate the cassette to the collection of the library media center.

Work with the library media specialist to prepare a large display of paperback books of the humor genre. Arrange the collection in a highly visible area of the library media center. Hold a contest for the students with amusing clues given for books in this genre. Let students read the clues over the school intercom system.

Students listening to the announcements can go to the library media center and browse through the display of humor books. They can register their answer by placing it in a specially prepared box displaying humorous slogans. The first correct answer drawn will receive a paperback copy of the book. Students who read humorous books for the humor unit can assist in preparing clues for the book that they read.

Read a humorous folktale to the class that contains dialect. Discuss ethnic and regional speech patterns.

Listen to a humorous recording of Bill Cosby such as *Wonderfulness*. Let students identify the speaker's method of appeal.

View and listen to the sound filmstrip series *Meet the Newbery Author: Beverly Cleary*. Ask students to identify the content of the information presented by the author by determining fact from opinion.

Ask students to locate a humorous poem or section from one of the books they read for this unit that contains descriptive language, imagery, or figures of speech.

As a culminating activity, tell the students that they are going to participate in a joint oral creative storytelling session. The story can be slapstick, nonsense, exaggerated humor, or a tall tale. The students are to brainstorm ideas for the story, create characters, and provide amusing incidents. The brief story should be about students their age. Remind them to listen carefully to the brainstorming ideas, because they cannot take or use notes. Record the brainstorming session and the students' creative story. Play both recordings and ask students to compare the two.

Additional Activities

Allow interested students to record picture storybooks to be used by primary grade students as read-alongs.

Ask students to find an amusing comic strip or cartoon to share with the class.

To illustrate the importance of listening and hearing, show a videotape or sound filmstrip *with the sound turned off*. Discuss the result with the students. Talk about the meaning of "Closed-Captioned TV." This may lead to a discussion of the hearing impaired and signing.

Let students create original riddles using the computer program *Riddle Magic,* produced by Mindscape. An excellent guide for this activity is Ron Martin's "Reveling in Ridiculous Riddles" in *Media Production & Computer Activities.*

NONPRINT RESOURCES

Audiocassettes

How To Eat Fried Worms by Thomas Rockwell. Cornerstone Large Print Read-Alongs.
There's a Bat in Bunk Five by Paula Danziger. Caedmon Records.

Computer Program

Riddle Magic. Mindscape Inc.

Record

Wonderfulness: The Amazing Comedy of Bill Cosby. Warner Brothers Records.

Filmstrips

The Cat Ate My Gymsuit by Paula Danziger. Cheshire.
Dear Mr. Henshaw by Beverly Cleary. Random House Media.
The Divorce Express by Paula Danziger. Cheshire.

Videotape

New Adventures of Pippi Longstocking. RCA.

References

Anderson, Celia, and Marilyn Apseloff. *Nonsense Literature for Children.* Hamden, CT: Library Professional Publications, 1989.
Barnet, Sylvan, Morton Berman, and William Burto. *A Dictionary of Literary, Dramatic, and Cinematic Terms.* 2d ed. Boston: Little, Brown & Company, 1971.
Bauer, Caroline Feller. "What's So Funny? Humor in Children's Books." In *Prelude: Mini-Seminars on Using Books Creatively.* Series 3. New York: Children's Book Council, 1977, p. 17.

Carter, Candy, and Zora Rashkis, eds. *Ideas for Teaching English in the Junior High and Middle School.* Urbana, IL: National Council of Teachers of English, 1980.

Cleary, Beverly. "The Laughter of Children," *Horn Book Magazine* 58 (October 1982): 555–564.

Donelson, Kenneth, and Alleen Nilsen. *Literature for Today's Young Adults.* Glenview, IL: Scott, Foresman and Company, 1980.

Hearne, Betsy. *Choosing Books for Children: A Commonsense Guide.* Rev. ed. New York: Delacorte Press, 1990.

Keller, Charles. *Driving Me Crazy: Fun on Wheels Jokes.* New York: Pippin Press, 1989.

Lukens, Rebecca. *A Critical Handbook of Children's Literature.* Glenview, IL: Scott, Foresman and Company, 1981.

Martin, Ron. "Reveling in Ridiculous Riddles." In *Media Production & Computer Activities,* edited by H. Thomas Walker and Paula Montgomery. Santa Barbara, CA: ABC-CLIO, 1990.

Norton, Donna. *Through the Eyes of a Child: An Introduction to Children's Literature.* 2d ed. Columbus, OH: Merrill Publishing Company, 1987.

Rosenbloom, Joseph. *Twist These on Your Tongue.* New York: Thomas Nelson, 1978.

Sandburg, Carl. *Rootabaga Stories.* New York: Harcourt Brace Jovanovich, 1951.

———. *The Sandburg Treasury: Prose and Poetry for Young People.* New York: Harcourt Brace Jovanovich, 1970.

Walker, H. Thomas, and Paula Montgomery, eds. *Media Production & Computer Activities.* Santa Barbara, CA: ABC-CLIO, 1990.

3

Mystery

"Crime fiction has always been, and will remain primarily an entertainment created by popular demand, whether its form is that of detective story, spy, or crime novel."
Julian Symons
"Life of Crime and Detection"

INTRODUCTION

The mystery genre is very popular with children and young adults as well as adults. The whodunits are well established in television series and capture a good share of the best-seller market. Detective stories, mystery and terror, crime, espionage, supernatural, horror, and ghost stories are all part of the mystery genre. They are often described as thrillers, spine-chilling, horrifying, suspenseful, shocking, hideous, entertaining, and mysterious. In general, the genre contains fast-moving stories that maintain interest to the end.

Mystery and detective stories contain some elements of conflict, danger, and revenge. Actions are resolved or explained by clues and discoveries. Ghost stories and horror stories include supernatural characters or events couched in suspenseful plots. Crime and espionage stories contain anything from simple petty thefts and uncomplicated spy adventures to violence and complicated international intrigue, depending upon the intended audience. In most stories of this genre for children and young people, there is triumph of good over evil.

The plot is all-important in mysteries; it carries most of the stories. The arrangement of the story or sequence of events usually has a rising action, a climax, and a falling action. In simplified terms, the protagonist becomes involved in a conflict, struggles against opposing forces, helps make discoveries or find clues, and contributes to the resolution of the conflict. Great excitement, drama, and suspense unfold in fast-paced plots that interweave suspicion, motives, and clues.

To young thrill-seekers reading mysteries, action and adventure absorb and hold their interest. Nancy Larrick states that books with "mystery, secret, or ghosts" in the title have a magnetic effect on children. Young readers get involved with the story, solve baffling cases, find answers for puzzling mysteries, and genuinely relish chilling stories of ghosts and supernatural beings. They want to be scared, awed, and stimulated. Donna Norton stresses this in her book, *Through the Eyes of a Child,* stating that an eleven-year-old girl who is an avid reader of mysteries lists the following characteristics that make mysteries enjoyable to her: exciting plot that holds interest, suspense, and many well-written clues to enable the reader to follow the action. Readers like to become involved in the solution. The mystery genre promotes rapid silent reading as readers speed up their reading to find answers and solve mysteries.

The age-old question still persists: Is it wrong for books to contain frightening or scary incidents and pictures? There remains controversy over some nursery rhymes, such as *Grimm's Fairy Tales, Hansel and Gretel, Bambi, The Adventures of Tom Sawyer,* and *Where the Wild Things Are.* Of course, some of the problem deals with using these books with young children, but there is enough debate over the issue of using scary books with older children to warrant a close look at books in the mystery genre. Stephen King, a well-known author in this genre, discusses this question in an article entitled "Let's Scare Dick and Jane" in the May 11, 1986, edition of *Book World.* He argues that the idea many people have that "it is wrong to scare the kids" is a judgment by people who want children to remain childlike for as long as possible. He expresses the idea that children have a great mental stability and their own set of "emotional muscles" to develop. He agrees that to children terrors are black indeed and that these terrors need to be faced. His advice is to discuss such a story after it is read, asking "What was the best part?" but never asking "What was the scariest part?" He believes that "children need make-believe fears in their lives." Of course, most of Stephen King's horror novels with violence, monsters, blood, and chaos are not children's stories. Other writers suggest that frightening topics can help children rather than hurt them, if everything is safely resolved in the end or if frightening things are brought out into the open and named and discussed. Betsy Hearne, in *Choosing Books for Children*, says that one big objection in children's books during the 1980s was to anything supernatural. She cites criticism of her positive review of Eve Bunting's *Scary, Scary Halloween*, in which she claims the story "will inspire shivers of delight in any darkened room." One critical response said that this type of book will frighten and corrupt young children. Betsy Hearne emphasizes that parent and adult involvement with children's reading concerning what is good, bad, evil, cruel, upsetting, or worthwhile is a viable alternative to censorship. By skillful reading, talking, and communicating with students and parents, problem elements in mystery stories can be overcome or lessened.

Well-written mysteries have dialogue that is credible, fast-moving plots, suspenseful moods, incidents that must be puzzled over, foreshadowing, and language that is picturesque. They move quickly to a satisfying conclusion. Some good mysteries leave unexplained incidents and open-ended solutions to heighten the effect of the story.

Poorly written mysteries have contrived plots, actions, and events that are not accounted for or resolved, boring details, flat characters, inferior style, "pat" solutions, and sensational details. Many series books, like the Nancy Drew and Hardy Boys books, contain some of the elements of poorly written mysteries. Other poorly written mystery stories contain violence and sensational material that is exploitive and mindless. A careful reading and screening of mysteries not on recommmended or suggested reading lists is especially important for books that are chosen for class study.

Mysteries cut across other genres in that some of them are stories of animals, historical fiction, fantasy, science fiction, adventure, or realistic fiction. The elements of suspense, danger, whodunits with cases to be solved, ghosts, and supernatural happenings requiring solutions solidify the components of the mystery genre.

Mystery writers of special appeal to children and young people include Joan Aiken, John Bellairs, Ellen Raskin, Eve Bunting, Avi, Donald Sobol, Virginia Hamilton, Joan Lowry Nixon, and Mary

Stewart. Short stories selected by Alfred Hitchcock also are very popular.

ELEMENT OF LITERATURE: FOCUS ON PLOT

Plot is defined in various ways as the author's plan for presenting the essential facts, sequence of events, action, or arrangement of the story. It is a controlling frame or pattern showing the relationship among the incidents that give the story structure and unity. Plot refers to any narrative pattern in which things move and happen. The happenings are connected for a reason, motive, or purpose. The emphasis is on the cause of the events in the narrative. Plot is the sequence of events showing the actions of the characters. Things happen in fiction to characters who have certain personalities as they respond to other people with different personalities. A good example of this is *Devil's Race*, by Avi, where John Proud responds to a demon ancestor who has the same name. Plot can be described as a series of happenings that reveal and influence character. The story has an introduction, complication, and resolution.

The patterns of action define the plot. The action can move from one incident to another, building to one or more crises. This can be diagrammed as a line moving diagonally upward, crossed by points of climax. The plot or arrangement of happenings often has a rising action, climax, and falling action. This sort of plot can be diagrammed as a pyramid with the crises rising to a climax and then descending. A good plot has its moments of tension produced by conflict. An example of a good plot in a mystery book is Ellen Raskin's *The Westing Game*. It is wildly imaginative, full of exciting clues, tricky, word-twisting, and moves rapidly from one incident to another to a satisfying conclusion.

The arrangement of the episodes in a narrative helps to build or create the plot. The most common arrangement is chronological order. Other ways of relating events are through dreams, daydreams, memories, and flashbacks. Chronological order, or the relating of events in the order that they happen, is generally used in stories for young children since flashbacks can be confusing. An example of a mystery story with chronological order is Mary Downing Hahn's *Following the Mystery Man;* one with flashbacks is *Night Fall*, by Joan Aiken, in which a frightening dream keeps recurring.

Conflict of opposing forces or wills occurs when some problem or difficulty arises. Tension, friction, struggles, clashes, discovery, strategies, and resolutions are parts of conflict. The conflict can be person-against-self, person-against-person, person-against-society, and person-against-nature. The protagonist struggles against one of the types of conflicts and usually is successful in overcoming, outwitting, or overthrowing the antagonist or opposing force.

Plots can be simple or complex. The simplest of plots is found in short stories where a single character or characters are involved in a single incident or crisis. In longer narratives, one or more characters are involved in a number of experiences that bring about a climax and resolution. In a dramatic plot, the protagonist is a central character with whom the reader may identify or sympathize. To solve the problem or conflict the protagonist may encounter difficulties, hardships, unexpected happenings, reversals, and complications. These lead to a climax where the protagonist succeeds or fails. In an episodic plot, the protagonist moves through a series of episodes or loosely connected actions or adventures toward an objective or goal. Complex plots involve multiple-plot narratives. They are very difficult to follow and are not usually a part of stories for children.

Subplots are secondary plots that may add variety and detail to the story. They are often used to describe the actions and conflicts of less important characters. They help to create mood, suspense, and excitement.

Good plots are convincingly real, gripping, and satisfying. They help the readers to lose themselves in the story. They answer questions and show the outcome of a series of events.

Plots in mystery stories for children and young people contain action and suspense; they "grab the reader." The plot is an all-important ingredient in mystery stories, from the simple plot that asks "what next?" to the complex plot with subplots. The following plot summaries range from humorous animal detectives, musical sleuths, and a haunted house, to a race with a demon.

RECOMMENDED LISTS

Recommended Titles for Teaching the Mystery Genre Unit

There are many books in the mystery genre that are suitable for this teaching unit. These include paperback and large-print editions. Choosing the right book or books for a particular class will depend on the reading levels, grade levels, grouping methods, methods of presentation, and time allotted for the unit. The suggested titles allow for the whole language approach, reading groups, and students with special needs. The reading levels *and* the interest levels serve as clues to picking the right books.

Aiken, Joan. *Night Fall.* New York: Holt, Rinehart and Winston, 1969. RL: Grade 7. IL: Grades 7–12. PB: Dell.

When Meg is nine years old, her mother and stepfather, famous movie stars, are killed in an automobile accident. Meg is sent to England to live with her father, a doctor. He is cool and aloof. Meg is miserable and lonely until she makes friends with neighbors, Polly and George. Meg has nightmares; each one is exactly the same. She sees a very steep cliff, she feels herself falling, she is badly hurt, and she sees the face of a man. The recurring nightmares persist into her adult life. Meg becomes a portrait painter and is engaged to George, a successful businessman. Because of the nightmares, Meg decides to talk to her mother's sister about them. Her aunt explains that when Meg was five years old, she was badly hurt in a fall. This happened in a small village in Cornwall where Meg and her mother were staying. Meg decides to visit the village in an attempt to discover the source of her nightmares. The village is almost deserted. It is under the control of one man who will not let any changes be made or businesses be established. Meg finds the cliff where she fell but also finds information about a murder that took place around the same time. It involved twin brothers; one was murdered, and the other one is the man who controls the town. Meg meets Mark, the son of the murdered man, and he escorts Meg around the area. Meg draws the portrait of the man in her nightmares, and Mark is astonished because it is a portrait of the twins. Strange things begin to happen to Meg to frighten her into leaving. She and Mark are invited to dinner in the family mansion high on the cliff where Mark's uncle lives. Mark gets called away on an emergency, and Meg goes to the mansion alone. Meg has a very frightening experience as she unravels the clues to her nightmares and to the murder as well.

The plot is a complicated one with subplots. It is told as a memory, in dreams, and in flashbacks. It is very suspenseful and intriguing. Since the protagonist is a young adult, it is more suitable for older students, grade 8 and up.

Avi. *Devil's Race*. New York: Avon, 1984. RL: Grade 5. IL: Grades 8–10.

Sixteen-year-old John Proud begins to research his family history for a school assignment. He learns from elderly Uncle Dave that he has the same name as his great-great-great-grandfather who was hanged in 1854 for murder. Just before his death, he told the people that he was a demon and that he would return. The young John Proud begins to have very strange feelings and decides to visit his Uncle Dave to find out more about the other John Proud. They travel to the Proud family home place and visit with distant cousins. John wants to go to the cemetery to see the grave, but the family discourages this. Finally John, accompanied by Ann, gets to the cemetery and sees and talks with the first John Proud. The two Johns are mirror images. The demon, John, tells the young John that he is needed to provide him with shape, size, and being. The young John will remain in control, but everything he wishes for will be carried out by the demon, John. Young John Proud finds himself in deep trouble as his nightmares become realities. He is accused of crimes that he did not commit and causes things to happen that he does not like. Ann becomes deeply involved with both John Prouds. The confrontation and resolution takes place at Devil's Run.

The plot in *Devil's Race* is a complex plot told in chronological order by the protagonist. It actually involves two protagonists, one a mortal and one a demon. The interweaving of the two John Prouds and incidents involving each of them are gripping and suspenseful. The underlying theme is complex. The climax and surprising resolution are interesting and well done. The story is suited for older children and young adults.

Bellairs, John. *The Spell of the Sorcerer's Skull*. New York: Dial Press, 1984. RL: Grade 5. IL: Grades 7–10.

Young Johnny Dixon goes on a trip with his friend, Professor Childermass. An innkeeper where they are staying tells them about a clock he has that is called the Childermass Clock. The clock has a tiny room that is a replica of a late-1800s Victorian room in the Childermass family home. The room is complete with shelves, books, and a miniature skull. The professor accidentally touches the skull and receives a bad shock. Later, Johnny is mysteriously drawn to the little room and picks up the skull when it rolls on the floor. He puts it in his pocket and takes it home. He tries but is unable to talk about the skull. One night, Johnny and his friend, Fergie, see a weird jack-o'-lantern in the professor's window. Johnny investigates and sees the professor's face in an image in a mirror, silently mouthing the words "help me." The professor then disappears. Johnny enlists the aid of the parish priest, St. Anthony, and Fergie to locate the professor. A vision he sees while on a ferryboat to Maine makes Johnny throw the miniature skull overboard. Clues lead Johnny, the priest, and Fergie to a clock museum where they again see the Childermass Clock. Research at the library provides additional clues. Sinister things happen as they discover the bewildered professor on an island. There is a real battle when black magic is confronted with a crucifix, prayers, and words from the mass. The secret of the Childermass Clock is revealed after a terrifying experience involving all of the characters.

The plot is a complex plot told in chronological order, with some incidents in the past told from memories. The plot is involved with many facets. The priest adds a different element. The incidents are entangled with weird and bizarre happenings, including the unleashing of demonic forces. The climax is spine-chilling, and the resolution answers many questions.

Brittain, Bill. *Who Knew There'd Be Ghosts?* New York: Harper & Row, 1985. RL: Grade 5. IL: Grades 4–7.

Tommy Donahue narrates his ghostly tale of the old Parnell House in Bramton. He and his friends, Harry the Blimp and Wendy the Books, love to play imaginative games on the grounds of the deserted house. The town had wanted to make it into a museum but did not have the money. Tommy, Harry, and Books go into the house a couple of times but feel like they are being watched, so they decide to play outside. When Tommy overhears his father, a real estate agent, say that someone might buy the old house, the trio tries to think up ways of saving their playground. They spy on two men who are looking over the Parnell House and discover that the men want something hidden in the house rather than the house itself. They plan to search the house at night. One of the men is an antique dealer, Avery Katkus. To protect their playground, Tommy, Harry, and Books decide to take turns in the Parnell House at night. Tommy spends the first night in the house and is terrified when he meets the head of a man who talks to him. He learns that Horace and his sister, Essie, are ghosts whose bodies were not returned to the home place for burial in the family cemetery. Their spirits were condemned to abide in the house forever. Tommy becomes friends with both Horace and Essie and is more determined than ever to protect the house. Harry and Books do not believe Tommy's story until they meet the ghosts. The ghosts assist the trio in fighting off the intruder as he tries to search the house. The ghosts cannot think of anything valuable that is stored in the house; the only things they remember are a ring, notes, and a journal from 1776. Avery Katkus still tries to buy the house, but Tommy, Harry, and Books try to block the sale. They trick Avery Katkus into the Parnell House, where Horace and Essie terrify him and hold him captive. The mayor and city council are ready to vote for the sale when Tommy raises the question of where the ghosts will live if the house is sold. The mayor, council, police, and townspeople accompany the young people to the Parnell House, where they confront Avery Katkus and meet the ghosts. They find the valuable hidden object and make the house into a museum. People come from far and near to see the house and hear about the ghosts.

The plot is a simple plot told as a memory of last summer by the narrator. The conflict is person-against-person and person-against-spirits. The incidents, even with the ghosts, are exciting and believable. The clues are easy to follow. The resolution is satisfying and open-ended.

Hahn, Mary Downing. *Following the Mystery Man.* New York: Avon, 1988. RL: Grade 5. IL: Grades 6–9.

Madigan, who is 12 years old, lives with her grandmother in a small town in Maryland. Her mother is dead, and she does not know anything about her father. She keeps daydreaming that someday her father will come and take her to his home. Angie is Madigan's best friend. Madigan and Angie want to become private investigators when they are grown so that they can lead exciting lives catching criminals. One day, a handsome stranger comes into the drugstore where Madigan and Angie are hanging out. He asks for directions to the house of Mrs. Porter, Madigan's grandmother. He wants to rent a room there. His name is Clint James. As future detectives, Madigan and Angie are determined to find out as much as they can about him. Clint is very friendly and very pleasant and seems to be enjoying the atmosphere at the Porter's. He does not reveal much of his background, but his kindness to Madigan makes her believe that he is her father. Angie is not so sure. Clint keeps very late hours; he drives away each night in his old van. He takes Madigan fishing one day and asks a lot about the houses in the wealthy part of town as they pass by. A number of burglaries take place in the town that summer. Madigan and Angie decide to look through Clint's room when he is not there. They find a pistol in one of his boots. They do not intend to tell, but Clint suspects that someone has been in his room and tells about the pistol. Grandmother Porter advises him to get rid of the gun. Angie's older sister, Alice, has a young son named Chad. Alice is estranged from her family because she has never given the name of Chad's father. Angie and Madigan sometimes babysit for Chad without approval from Angie's family. Madigan and Angie suspect that Alice is involved in some way with Clint. Madigan spies on a secret meeting between Clint and Alice and learns that Clint is both the burglar and Alice's husband. When Madigan is discovered, Clint kidnaps her and takes her away with Alice and Chad. Alice finally helps Madigan to escape.

The plot is a simple plot told in chronological order. The subplots involve Alice and Clint and Madigan's search for her father. There are a number of clues provided throughout the story. Foreshadowing is used to reduce some of the surprise. The incidents involve person-against-person and person-against-self. The resolution fulfills the reader's expectations. This is an easy-to-read, suspenseful mystery.

Howe, James. *Howliday Inn*. New York: Avon, 1982. RL: Grade 6. IL: Grades 4–7.

Chester, the cat, and Harold, the dog, are taken to a special pet-boarding establishment when their owners go on vacation. Chateau Bow-Wow consists of nine bungalows housing an assortment of dogs and a cat. Dr. Greenbriar leaves Jill and Harrison, two young people, in charge of the pets. Jill is very devoted to her work, but Harrison is lazy and greedy. Harrison is left alone when Jill becomes upset and goes home early. Louise, a French poodle, disappears after a jealous argument with Max. Clues lead to possible poisoning and murder. A pair of howling dachshunds are suspected of being werewolves. When Chester and Harold try to solve the mysteries of the missing Louise and the strange dachshunds, Chester also disappears. Alone, Harold is not much of a private eye. When Chester is returned to his bungalow after being abducted by Harrison, the two of them are able to solve the case.

The plot of *Howliday Inn* is a simple plot told in chronological order. The clues are easy to follow, and the climax and resolution bring a satisfying conclusion for young readers.

Kidd, Ronald. *Sizzle and Splat.* New York: Dell, 1983. RL: Grade 6. IL: Grades 6–10.

Sizzle is a star trumpet player who plays in the high school band and in the Pirelli Youth Orchestra. She is also the chairperson of the musicians' steering committee. Splat is a high school senior who transfers to Westside High. He plays the tuba and wants to join the youth orchestra. The youth orchestra is in financial trouble. Sizzle and her committee visit a famous composer and ask him to compose a piece for their orchestra to play at their fund-raising concert. The composer, Mr. Klieman, loves games and puzzles. He is ill with cancer, but before he dies, he composes a Trumpet Concerto and sends it to the youth orchestra conductor, Mr. Pirelli. He secretly sends Sizzle a copy and a letter explaining a game in the message of a cryptogram. The cryptogram is to be solved during intermission and provides a large monetary prize for anyone solving the puzzle. The concert is a guaranteed success until there is a kidnapping and a message that the concerto must not be played at the concert. Sizzle and Splat get involved in solving the kidnapping and strange request. Their assumptions of the guilty parties lead them into some hilarious, hair-raising, and dangerous experiences. After solving the cryptogram, they have the needed clues to solve the mystery. Even then, the solution contains a surprise for them.

The plot in *Sizzle and Splat* is simple with several subplots told in chronological order. The conflict is person-against-person. The minor characters are involved in the subplots and create incidents that entangle Sizzle and Splat. The protagonists proceed from one crisis to another, creating excitement and entertainment. The clues are disguised and involved. The resolution is credible and the conclusion fulfilling.

Raskin, Ellen. *The Westing Game.* New York: E. P. Dutton, 1978. RL: Grade 7. IL: Grades 7–10. PB: Avon. Cornerstone.

Six families receive letters inviting them to move to Sunset Towers Apartments. Unbeknownst to them, they are chosen tenants-to-be, except for one who is a mistake. Office space and restaurant space is also rented to them. The intricate plot follows different characters for short periods of time. An eccentric millionaire businessman, Samuel W. Westing, dies or is murdered and leaves a fortune to 16 heirs. Instructions are left that include pairing the heirs to form eight pairs, a different set of clues for each pair, and a sum of $10,000 to each pair. The heirs must uncover the circumstances of Sam Westing's death before they can claim the inheritance. They are told that it is not what they have but what they don't have that counts. Notes are exchanged as they are tacked to the elevator's back wall. Each pair of heirs tries to get information from the other heirs. Accidents, bomb scares, and fires all reflect the warning of Sam Westing's "heir's beware." Young Turtle Wexler, known variously as the "kicking witch," "stock market genius," "mischievous daughter," and "understanding sister," is the zany character who finds the clues and helps the reader put the pieces of the puzzle together.

The plot is described as a "puzzle-knotted, word-twisting plot." It is a complex plot using chronological order. The many characters, unusual clues, and exciting and dangerous incidents lead to a very interesting climax and unique resolution.

This is an excellent story for sharing. It can be read to a class or by individuals and discussed and shared by the entire class. The sharing will assist readers in keeping up with all of the characters and clues.

Recommended Titles for Individual or Group Study

Bellairs, John. *House with a Clock in Its Walls.* New York: Dial Press, 1973. RL: Grade 5. IL: Grades 5–7. PB: Bantam.

Lewis goes to live with his uncle Jonathan in an old mansion with many rooms. It is a mysterious house with many hiding places and a secret passageway. Uncle Jonathan practices white magic, which is fun but not harmful. The former owner of the house, Issac Izard, practiced black magic that was evil. Before he died he made a doomsday clock that would bring about the end of the world. The clock constantly ticks, but Lewis and Uncle Jonathan cannot find it. Strange problems arise when Lewis brings Selena Izard back to life, since she has a special connection to the clock.

Garfield, Leon. *Smith.* New York: Pantheon, 1967. RL: Grade 8. IL: Grades 7–10. PB: Dell. Yearling.

The perils of street life in eighteenth-century London are the background for this story about the life of a young pickpocket, Smith, who steals a document from a man who is murdered soon afterward. The murderer pursues Smith, who is given sanctuary by a judge. Smith goes to prison but escapes into a trap. This well-written, exciting, and suspenseful story is recommended for advanced readers.

Hamilton, Virginia. *The House of Dies Drear.* New York: Macmillan, 1968. RL: Grade 5. IL: Grades 5–9. PB: Macmillan.

Thomas is told by his professor father about the history of the house they are about to rent. The house was once a station on the Underground Railway and belonged to Dies Drear, an abolitionist. Secret tunnels, movable wall panels, buried treasure, and rumors of ghosts create excitement, drama, and suspense.

Peck, Richard. *The Ghost Belonged to Me.* New York: Viking, 1975. RL: Grade 6. IL: Grades 5–8. PB: Dell. Cornerstone.

Young Alexander's life changes drastically when he meets the sobbing, restless ghost Inez and begins to believe in the reality of ghosts. Blossom Culp and her spiritualist mother force Alexander to listen to the predictions. Alexander tries to prevent a serious accident from happening and involves the town in his ghost story. It is a scary but humorous story.

Raskin, Ellen. *Mysterious Disappearance of Leon (I Mean Noel)*. New York: E. P. Dutton, 1971. RL: Grade 5. IL: Grades 5–9.

False identity and mysteries are solved when the names of things are made clear and true. Wit and invention aid in this solve-your-own mystery with many clues and instructions.

Sobol, Donald. *Encyclopedia Brown Sets the Pace*. New York: Scholastic, 1982. RL: Grade 5. IL: Grades 5–7. PB: Apple.

This collection of ten mysteries is a new series of cases featuring Encyclopedia Brown, who is filled with facts that he uses to solve crimes. He helps his father, the police chief, by unraveling the clues. Mysteries involving a thief and a bully are solved by detective Encyclopedia Brown and his partner, Sally Kimball. Readers are invited to use the clues to solve the mystery.

Picture Storybooks for Teaching Plot

The plots in picture storybooks are very simple and very easy to read. They can be used to help students understand the meaning of a plot and to share an example of a plot. Reading easy storybooks where word recognition and comprehension are not a problem can facilitate the understanding of the plot. This can also be a confidence builder for students when they read more complicated books and search for the plot.

Bennett, Jill. *Teeny Tiny*. Illustrated by Tomie de Paola. New York: G. P. Putnam's Sons, 1986.

This short, suspenseful story is an old folktale about a teeny tiny woman who finds a teeny tiny bone. She places it in her cupboard while she tries to take a nap. She hears a soft voice cry, "I want my bone." Trying to hide from the voice, she ducks under the cover. She trembles as the voice gets louder and louder, demanding the bone. She becomes very frightened when the voice screams, "Give me my bone!" In reply, she throws off the covers and yells, "Take it!"

Kellogg, Steven. *The Mystery of the Stolen Blue Paint*. New York: Dial Press, 1982.

Belinda has her room all fixed up with blue and white accessories. She needs a blue picture to hang over her desk. She decides to take her painting supplies, blue paint, and her dog outside to paint her picture. She and Homer hide as Belinda sees her pesky cousin, Jason, coming out of the library. Jason thinks that Belinda is playing cops and robbers. Belinda tells Jason that she is on her way to paint a picture. Jason asks if she wouldn't rather read to him. Jason finds Simon and LouAnne, and the three of them bring all kinds of paintbrushes. Belinda tells them that she only has one little jar of blue paint and that there is not enough for four artists. She tells them that if they go and play she will read to them later. They decide to stay and watch. It gets very windy, and Belinda's picture is blown away. She chases it and returns to find that her blue paint is gone. She decides that this is a case for Inspector Belinda Baldini and her trusty police dog. She is sure that one of the little kids took it. Inspector Belinda goes to the apartment building where the little kids live and asks what happened to her paint. She tells them that if they do not confess, she will not read to them again. She asks the kids to line up for an inspection as she looks for traces of blue paint. She decides to ask Homer, her trusty police dog, which one is the culprit. Homer licks the kids and gets blue paint on all of them. He has a blue tongue. He is the guilty one; Homer ate the paint.

The plot can be simplified by stating that Belinda is painting a picture with blue paint. The paint disappears. The suspects are the kids who are watching Belinda as she paints. The motive appears to be that the kids are mad because Belinda will not read to them or will not share her paint with them. The clues are the empty jar, the sleeping dog nearby, and the kids leaving the scene of the crime. The kids are confronted and searched for evidence—traces of blue paint. The suspects are cleared after Homer, the police dog, is found with blue paint on his tongue. The solution is satisfying: Belinda admits that she was wrong and agrees to read to the suspects.

Viorst, Judith. *My Mama Says There Aren't Any Zombies, Ghosts, Vampires, Creatures, Demons, Monsters, Fiends, Goblins, or Things.* Illustrated by Kay Chorao. New York: Macmillan, 1973.

Nick is afraid of all kinds of wild creatures he creates with his vivid imagination. He keeps telling his Mama about them, but she keeps telling him that these creatures do not exist. Nick is not reassured, because he keeps recalling instances when his mother was wrong. The climax is reached when he finally decides that, even though mamas do make mistakes sometimes, they are sometimes right.

TEACHING TIPS: THE MYSTERY GENRE AND PLOT

Mystery stories used in teaching literature can provide pleasurable experiences for students and teachers. Whodunits, ghosts, and spine-chilling stories appeal to most students on the reading grade levels of 5–9. Good reading experiences with mystery stories build the foundation for good experiences with books in other genres. Begin the unit by reading or telling a scary short story, showing a sinister videotape or filmstrip, or playing a shivery recording of a ghost story. If the unit is started around Halloween, make use of decorations, costumes, sound effects, and an eerie atmosphere. Ask the library media specialist to tell a story or to suggest a recorded one. Suggestions for read-alouds include stories from *Spirits, Spooks, and Other Sinister Creatures,* compiled by Helen Hoke, and *Alfred Hitchcock's Ghostly Gallery* or *Alfred Hitchcock's Supernatural Tales of Terror and Suspense,* edited by Alfred Hitchcock. An excellent source for scary stories to tell is Margaret MacDonald's *When the Lights Go Out: Twenty Scary Tales To Tell.*

Tell the students that this unit of study will feature mystery stories and their plots. Using the introductory material and other resources, discuss the mystery genre. Students may want to share titles or authors of favorite mysteries. Inform the students that they will be learning about plots and critical-thinking skills throughout this unit. Use picture storybooks to introduce the study of plot. Read and show the illustrations of one or more of the suggested mystery picture storybooks, and ask the students to recall the plot. Discuss the principles of plot using the background notes and other supporting data. Borrow enough mystery storybooks for each student to have a copy or enough for small groups of students to have a copy. Let the students read the story and tell the plot. To review the elements of mysteries and plots with the entire class, use a large paper skeleton. Explain that the plot is like a skeleton on which the other story elements can be built. Help the students give "flesh" to the bones as they relate incidents and story elements.

Depending upon the method selected for grouping students for the mystery study unit, carefully choose or let students choose the stories. See the recommended titles for mystery teaching units and additional suggested titles already provided. If students are to select a mystery story of their choice, provide assistance by asking the library media specialist to reserve and display mystery stories. Review the card catalog subject headings such as: MYSTERY AND DETECTIVE STORIES—FICTION and SUPERNATURAL—FICTION. If the computer programs *BookWhiz* or *BookBrain* are available, students can use them to assist in their selection of a mystery story.

The activities before, during, and after the mystery unit study will vary according to the goals and objectives and the methods of teaching. If all students read the same story or have the story read to them, plan to ask questions at intervals that encourage understanding of the plot, infer meaning, and predict outcomes. If students work in small groups, prepare questions that they can discuss with other group members. If students read individual titles, plan to hold individual conferences during silent reading time in class. Ideas for other activities are included in this chapter.

FOCUS ON CRITICAL-THINKING AND COMMUNICATION SKILLS: READING CRITICALLY

The poor performance of students in 1988 on a test for the National Assessment of Educational Progress points to the need for greater emphasis on critical-thinking and communication skills in all grade levels. In this information age, students must have many opportunities to practice comprehension and abstract reasoning skills and to communicate facts, information, ideas, and concepts. By integrating these skills through activities into literature units like the mystery unit, students can develop some of these skills in a meaningful and enjoyable way.

Since this mystery unit focuses on the plot of the story, the following critical-thinking skills can be successfully emphasized:

1. Identify and explain cause-and-effect relationships
2. Detect plotting structures such as foreshadowing, flashback, climax, and resolution

3. Make inferences and generalizations
4. Separate fact from opinion
5. Make predictions
6. Draw conclusions

By using the suggested mystery unit activities and adding relevant teaching strategies, students can be guided toward meeting these competencies.

ACTIVITIES

Activities Related to Teaching the Mystery Genre

To provide one of the best examples of the mystery genre, read aloud one of Edgar Allan Poe's short stories to the class or provide a listening tape. *The Purloined Letter* is an excellent choice. In a large discussion group, review the story and help students to understand the plotting structures of foreshadowing, climax, and resolution. Let a small group of students locate biographical information on Poe. Include information concerning the continuing mystery of the unknown person who puts a flower and a bottle of whiskey on Poe's grave on his birthday.

Obtain several copies of *Two-Minute Mysteries* by Donald Sobol. Randomly assign students to small groups. Let group members take turns reading one of the short mysteries aloud to the group, while the other members try to solve the case by making predictions and drawing conclusions.

Discuss the controversy of scary books for children. Include the censorship issue and banned books like Sendak's *Where the Wild Things Are* or Eve Bunting's *Scary, Scary Halloween*. Ask students to list reasons both pro and con concerning the use of scary books for children. Combine the lists and make copies for each student. Ask students to review the list and determine if the reasons are based on fact or opinion. Remind them that facts can be verified, but opinions cannot. Discuss the answers.

Ask students in upper grades to obtain permission from their parents to watch a detective/mystery story on television such as *Murder, She Wrote* or *Matlock*, or a current program of this type. Tell students to write a generalization of the program in one paragraph, dealing only with the main elements. If students need help with this activity, provide a written example for them.

The mystery genre includes numerous series of books. Most students will be familiar with these mystery series: Nancy Drew, Hardy Boys, Three Investigators, Great Brain, and Encyclopedia Brown. Plan an activity that will let students form their own critical evaluation of the series. Obtain copies of series books and divide students into groups so that each group will take one series to study. For example, one group will have the Nancy Drew books, and another group the Hardy Boys books. Include books from the old series and the new series, "Nancy Drew Case Files" and "Hardy Boys Case Files." Other groups can read books from the Great Brain or Encyclopedia Brown series. Ask each student to read one book from his or her group's series and make a written summary of the plot. Give the students group time to discuss the book they read with other group members. Encourage the students to discuss the similarities of all the plots in the series. Ask the group to write a critical analysis of the series to share in large-group time. While the group members are working on the critical analysis, tell them to have one or two students go to the library media center to compile information about the author of the series. Some students will be surprised to find that both Carolyn Keene and Franklin Dixon are pseudonyms that were begun under the Edward Stratemeyer Syndicate. In large-group sharing time, allow each group to present their critical analysis and present information on the authors. Ask students to relate some of the changes in the new Nancy Drew and Hardy Boys series. Discuss the Stratemeyer Syndicate and the *formula* writing that is predictable, patterned, and success-oriented. Discuss other series books by such authors as Donald Sobol and John Fitzgerald and compare them with formula writing. Draw an analogy between Ellen Raskin's books and series books. Let students draw their own conclusions about series books.

Activities Related to Teaching Critical-Reading Skills

To strengthen skills of analyzing, inference, generalizing, and drawing conclusions, ask students to bring a newspaper article to class about some recent crime or mystery. Review the articles and let students tell what questions are answered in the article. Assist them in determining answers to what, where, when, who, and why.

Ask students to write a newspaper article about the mystery, crime, or supernatural event that they read about in one book they read during this mystery unit. Tell them that they are to write the article as if it actually happened. If the setting is in ancient times, the students are to write the article for a journal rather than a newspaper. The students are to include the following information in their article:

WHAT: What crime, murder, kidnapping, mystery, disappearance, or unusual occurrence takes place

WHERE: Specific details of place: city, town, country, home, school, train, garage, gym, graveyards, or abandoned house

WHEN: Time of occurrence: night, day, day of week, month, or year; period of time covered in kidnapping, hunt for suspects, or tracking clues

WHO: Who are the victims, the detectives or crime solvers, the witnesses, the main characters involved, and the supporting cast

WHY: Why the crime was committed: reward, treasure, revenge, money, or supernatural involvement

Tell the students that they can also add information about clues that assisted in solving the mystery. Be sure to remind students to include the author, title, publisher, and copyright date for the book they read. Choose the best articles and post them on a bulletin board or publish them in a class newspaper.

To assist students in making predictions and drawing conclusions, select short mystery stories to read to the class. A suggested title is *Tales from Alfred Hitchcock's Mystery Magazine,* compiled by Cathleen Jordan and Cynthia Manson. Read a section, then stop and ask students to predict what will happen. After completing the story, let students draw conclusions about the outcome, the credibility of the story, and the significance of the clues.

To reinforce the significance of the plot, ask students to write a brief paragraph describing the plot of one mystery story read during the unit. Remind them to include the beginning, the episodes, the climax, and the resolution. More advanced students can include plotting structures of foreshadowing and flashback.

To allow creativity, divide the class into several small groups.

Ask each group to make an outline of a mystery story with a teenage protagonist that they would enjoy reading. As a guide for the outline, the students should use the Ws: WHAT, WHERE, WHEN, WHO, WHY. As a group they will decide on the crime, the setting, the characters, and the motive. Tell the students that they do not have to write the story, but they should have an idea of the plot. Encourage them to think of creative ways to present the outline to the class using props and audiovisual aids. Allow all groups to present their outlines to the class.

Additional Activities

Plan a bulletin board featuring the mystery genre with articles, annotations, mystery writers, and clues. Ask students to contribute items for the display.

Ask students to select a favorite mystery author for whom they will compile an annotated bibliography of books and a bibliographic sketch.

Let students select a short mystery story to record using sound effects. They may want to divide the parts using a narrator and different students to read the dialogue of each character.

Encourage students to act out and videotape one of the mystery stories from the children's picture storybooks, such as *Teeny Tiny,* to show to elementary students.

NONPRINT RESOURCES

Audiocassette

The Purloined Letter by Edgar Allan Poe. Caedmon Records.

Computer Programs

BookBrain, Grades 4–6. Apple. Version 3.0.
BookBrain, Grades 7–9. Apple. Version 1.1.
BookWhiz, Grades 6–9. Apple, IBM.

Filmstrips

The Case of Bugs Meany's Revenge by Donald Sobol. Encyclopedia Brown Series. Random House.

The Case of the Hungry Hitchhiker by Donald Sobol. Encyclopedia Brown Series. Random House.
The Case of the Kidnapped Pigs by Donald Sobol. Encyclopedia Brown Introduces Report-Writing Skills Series. Society for Visual Education.

Videotapes

Blackbeard's Ghost. Walt Disney Educational Media Company.
The Ghost Belonged to Me by Richard Peck. Live Oak Media.
Ghosts I Have Been by Richard Peck. Children's Television International.

References

Donelson, Kenneth, and Alleen Nilsen. *Literature for Today's Young Adults.* Glenview, IL: Scott, Foresman and Company, 1980.
Fox, Barbara J. *PX for Reading.* New York: Penguin, 1989.
Hearne, Betsy. *Choosing Books for Children: A Commonsense Guide.* Rev. ed. New York: Delacorte Press, 1990.
Hitchcock, Alfred, ed. *Alfred Hitchcock's Ghostly Gallery.* New York: Random House, 1984 (orig. 1962).
——, ed. *Alfred Hitchcock's Supernatural Tales of Terror and Suspense.* New York: Random House, 1973.
Holman, C. Hugh, and William Harmon. *A Handbook to Literature.* New York: Macmillan, 1986.
Jordan, Cathleen, and Cynthia Manson, comps. *Tales from Alfred Hitchcock's Mystery Magazine.* New York: Morrow, 1988.
Larrick, Nancy. *A Parent's Guide to Children's Reading.* 5th. ed. New York: Bantam, 1982.
MacDonald, Margaret. *When the Lights Go Out: Twenty Scary Tales To Tell.* New York: H. W. Wilson Company, 1988.
Malless, Stan, and Jeff McQuain. *The Elements of English.* New York: Madison, 1988.
Sobol, Donald. *Two-Minute Mysteries.* New York: Scholastic, 1986.
Symons, Julian. "Life of Crime and Detection." In *The Literature of Crime and Detection,* edited by Waltraud Woeller. New York: Ungar, 1988.

4

Fantasy

"Sometimes heartbreaking, but never hopeless, the fantasy world as it 'should be' is one in which good is ultimately stronger than evil, where courage, justice, love, and mercy actually function. Thus, it may often appear quite different from our own. In the long run, perhaps not. Fantasy does not promise Utopia. But if we listen carefully, it may tell us what we someday may be capable of achieving."
   Lloyd Alexander
   "The Flat-Heeled Muse"

INTRODUCTION

   The fantasy genre encompasses some of the richest, most memorable, enjoyable, and intriguing books ever written for children and young people. These include the beloved classics of Lewis Carroll's *Alice's Adventures in Wonderland,* L. Frank Baum's *Wonderful Wizard of Oz,* J. R. R. Tolkien's *The Hobbit,* E. B. White's *Charlotte's Web,* Norton Juster's *The Phantom Tollbooth,* and the amusing antics of Astrid Lindgren's *Pippi Longstocking.* John Farrar, the poet, says that the creations of the great authors of fantasy spring from the deepest imagination.
   Fantasy literature is defined as imaginative, fanciful, visionary, impossible, and dealing with things that cannot be. Constantine Georgiou describes fantasy as literature that brings the "magical and irrational into a world of reality." It has a convincing reality of its own, whether it is mysterious, supernatural, otherworldly, or magical. It concerns things that cannot really happen, with characters who often accomplish superhuman feats in imaginary places.

Fantasy creates an extension of reality while providing glimpses of other worlds. Donna Norton, in *Through the Eyes of a Child*, says that fantasy opens doors to the world of imaginative delights and "takes children into imaginative worlds where animals and dolls can talk, where wizards cast their spells" (p. 297). According to Ruth Lynn in *Fantasy For Children*, definitions of fantasy vary from the ambiguous to the obscure and from one fantasy writer to another.

The traditional elements of folklore, myths, legends, and fairy tales that were anonymous creations handed down through oral tradition linger in modern fantasy. They are reminiscent of witches, giants, elves, dwarfs, transformations, magical objects, enchantment, wishes, marvels, power, quests, and the supernatural. They provide bridges to fantasy based on high adventure, talking animals, time warps, miniature people, and mythical quests.

Modern fantasy is the work of known authors who use plots that are well-knit and balanced to make the unreal seem real and the incredible seem credible. Fantasy carries the reader to unknown realms where familiar settings are reshaped and rearranged beyond everyday reality. Many fantasy stories begin dramatically and flow with storytelling ease. They are filled with imagination and wonder, highly original, and based on fundamental issues of universal truths. Themes and motifs include good over evil, faithfulness and unfaithfulness, man against unknown forces, morals and ethics, rightings of wrongs, powers beyond, humor and nonsense, extension of joy and hope, and powers of darkness overcome by intellect and magic. Significant details include dramatic ingredients, foundation on truth, wide range of human emotions, magical power, strange happenings, memorable characterization, wholeness of conception, moral soundness, zestfulness, and satisfying endings. Important ingredients in fantasy are a clarity of purpose and respect for the reader.

Fantasy for children and young people provides pleasure and escape as well as personal insights and understanding of the world. The purpose of fantasy as described by critics and writers of fantasy is to provide an extension of reality, to evoke wonder and hope, "to refresh the heart, to intensify experience, to demonstrate immutable truths, to stretch the mind and imagination, to sharpen sensitivities, to derive a sense of beauty, and to spread joy." In *Touch Magic,* Jane Yolen expresses an author's desire in writing fantasy: "To write with as much honesty and love as she can muster in hopes of 'touching magic' and passing it on" (p. 20).

Types of fantasy, with examples based on the reading levels of grades 5–9, include the following:

1. Strange Worlds: Le Guin, Ursula. *The Tombs of Atuan*
2. Little People: Norton, Mary. *The Borrowers Afloat*
3. Humorous and Preposterous Characters: Lindgren, Astrid. *Pippi Longstocking*
4. Talking Animals: White, E. B. *Charlotte's Web*
5. Imaginary Kingdoms: Tolkien, J. R. R. *The Hobbit*
6. Incredible Creatures: Yolen, Jane. *Dragon's Blood*
7. Toys: Banks, Lynne. *The Indian in the Cupboard*
8. Spirits: Garner, Alan. *The Owl Service*
9. High Fantasy: Cooper, Susan. *The Dark Is Rising*
10. Time Warp: Voigt, Cynthia. *Building Blocks*

Fantasy stories should not be confused with science fiction stories. Sylvia Engdahl states in "The Changing Role of Science Fiction in Children's Literature" that the line is difficult to draw. Her personal view is that science fiction differs from fantasy "not in subject matter but in aim," which is to express ideas about the future and things that are now unknown. Ruth Lynn, in *Fantasy for Children*, distinguishes the two by stating that science fiction involves scientific and technological advances that make the future seem more or less possible. Fantasy includes things that cannot happen and characters and creatures that do not exist.

There are many outstanding fantasy writers in addition to those already mentioned. Among them are: C. S. Lewis, Lloyd Alexander, Patricia McKillip, Robin McKinley, William Mayne, Philippa Pearce, William Pene DuBois, and Natalie Babbitt.

ELEMENT OF LITERATURE: FOCUS ON DESIGN/ILLUSTRATION

Design and art play an important part in all children's books, but they are especially significant in fantasy literature. Although students notice illustrations, jacket covers, and overall design, they do not analyze and talk about them because they have not been asked to do so. In today's highly visual society, the elements of design, illustration, and visual communications form the nucleus for the study of visual literacy. Nathan Knobler, in his *The Visual Dialogue,* states that there is a widespread "visual illiteracy"—most of the public is incapable of "reading the current visual language." Lyn Ellen Lacy states in her *Art and Design in Children's Picture Books,* "The world can be a visual delight—and so can the works of art that mirror it. The visual arts can be a lifelong wonderment and source of pleasure" (p. 1). She stresses that more than ever, students must be taught not only the basic skills of reading, writing, and computing, but also "to see, feel, and think creatively in order to contribute in a complex world ahead" (p. 2). An editorial in the March/April 1990 issue of *Horn Book Magazine* entitled "Visual Literacy" reinforces the need for education about the art in children's books and the need for ensuring that working with the art in picture books is a learning process.

Design complements the text with particular attention to all of the details. Howard Greenfeld shows the relationship of graphic design and illustration in his excellent compilation, *Books from Writer to Reader*. He explains that design is concerned with the physical appearance of the entire book. The nature of the manuscript must be understood so that the design extends the meaning of the text. With an artist's eye for detail, the designer is concerned with the appearance and readability of the entire page, including the typeface and the size of the type, which is measured in points. The design of the title page, part title, and chapter openings set the mood for the entire book. There is great freedom in these designs allowing for the creative vision of the designer. An eye-catching and informative jacket design is very important because the jacket is an effective medium in selling the book to both the buyer and the reader. Once the jacket served as a "dust jacket" to protect against dust and dirt; now it is used to attract readers.

Illustration provides a visual statement by the artist to add to the written text or narrative statements by the author. The medium, whether line drawings, paintings, photographs, collage, or decorative patterns, determines how the artist's image is transferred to the page. The harmonious blend of illustrations and text allows the artist to express through images what a writer has expressed through words. In children's picture storybooks, the illustrations are as important as the text. They must complement and extend the text. Of course, the author also provides text that creates its own pictures in the minds and hearts of its readers. In wordless storybooks like *Anno's Flea Market,* the illustrations take the place of text.

Illustrators hold to the tenets of art to enhance and enliven the author's concepts. They capture picturesque scenes, unique characters, strange and monstrous creatures, make-believe lands, and glorious landscapes, as well as everyday scenes of contemporary life. They reflect behavior characteristic to the theme and mood of the story. They use their artistic integrity to make their illustrations believable. Yet, in all this they are cognizant of the developmental stage of the reader for which the book has the greatest appeal.

The artistic elements of design and illustration are line, color, texture, pattern, composition, perspective, shape, and form. Popular techniques and media include pen and ink, pastels, charcoal, colored pencil, collage, and wood block. An understanding of these elements can assist in the understanding of the visual images in illustrations. Resources to consult include the art teacher, art history books in the library media center and public library, art students, and local artists.

An example of the blending of design, illustration, and text that illustrate the theme of visual understanding is Cynthia Rylant's picture storybook *All I See* with illustrations by Peter Catalanotto. The jacket design sets the mood of the story with strong composition illustrating the rule of thirds and with an overhead point of view. A man with blotches of paint on his coat is shown relaxing in a canoe out on the lake. A white cat is curled up on his chest. The man is gazing upward. A small boy is shown on the bank looking toward the canoe. The title *All I See* is printed in bold red letters. The jacket painting is by the illustrator of the book. The title page is in full color with a spotlight highlighting a chair holding a jar of artists' brushes and paint tubes. A gray raincoat with splotches of paint is draped over the chair. Green leaves of trees form the backdrop. The title and names of the author and illustrator are in bold red letters, while publication data is in smaller black letters. The verso, giving the copyright information in small black letters, cites Mina Greenstein as the book designer. Other data informs us that the illustrations are watercolor paintings reproduced in four-color halftone with text set in 21pt. Perpetua. The dedication by the author is to Scott Savage, "who loves the light"; the dedication by the illustrator is simply to Ginny and Tony. The provocative illustrations covering a two-page spread provide the visual statement that accompanies and enhances the written narrative.

The story is about an artist who spends his days painting beside a lake. His name is Gregory. He likes to whistle Beethoven's Fifth Symphony while he works. When he becomes tired, he takes his cat out on the lake in his canoe. He likes to lie down in the canoe and look up into the sky. Charlie, a young boy who spends his summers at the lake, watches Gregory painting and drifting in his canoe. Charlie sneaks a look at the painting on the easel one day when Gregory is in the canoe. Charlie is surprised when he sees that it is a picture of a blue whale. After that, every time Charlie looks at the latest painting, it is always a picture of a blue whale. Charlie likes the artist but is too shy to talk to him. One day Charlie leaves a drawing on the easel that depicts the actual scene that he observes day after day. The scene shows the artist painting a blue whale by the lake while the cat is stretched out nearby. Musical notes whirl around the painter. Gregory looks at the painting and ponders it. After an exchange of notes on the easel, Gregory leaves a note that says "PLEASE STAY!" Charlie and Gregory become friends, and Gregory teaches Charlie to paint and gives him a gift of paints, brushes, and an easel. Charlie always paints exactly what he sees and Gregory always paints blue whales. When Charlie asks Gregory why he paints only whales, Gregory replies, "It is all I see." This profound statement sums up the "mind's eye," or imaginative perception, of the artist and illustrates the fact that not everyone sees things in the same way. It is a matter of the senses, experience, emotions, judgment, training, and artistic or poetic license.

To help students understand illustrations from an artist's point of view, use the picture storybook *The Sleeping Beauty*, retold by Jane Yolen and illustrated by Ruth Sanderson. This fairy tale has many elements of fantasy. The design and illustrations are superb. The motif of the heroine, Briar Rose, is carried out in the rose pattern throughout the book until the roses become briars when the spell encases the princess and the entire castle. The illustrator, Ruth Sanderson, includes a note explaining how she created the illustrations. She says that she has always been fascinated by the fantasy world of faraway kingdoms, princes, and princesses. For inspiration she studied the work of Pre-Raphaelite artists, and she consulted reference books. She sought out models who embodied her conceptions of the characters, had costumes made for the models, photographed them, drew sketches, and painted the illustrations in oil. The original paintings are about three times the size of the illustrations in the book.

A videotape that provides insight on design and illustration, produced by The American Library Association, is *Picture Books: Elements of Illustration and Story* by Betsy Hearne. It is excellent source material for teaching this unit. Demonstrations of visual, verbal, and artistic elements are presented as well as literary elements. Videotapes of picture storybooks and filmstrips of children's literature produced by Weston Woods are a hallmark in the field. Gene Deitch of Weston Woods is a master of the animated adaptation of picture storybooks.

The captivating designs and imaginative strength of illustrations are marvelously displayed in fantasy literature. Brilliant colors or black and white line drawings depicting heroic actions or quiet contemplation blend with the aura of high adventure or magical happenings. The artist and author conjure up scenes of enchantment, supernatural creatures, talking animals, spells, demons, quests, lively toys, and humorous adventures.

The importance of illustration in fantasy books is underscored by the experiences of John Tenniel, who illustrated Lewis Carroll's *Alice's Adventures in Wonderland* and *Through the Looking Glass*. Lewis Carroll was a perfectionist and expected perfection in the illustrations of his books. He insisted that Tenniel portray the characters and settings to conform with Carroll's own mental visions. It was a very trying experience for Tenniel as he created his illustrations to the exact detail demanded by the author. Tenniel was dissatisfied with the reproduction of his illustrations in the first printing of *Alice*. Carroll agreed and had an improved edition published. Tenniel at first refused to illustrate the sequel, *Through the Looking Glass*, because it was so difficult to work with Carroll. However, when Carroll could not get another illustrator, Tenniel agreed. After this experience, Tenniel later said that his desire to illustrate books had left him and he had done nothing in illustrations since that time.

Lewis Carroll was not the only author of fantasy literature to be involved with and critical of the illustrators of his books. J. R. R. Tolkien did not like any of the illustrations of *The Hobbit* except his own. According to Natalie Babbitt in her review of *The Annotated Hobbit*, edited by Douglas Anderson, Tolkien called the illustrations in some of the foreign editions "foul" and "frightful." Natalie Babbitt says that the illustrations presented by Anderson in *The*

Annotated Hobbit are very interesting, but the best illustrations are drawn by Tolkien himself. She also writes, "*The Hobbit* really requires no pictures at all. The prose alone is quite provocative enough" (p. 19).

In many fantasy books, design, jacket cover art, and one or two pages of illustrations form the whole of the illustrations. This is the case in *Building Blocks* by Cynthia Voigt and in *Heart's Blood* by Jane Yolen. In the latter the jacket design, by Gus Papadopoulos, and the jacket illustration, by Julek Heller, captivate attention with a bold red dragon carrying a knotted shirt with a young man clinging to it. The white cover with borders of red and yellow and background of yellow with a touch of green bring out the fierceness of the snorting dragon. The endpapers are bright red. Two double pages of black and white drawings complete the illustrations. One of these drawings shows a large dragon, a picture of barns, an incubarn, a bond house, and a map of the journey into the mountains. The other drawing shows a close-up of a fertilized dragon's egg through the stages of growth into a hatchling. This is the second book in Jane Yolen's Pit Dragon trilogy. It is the story of Jakkin after he becomes a young dragon master. His red dragon produces five hatchlings and wins exciting victories in the gaming pits. Jakkin travels through the underworld to find his beloved Akki. In Jakkin's attempt to climb a cliffside, his great dragon, Heart's Blood, flies to his rescue. The cover painting illustrates Heart's Blood carrying Jakkin in the knotted sling made by Jakkin.

Other examples of design and illustration in fantasy literature that beautifully complement the entire text are the reissued series of C. S. Lewis's *Chronicles of Narnia,* published by Macmillan in 1988, and *The Tombs of Atuan* by the masterful storyteller, Ursula Le Guin.

RECOMMENDED LISTS

Recommended Titles for Teaching the Fantasy Genre Unit

The following books are recommended for teaching units dealing with the fantasy genre. They can be used for reading and study by an entire class or by small groups. Some of them are suitable for reading aloud to an entire class.

Babbitt, Natalie. *Tuck Everlasting*. New York: Farrar, Straus & Giroux, 1975. RL: Grade 5. IL: Grades 4–7. Cornerstone.

Winnie Foster, a lively ten-year-old, is bored with life in the summertime in her little town of Treegap. She considers running away, but then she meets an unusual family, the Tucks. When Winnie sees Jesse drinking water gushing from the ground in her family's grove of trees, she is kidnapped by the family because she has seen the magic fountain. Mr. and Mrs. Tuck, Jesse, Miles, and their horse all drank from the fountain 87 years ago. They all have remained the same age they were when they drank the water, and they cannot die. The Tucks are kind and loving to Winnie. The tale becomes complicated when a man overhears the story and his greed gets the best of him. Winnie has some choices to make when the family gets in trouble.

Since this book does not have any illustrations, it is an excellent source for students to imagine the characters and the setting. Let them visualize each character in the context of the opening of the story and again at the closing of the story.

Cooper, Susan. *The Dark Is Rising*. New York: Atheneum, 1973. RL: Grade 8. IL: Grades 6–10. Windrush.

Will Stanton begins a dark adventure on his eleventh birthday when he discovers that he is the last of the Old Ones. The Old Ones are immortals dedicated to fighting the force of evil, the Dark. It becomes Will's task to take up their quest. He must find and guard the six great magical Signs of Light. Will continues his everyday life with his family but is drawn away for intervals of time as he faces untold dangers and adventures across time and space. He is aided by Merriman, who helps him understand and use the special gift of power from the Old Ones. After Will learns to use his powers, he is tested again and again by the Black Rider.

The impact of the design of *The Dark Is Rising* begins with the oversize height of the book. The black jacket is illustrated as a two-page spread; it shows the opposing forces of good and evil, with evil symbolized by the black horse and its red rider, and good by the magical white horse, the Walker, and the Hooded helper. The illustrations and jacket are by Alan E. Cober. The three black-and-white illustrations represent the finding, the learning, and the testing. They show Will, his mother, and the Walker in the background, Will soaring as a great white eagle, and the beautiful white horse carrying the Hunter who is wearing the mask that makes him half man, half beast.

Garner, Alan. *The Owl Service*. London: Collins, 1967. RL: Grade 6. IL: Grades 8–10. Windrush.

In the Welsh countryside, three young people become involved in a powerful reenactment of an ancient conflict of Blodeuwedd caused when the wizard, Gwydion, made a wife out of flowers for a princeling. The flowers are changed by a destructive force, bringing death. The legend is entwined within a set of dishes called the owl service. The three young people are Alison, who has been left the house by her father; Roger, her step-brother; and Gwyn, whose mother returns to her native valley to cook for Alison's family. Other characters include Alison's mother and stepfather, Nancy the cook, and strange Huw Halfbacon, the gardener. The destructive spirit works through the images of flowers and owls and nearly destroys Alison's family.

The jacket cover displays the same illustration of an owl on the front and the back. The front illustration is in muted shades of yellow and green, while the back cover is stark white. The owl with clenched claws is shown against a round backdrop. The cover is framed with four unusual winged mystical beasts. It reflects the mood and text of the book. The motif of the book is cleverly hidden in the design of the dishes that are displayed on the double-page endpapers at the beginning and end of the book. The hidden design on the dishes, called the owl service, is intermingled with the tragic Welsh legend.

Juster, Norton. *The Phantom Tollbooth*. New York: Random House, 1961. RL: Grade 8. IL: Grades 6–9.

Milo suffers from boredom. He considers learning a waste of time. He receives a mysterious package that contains a magical tollgate, complete with a small electric car. The car takes him to a "land beyond." He leaves Reality for some outrageous puns and fun. He meets some crazy creatures. He is joined by Tock and Humbug. His new friends add to the rollicking adventures with words. The three try to avoid the forbidden Mountains of Ignorance. They enter the Kingdom of Wisdom and are involved in bringing back Rhyme and Reason.

The illustrations by Jules Feiffer add to the zany, fast-paced story. The cover contains a picture of Milo and the dog, Tock, who is larger than Milo. Tock has a huge clock as part of his body. The technique of pen-and-ink line drawings is used by the illustrator, with hatching and cross-hatching. Illustrations abound throughout the book. The incidents at the Mountains of Ignorance are depicted with a double spread. The large map entitled "The Lands Beyond" adds to understanding the places and events described in the text.

Le Guin, Ursula. *The Tombs of Atuan.* New York: Atheneum, 1970. RL: Grade 7. IL: Grades 8–12. PB: Bantam.

The illustrations, including the jacket, are by Gail Garraty. The story is about a young girl, Tenar, who is taken to Atuan to become the high priestess of the dark and foreboding underworld beneath the Tombs of Atuan. She is given the name Arha, the Eaten One, and is to serve the nameless Powers of the Earth. Each chapter begins with a bold, black-and-white block-print illustration depicting an important person, place, thing, or event from that chapter. Illustrations of important people include Arha's kindly warden, Manan; the evil priestess, Kossil; the understanding priestess, Thar; and the handsome stranger, Ged. Illustrations of important things include the huge key ring with fascinating keys and the large broken-arm Ring of Erreth-Akbe that plays a significant role in the story. The story is summed up by the illustrations showing Tenar and Ged overlooking a city beyond the mountains and showing them in a boat on a voyage. Maps at the front of the book depicting The Labyrinth of the Tombs of Atuan and The Place of the Tombs of Atuan add to the understanding of this intriguing story.

McKinley, Robin. *Beauty: A Retelling of the Story of Beauty and the Beast.* New York: Harper & Row, 1978. RL: Grade 7. IL: Grades 7–10. PB: Pocket Books.

Beauty's father, a merchant, returns from a trip and tells a strange tale. He was caught in a blizzard in a thick forest and found a walled castle where he took refuge. He and his horse were well-cared for and fed by invisible hands. As he left the next morning, he picked a rose from the garden to give to one of his daughters. Immediately a huge beast captured him. He was released on the condition that he would give the Beast one of his daughters. The Beast declared she must come of her own free will out of her love for her father. After the father tells the story, the three daughters discuss what must be done. Grace, Hope, and Beauty all have different ideas. Beauty, whose real name is Honour, insists that she is the one to go. She says that anyone who loves roses as much as the Beast cannot be so bad. The girls find beautiful gifts and money from the Beast in their father's saddlebags. Each daughter gets a wooden box with her initials on it. Two are filled with precious stones and gems, but Beauty's is full of rose seeds. Beauty goes to the castle and the Beast tells her she has nothing to fear. Magic and enchantment in the castle fill Beauty's life, but she misses her family. The Beast tells Beauty that she can never leave. The Beast keeps asking Beauty to marry him, but she refuses. Her father dreams about her and notices that she is changing. Her sisters notice that the roses in their garden are always blooming and do not require any care. The Beast tells Beauty that he sends the dreams and cares for the roses to offer hope to the family. Beauty's inner values change as she gets to know and understand the Beast. She begins to love the Beast, and this love brings about startling changes.

The jacket art by David Palladini is the single illustration for the book. It reflects the artistic style of the writing. A close-up of a single beautiful red rose with two rosebuds of different stages of development is depicted against a black backdrop of a house or castle and trees. The trees are barren, yet the rose is mysteriously in full bloom. The illustration is framed on the white cover with black lettering. The title page and beginnings of each chapter have a flowing geometric design. The format is by Harriett Barton. It is set in 11/14pt. Video Garamond type.

Lewis, C. S. *The Last Battle*. New York: Macmillan, 1956. Reset and reissued in 1988. RL: Grade 6. IL: Grades 5–9.

In *The Last Battle*, the lovely pen-and-ink illustrations are by Pauline Baynes, the colorful jacket painting is by Daniel San Souci, and the flowing jacket calligraphy is by Leah Palmer Preiss. The overall design, from the inviting open door on the cover, the mottled blue and white endpapers that are an extension of the cover, the half-page and title page layout, the chapter beginnings with the tiny star designs, the 11pt. Palatino typeface and type, to the size of the book, faithfully carries out the author's message of magic and wonder. *The Last Battle* is the seventh and last book in the series *Chronicles of Narnia*. The King of Narnia, Tirian, calls the children who are friends of Narnia to come from across the worlds to join him in the battle against the evil Calormenes. He is joined by Jill and Eustace, and later by Lucy, Peter, Edmund, Polly, and Digory, who are characters from the other books in the series. Aslan, the Eagle, the talking dogs, the Bear, the Unicorn, and Jewel also join the king in the battle. Small pen-and-ink drawings are interspersed throughout the text to illustrate the happenings. The placement of the illustrations coincides with the text, adding meaning and enjoyment.

Saint-Exupery, Antoine. *The Little Prince*. New York: Harcourt Brace Jovanovich, 1943. RL: Grade 9. IL: Grades 8–10.

The narrator of *The Little Prince* is an aviator who is forced down on the Sahara Desert. He is astonished to be joined by the delightful and profound little prince. Their conversations are "matters of significance." The little prince never answers questions about himself directly but eventually shares his story with the aviator. The little prince tells about living alone on a tiny planet or asteroid where he owns a flower of great beauty and inordinate pride. This pride ruins the serene life on his planet and starts the prince on his travels. He visits other asteroids with strange characters like the king, the conceited man, the tippler, the businessman, the lamplighter, and the geographer. Finally the little prince visits the planet earth, where he lands in the Sahara Desert. After his experiences with a snake, an echo, and many beautiful flowers, he learns what is really important in life from a fox. He and the aviator become very special friends.

The lyrical and sensitive illustrations by the author blend with the text to produce a classic book in the fantasy genre. The illustrations frequently express a special vision held by its readers, both children and adults. The story was written for adults but it may be read on several different levels: by children as a delightful story and by adults as a satiric allegory. This book is an exceptional example of design, illustration, and visual communications. The narrator communicates through art with the little prince. But visual communication is not as important as seeing with the heart. "What is essential is invisible to the eye." Since the reading level is grade 9, it is a good choice for reading aloud to students.

Voigt, Cynthia. *Building Blocks.* New York: Atheneum, 1984. RL: Grade 5. IL: Grades 7–10. PB: Ballantine.

The jacket painting by Eileen McKeating visually focuses on Brann, who stands in front of a big pile of wooden blocks. In the background behind the blocks is a thoughtful little boy wearing overalls. The jacket illustration raises questions concerning the two boys and the building blocks. The only other illustration is the picture of a farm on the back cover. In this fascinating time warp, Brann enters his father's world of 37 years ago through the handmade building blocks in his room. Brann becomes friends with Kevin, who is younger than Brann. Kevin turns out to be Brann's father.

Yolen, Jane. *Dragon's Blood.* New York: Delacorte Press, 1984. RL: Grade 7. IL: Grades 7–12. PB: Dell.

In this first book in the Pit Dragon trilogy, Jakkin is in bondage to Master Sarkkhan. He works in the dragon nursery and longs for the day when he can own and train his own dragon. The long, arduous training process brings its rewards as Jakkin experiences victory in the gaming pits. An unusual happening in the nursery gives him the opportunity to take a dragon hatchling for his own. He is helped in his ventures by a young girl, Akki. Jakkin is able to pay his bond-price and begin the life of his dreams.

The book design complements the theme. The composition of the cover design, by Jo Anne Bonnell, and the jacket illustration, by Jean-Louis Huens, draws attention to the small, fierce dragon and the main character, Jakkin. Akki, a secondary character, is in the background watching the action. The red color of the wings, the outline of the dragon, and the title are contrasted with the light-green background. They make a bold statement. The panoramic format of the two illustrations at the beginning of the book provides an excellent visual statement of Sarkkhan's Nursery and Heart's

Blood's Line. They are instructional illustrations that offer information vital to the text.

Recommended Titles for Individual or Group Study

Alexander, Lloyd. *Castle of Llyr.* New York: Holt, Rinehart and Winston, 1966. RL: Grade 5. IL: Grades 5–8.

Princess Eilonwy of the red-gold hair is abducted by the forces of evil in this third volume in the Prydain Chronicles. Taran, the hero, is the Assistant Pig Keeper. He does not have much status but goes forth as a warrior to fight just causes. Taran realizes that he loves the capricious Princess Eilonwy and must find some way to rescue her from an evil enchantress. The dangerous power of magic brings triumph after many struggles and adventures.

Banks, Lynne. *The Indian in the Cupboard.* New York: Doubleday, 1981. RL: Grade 6. IL: Grades 5–7. PB: Avon. Cornerstone.

Ormi gets a little plastic Indian as a birthday present from his friend Patrick. His brother gives him a wooden cupboard. He decides to put the tiny Indian in the cupboard overnight. He locks the cupboard with a very old key that he finds in a collection of keys. He is surprised that the key fits the cupboard lock. The next morning, Ormi hears a noise coming from the cupboard. He opens the cupboard and finds that the Indian has come to life. His name is Little Bear. Ormi likes Little Bear and tries to provide him with many things to make him comfortable. Ormi tries to keep the truth of Little Bear from everyone, but Patrick discovers the secret and causes problems when he brings his plastic cowboy to life.

This delightful book is an excellent choice for reading aloud.

McKillip, Patricia. *Heir of Sea and Fire.* New York: Atheneum, 1977. RL: Grade 6. IL: Grades 7–11. PB: Ballantine.

In *The Riddle-Master of Hed,* the first book in this trilogy, Morgan and Raederle are on a quest to learn the significance of the Star-Bearer. Morgan bears three stars on his forehead. He must find the answer to the riddle of the stars, a harp, and a sword. In *Heir of Sea and Fire,* the second book of the trilogy, Raederle is the heroine and the story is seen through her eyes. When Morgan does not return, Raederle cannot believe that he is dead. She is determined to find him and begins her quest. She finds that she has magical powers that could bring tragic results to the one she loves.

Norton, Mary. *The Borrowers Afloat.* New York: Harcourt Brace Jovanovich. 1959. RL: Grade 5. IL: Grades 4–7. PB: Voyager.

The history of the Borrowers is reviewed by Mrs. May as she tells Mr. Beguid, the lawyer, about the little people who inhabited Firbank. She tells of Pod, Homily, and Arrietty, the little people who had nothing of their own but borrowed everything from the places they lived. The Borrowers have been rescued by Spiller and taken to their cousins, Uncle Hendreary and Aunt Luppy. When the humans move out of the house, the Borrowers must go also because they can't live without humans. Spiller comes to the rescue and suggests that the family go to the town of Little Fordham. They go by boat through the drain. The drain branches out and brings a collection of soap, tea leaves, and hot-scented bathwater. The water in the drain is sometimes slow and peaceful, and at other times it rages like a torrent. After escaping from the drain, the family uses Spiller's kettle to travel down the river. New adventures await them at every turn.

Selden, George. *The Cricket in Times Square.* New York: Farrar, Straus & Giroux, 1960. RL: Grade 4. IL: Grades 4–6.

Chester, the cricket, is carried to Times Square in a picnic basket from his home in Connecticut. In a wry and humorous way, Chester Cricket becomes a part of the hustle and bustle of Times Square. He joins Tucker Mouse and Harry Cat, who become special friends to him. He lends his talents to the Bellini family, owners of a newspaperstand that is nearly bankrupt. Chester becomes a hero as he helps save the business.

The delightful illustrations by Garth Williams portray the authentic background of the Times Square Subway Station. His characterization of Chester and his friends is realistic and memorable.

White, T. H. *The Sword in the Stone.* New York: G. P. Putnam's Sons, 1939. RL: Grade 9. IL: Grades 8–12. PB: Dell.

Set in the background of medieval England, this is the story of King Arthur's youth. The story is based on Malory's account. It is a book of mixed fantasy and realism. Merlin is the key to Wort's changing status as he turns out to be King Arthur.

This is a book for advanced readers who not only love knights and the romance of knighthood, but are willing to undertake the reading challenge. The Arthurian legends are exciting with quests, battles, and adventures. T. H. White's *The Once and Future King* series begins with *The Sword in the Stone* and ends with *The Book of Merlin,* the conclusion published after White's death by the University of Texas Press in 1977.

Picture Storybooks for Teaching Design/Illustration

The following picture storybooks are excellent examples of design and illustration in fantasy literature. They are designed with artistry and are well blended and balanced with the text. Students will recognize some of their favorites.

MacDonald, George. *At the Back of the North Wind.* Illustrated by Ernest Shepard. London: J. M. Dent & Sons, 1956.

The beautiful watercolor illustrations of Ernest Shepard are in keeping with the dreamlike qualities of the story. They catch the radiance and whimsical atmosphere of the author's style. The language is flowing, poetic, and magical. It is a deeply moving story of the young boy, Diamond, whose great love for the North Wind is told with romance and wonder. As Diamond travels, riding at the back of the North Wind, the reader is transported to a fantasy world of wonder and awe. The overall design and illustrations enlarge the vision and touch the heart.

Martin, Rafe. *Will's Mammoth.* Illustrated by Stephen Gammel. New York: G. P. Putnam's Sons, 1989.

The illustrations in *Will's Mammoth,* by Stephen Gammel, visualize the mammoth imagination of Will. The design, with large, bright letters of mixed sizes and shapes and unconventional spacing, creates a sense of the unusual. The luminous colors and delightful depiction of prehistoric herds of mammoths, wolves, wild ponies, and rhinoceros blend with the fantastic adventures of Will. The animals, despite their large size, are beautiful and appealing. Will's love for mammoths and prehistoric creatures is vividly shown in the two-page spread showing his room. Mammoths are everywhere, from his small models and his curtains to his large, stuffed, woolly ones. The prehistoric men, tigers, bats, and other animals add to the fun-filled room. The bookcase, with its books on mammoths, models, and the skull, suggests part of the source for Will's imaginative world. His determined look as he sits on the floor drawing his own illustrations suggests his intense involvement in a world of fantasy. His illustrations that he displays all over his room are an expression of this involvement. Rafe Martin blends the fanciful with the actual in this dramatic but uncomplicated story. In Will's actual world, his parents tell him that there are no more mammoths; they all disappeared 10,000 years ago. But in his magical world, Will knows that there are mammoths. He has his own special one who takes him for rides with exciting glimpses of other animals and even prehistoric family life. Through the movement and vitality of the illustrations, Will and his mammoth help rescue a baby mammoth, visit a prehistoric family, and wave goodbye to the prehistoric children he encounters. His special woolly mammoth picks a flower and gives it to him. Will is drawn back to the world of reality when his parents yell for him to come to supper. When asked what he did today, Will replies, "I rode my mammoth." As he gets in bed surrounded by his woolly mammoths, the illustration depicts Will's special mountain that he climbs to get to his imaginary world. In his hand is the flower given to him by his mammoth.

Sendak, Maurice. *Where the Wild Things Are*. Illustrated by the author. New York: Harper & Row, 1964.

Maurice Sendak is a master at artistic storytelling. His fierce and compelling Wild Things have captured the hearts and imaginations of children all over the world. His use of line, cross-hatching, and color show movement and excitement. His fantasy is spun with the stuff dreams are made of, albeit wild and unforgettable. When Max, who has been acting a little wild, is sent to bed without his supper, his powerful imagination lets him soar into the realm of the unknown where he takes charge of the Wild Things. On his island the wild, monstrous creatures crown him king. He is now the one who issues the commands, and the Wild Things dance at his bidding. His return to reality to find his warm supper waiting for him makes the incredible seem credible. The design of the book faithfully depicts the mood and tone of the story. Lyn Ellen Lacy in *Art and Design in Children's Picture Books* carefully explains the techniques used by Maurice Sendak in creating this book. The figures seem to grow by enlarging or diminishing according to the telling of Max's story. Page sequence and margins change with the action in the story. The double-page spread or panorama is used only for the Wild Things. The story unfolds as a stage and builds to a satisfying conclusion with its unique artwork.

Wiesner, David. *Free Fall*. Illustrated by the author. New York: Lothrop, Lee & Shepard, 1988.

Elements of traditional and modern fantasy blend in the mythical picture storybook *Free Fall*. A young boy dreams of exploring uncharted lands, reminiscent of high fantasy quests of nobility and grandeur. His adventures include the slaying of a dragon, visits to castles, meeting kings and queens, and climbing the highest mountain. The rich, graceful writing and the magic and marvels of the storyline are balanced by the colorful, inventive illustrations. An iconographic videotape, using the author's illustrations and adding music and sound effects to express the interplay of fantasy and reality, is available from American School Publishers.

TEACHING TIPS: THE FANTASY GENRE AND DESIGN/ILLUSTRATION

The aura of high adventure and imagination of fantasy literature combined with the creative vision and imaginative strength of illustrators make this unit a pleasurable one for teaching. Students grounded in folk literature and science fiction movies can be enticed to partake of the pleasures of fantasy literature. Adding the dimension of visual communication can enhance that pleasure. Many of the books that are recommended for study have been made into movies, videotapes, filmstrips, or audiocassette tapes. The audiocassette tapes help students visualize the stories in their own minds. Audio Book

Contractors and G. K. Hall Audio Publishers specialize in unabridged children's books. Recorded Books has recently issued a complete single-voice narration of Tolkien's *Lord of the Rings*. The trilogy consists of 38 cassettes or 53 hours of narration. Borrowing some of the tapes to use with advanced or gifted students or high school students can help with the understanding and pronouncing of the many original names, places, and variants of languages.

Before selecting the fantasy books for study, check the library media center, the public library, or interlibrary loan to learn the availability of the various media for fantasy literature. Based on the findings, include as many visual presentations as possible. A movie or videotape can take the place of reading a fantasy book, or it can be used for a comparison with the book after the book is read.

Become familiar with many fantasy authors and their works. Discuss fantasy literature with the library media specialist and obtain bibliographies. Use the suggested lists and resources included in this chapter. Additionally, two excellent source books are Ruth Lynn's *Fantasy for Children,* Second Edition, and *Fantasy Literature: A Core Collection and Reference Guide* by Marshall B. Tymn et al. If the entire class will read and study the same title, be sure to pick a title with which both the teacher and the students can relate. Carefully select fantasy books for class study based on reading levels, whole group, small group, or individual grouping methods, or according to the other preselected criteria. Find out which books are available in multiple copies, paperback, and large-print editions. Plan for advanced, less able readers, and special-interest groups. If books need to be ordered or placed on reserve, be sure to allow enough time for the books to arrive.

Begin the fantasy genre unit by reading one of the suggested picture storybooks, such as Rafe Martin's *Will's Mammoth* or David Wiesner's *Free Fall*. Tell the students that the skills emphasis will be on design and illustration and visual communications. Show examples of good design and illustration in the picture storybook being read. Ask students to share memories of special children's fantasy books. *Where the Wild Things Are* is sure to be one of their favorites. Have a copy of the book on hand to share. Discuss the genre and talk about some of the interesting books. Show a filmstrip or videotape as an example of the genre, if available. If students are to choose individual titles of fantasy books to read, ask the library media specialist or a guest from the public library to give book talks.

Suggestions for activities to use during and after the class study of fantasy books are included in this chapter after the next section.

FOCUS ON CRITICAL-THINKING AND COMMUNICATION SKILLS: VISUAL COMMUNICATIONS

Visual communications involve the senses, awareness, insight, judgment, discernment, appreciation, sharing, informing, and transmitting. *The Oxford University Dictionary* defines *visual* as connected to sight or vision, carried out or performed by means of vision, impressions received through the senses, nature of mental vision, and perceptible. The word *communications* is defined as the action of imparting, conveying, or exchanging ideas.

To help students understand visual communications, they must first understand how visual dialogue and meaning are communicated. Visual communications have much in common with all systems of communications: source, medium, and receiver. In art, design, and photography the source for communications is the artist, the medium is the work of art, and the receiver is the observer. The artist provides a visual statement in a work of art for a response or reaction from the observer. Many times the observer has a sense of confusion or inadequacy or a feeling of antagonism toward works of art because of a lack of communication.

As in verbal and written communications, there is a need for training, instruction, and practice in the field of visual communications. Lyn Ellen Lacy, in *Art and Design in Children's Picture Books,* says that the basic skills that need to be taught for evaluation of visual material are "to distinguish between reality and unreality, to appreciate use of details that contribute to the whole, to identify unique properties of the medium used, and to understand the main idea intended by the visual message" (p. 2). Students need to understand that their perception or awareness of the visual world around them is based on information that comes from the senses, and that everyone does not see the same thing. What they see is affected by their senses, experiences, emotions, and intelligence. To build their self-confidence, students need many opportunities to express their reactions and opinions of visual images in a nonthreatening atmosphere where there is no right or wrong. They also need opportunities to express themselves visually in creative media. Activities included in this chapter can provide students with some of these opportunities.

Objectives in visual communications include:

1. Discern between factual and imaginative symbols
2. Use picture clues or other elements of design to predict the outcome of the story
3. Prove or disprove predictions on the basis of subsequent pictures or text
4. State the main idea implied in a work of art
5. Explain the viewpoint of the artist
6. Rearrange a series of pictures so that they tell a story in a sequence
7. Express personal reactions to a work of art
8. Explain the meaning of visual propaganda
9. Define visual literacy
10. Express self through a visual medium: photography, drawing, super-8mm movie, diorama

The art teacher, library media specialist, local artist, or other staff member can assist with instruction and training in visual communications.

ACTIVITIES

Activities Related to Teaching the Fantasy Genre

To assure that students know the meaning, types, and elements of the fantasy genre, review each of these at the completion of the study. This can be done in the form of matching exercises, word scrambles, crossword puzzles, discussions, games, and questions and answers. Additional ideas include the following:

1. Using a number of fantasy books, let students locate types and elements of fantasy to share with the class
2. Plan a research activity in the library media center for students to locate information on important authors of fantasy
3. Help students plan and construct a bulletin board depicting the elements of fantasy literature
4. Invite a storyteller to tell a fantasy story that is representative of the genre

5. Read a short story from a fantasy story collection like Robin McKinley's *Door in the Hedge* and discuss the components of fantasy
6. Show a filmstrip or videotape of a fantasy story that was read in class and ask students to compare and contrast the two media

Activities Related to Teaching Visual Communications

While emphasizing design, illustration, and visual communications, review the parts of the book with students. Include the jacket, spine, call number, endpapers, blurb, half-title and title pages, copyright information, dedication, table of contents, and text. With the help of the library media specialist, collect a number of fantasy books. Divide the class into small groups. Let them work at small tables either in the library media center or conference areas, if available. This is a good time to organize the groups of students by criteria other than reading levels so that they have an opportunity to work with many different students. Give several fantasy books to each group, asking the students to look through each book and select the one that *best* exemplifies the criteria of overall design and illustration and the one that *least* exemplifies the criteria.

Review the ten objectives for teaching visual communications as stated in the Focus on Communication Skills. Intersperse the objectives into the teaching unit as applicable. Have on hand the materials or books needed as examples, such as picture clues, series of pictures or slides for arranging in sequence, definitions, and examples of propaganda and visual literacy.

Obtain fantasy literature in cartoon format, such as *Forgotten Realms* or *Spelljammer* comic books, published by D. C. Comics for more mature students. The students can probably supply these or other fantasy comic books. Let the students read the comic books during a class period. In a large discussion group, ask the students to explain why these comic books are classified as fantasy literature. Let them give examples of such elements as these from "Rivals" in *Forgotten Realms:* spell-casting talent, most-holy priests, sea of fallen stars, omens, key to extradimensional space, wizard, magical nation of Halruaa, flying ships, and winged humanoid. Explain the use of sensationalism and violence as seen in some fantasy comic books and television programs. Compare the comic books with fantasy writers such as Ursula Le Guin and Susan Cooper.

Use books on optical illusions to assist students in understanding visual symbols. Obtain books from the library media center and public library. Include works of M. C. Escher.

Plan a field trip to an art gallery. Work with the art teacher and staff at the museum to arrange a tour. Specify that the topics to be discussed and art objects to be viewed include the themes of fantasy and visual communications.

Let students produce a visual report on their fantasy book. They can make a collage, poster, papier-mâché characters, super-8mm animation film, cartoon, hand-drawn slides, transparencies, videotape, or sketches. The entire class can plan and make a mural of fantasy elements. Students interested in photography can make a photographic essay of fantasy books, including photographs of jackets or covers of books, illustrations, and pictures of authors. Enlist the help of the library media specialist in the productions.

Additional Activities

Ask students to compare the format and illustrations in a library edition and in a paperback edition of a single book.

For a fun activity with students, obtain a number of wordless picture storybooks such as *Anno's Flea Market* by Mitsumasa Anno. Let students work in groups to find how to tell the story as they perceive it. They can also make a list of the many details on each page, exchange books, and compare their lists with those of the other groups.

NONPRINT RESOURCES

Audiocassettes

The High King by Lloyd Alexander. Miller-Brody Productions.
Tuck Everlasting by Natalie Babbitt. Large-print read-along. Cornerstone.

Film

Milo's Journey. Films Inc. Based on *The Phantom Tollbooth* by Norman Juster. (16mm film)

Filmstrips

The High King by Lloyd Alexander. Miller-Brody Productions.
The Phantom Tollbooth by Norman Juster. Encyclopaedia Britannica Educational Corporation.
The Tombs of Atuan, Part 1 & Part 2, by Ursula Le Guin. Miller-Brody Productions.

Sound Filmstrips

Animating Picture Books: Gene Deitch. Weston Woods.

Videotapes

Free Fall by David Wiesner. Random House Media. (iconographic video)
Gene Deitch: The Picture Book Animated. Weston Woods.
Picture Books: Elements of Illustration and Story by Betsy Hearne. American Library Association.
Sword in the Stone by T. H. White. Walt Disney Educational Media Company.

References

Alexander, Lloyd. "The Flat-Heeled Muse." In *Children and Literature: Views and Reviews,* edited by Virginia Haviland. New York: Lothrop, Lee & Shepard, 1973.
Anno, Mitsumasa. *Anno's Flea Market.* New York: Philomel, 1984.
Babbitt, Natalie. "The Secret Life of Bilbo Baggins," *Bookworld* (November 6, 1988):19.
Engdahl, Sylvia. "The Changing Role of Science Fiction in Children's Literature." In *Children and Literature,* edited by Virginia Haviland. New York: Lothrop, Lee & Shepard, 1973.
Greenfeld, Howard. *Books from Writer to Reader.* New York: Crown Publishers, 1976.
Knobler, Nathan. *The Visual Dialogue.* New York: Holt, Rinehart and Winston, 1966.
Lacy, Lyn Ellen. *Art and Design in Children's Picture Books.* Chicago, IL: American Library Association, 1986.
Lynn, Ruth Nadelman. *Fantasy for Children.* 2d ed. New York: R. R. Bowker, 1983.

Pierpoint Morgan Library. *Early Children's Books and Their Illustration*. Boston: David R. Godine, 1975.

"Rivals." *The Forgotten Realms*. D. C. Comics, 1990.

Rylant, Cynthia. *All I See*. Illustrated by Peter Catalanotto. New York: Orchard, 1988.

The Sleeping Beauty. Retold by Jane Yolen and illustrated by Ruth Sanderson. New York: Alfred A. Knopf, 1986.

Tymn, Marshall B., Kenneth Zahorski, and Robert Boyer. *Fantasy Literature: A Core Collection and Reference Guide*. New York: R. R. Bowker, 1979.

"Visual Literacy." *Horn Book Magazine* 66 (March/April 1990): 132.

Wheeler, Jim. "Fantasy: A Bare Bones Collection." *The Book Report* 4 (January/February 1985):34–35.

Yolen, Jane. *Touch Magic*. New York: Philomel, 1981.

5

Science Fiction

"The world has caught up with science fiction, but science fiction is not there. It has rocketed on farther into the unknown, charting new territories of the imagination, expanding once more the frontiers of the possible."
James Gunn
Alternate Worlds

INTRODUCTION

The science fiction genre is a popular literary form with all ages. It has a long history, dating back to Jules Verne's *Five Weeks in a Balloon* in 1863. James Gunn discusses this history in his book *Alternate Worlds*. Forerunners of science fiction novels include the imagination and creativity of inventors, scientists, technologists, and writers who told of inventions, new technologies, far-reaching journeys, and flights to the moon. In 1911, Hugo Gernsback wrote *Ralph 124C 41+: A Romance of the Year 2660,* a Utopian vision of flying saucers, vending machines, fluorescent lighting, sleep learning, synthetic fabrics, plastics, solar energy, microfilm, and jukeboxes. In 1926, Gernsback started the magazine *Amazing Stories,* which carried stories by Edgar Allan Poe, Jules Verne, and H. G. Wells. In 1895, H. G. Wells wrote *The Time Machine,* followed by *The Invisible Man* and *The War of the Worlds.* Pseudo-scientific and pulp magazines led to the development of modern science fiction magazines. In 1939, the "golden age" of science fiction began with writers like Robert Heinlein, Theodore Sturgeon, A. E. van Vogt, and Isaac Asimov.

The term *science fiction* was coined by Hugo Gernsback when he began the magazine *Science Wonder Stories* in 1929. *Webster's Seventh New Collegiate Dictionary* defines science fiction as "fiction dealing principally with the impact of actual or imagined science upon society or individuals; *broadly:* literary fantasy including a scientific factor as an essential orienting component." According to James Gunn in *Alternate Worlds,* authorities differ on the definition of the term. It has been called speculative fiction dealing with the real world by Robert Heinlein; Isaac Asimov calls it a "branch of literature concerned with the impact of scientific advance upon human beings" (p. 31). Gunn himself writes, "In science fiction a fantastic event or development is considered rationally" (p. 32). *The Science Fiction Encyclopedia,* edited by Peter Nichols, after giving numerous definitions of science fiction, makes the statement that science fiction is so flexible in practice that it is "simply not capable of clear definition" (p. 161).

Science fiction is a literary genre combining the image of Utopia, imaginary voyages, and speculative accounts of the future. Science fiction stresses scientific laws and technological inventions, scientific plausibility, and "future history." It involves human beings with scientific laws and confronts the possibilities of human interaction with interplanetary voyages and future societies. Science fiction writers emphasize man's precarious place in the universe and are concerned with the social, psychological, and ecological implications of science and technology.

Fantasy and science fiction are related genres. It is sometimes difficult to distinguish between the two. However, the following guidelines generally apply. Fantasy deals more with the unreality of supernatural beings, dragons, magic, and talking animals. Fantasy is a recreating of old myths and is a rich source of human creativity. Fantasy could not happen in the past, nor can it happen in the present or in the future because it includes imaginary creatures. Science fiction writers seek to persuade the reader that their events could happen, or they present a rational explanation for future happenings. Science fiction sometimes tells what might happen in the future based on scientific knowledge. It often deals with the future of our planet and ways of preventing its destruction.

James Gunn says that we live in a science fiction world. Science fiction has influenced our world of today. We have seen the fulfillment of machines that fly, of men walking on the moon, of photographs of the surface of other planets, and of space shuttles. Mary Ann Paulin states in *Creative Uses of Children's Literature* that science fiction is often considered almost realistic because the predictions of robots, computers, and space travel have become a reality. What the future holds may be predicted by current science fiction writers as they focus on the long journey or on lands unknown.

Characterization is important to good science fiction. Rebecca Lukens says in *A Critical Handbook of Children's Literature* that readers must believe in the reality of the characters in order to believe in their experiences. Characters must remain consistent to their inner nature even when they show growth, change, and maturity. Kingsley Amis is quoted by James Gunn in *Alternate Worlds* (p. 239) as follows:

Cardboard spacemen aren't enough,
Nor alien monsters, sketched in rough,
Character's the essential stuff.

Many science fiction writers are now placing increased emphasis on characterization rather than on the plot.

Science fiction appeals to children and young people because it is exciting and entertaining. It explores unknown worlds, presents unusual aliens, promotes adventures, provides study of future societies, portrays heroes, and forecasts brave new frontiers to conquer. The appeal of science fiction has been promoted by the mass production of paperback books, movies, cartoons, magazines, and television programs.

Suggestions for evaluating imaginative literature are given by Kenneth Donelson and Alleen Nilsen in *Literature for Today's Young Adults*. In regard to science fiction, these include positive qualities associated with good literature, originality of concept, establishing a relationship with the real world to encourage new viewpoints, and stimulating readers to think creatively. Negative qualities of poor literature that apply to science fiction include stereotypes, awkward transitions, no relationship to human nature or the real world, inconsistencies throughout the story, and unexpected magical solutions.

Ursula Le Guin comments in *The Language of the Night* that the science fiction writer makes or uses a connection or bridge "between the conscious and unconscious—so that his reader can make the journey too" (p. 78). She states that science fiction should be taken seriously because it deals with important human concerns. Concepts that adults reject are often acceptable to children. Madeleine L'Engle, quoted by Donna Norton in *Through the Eyes of a Child*, says that there is "one very solid reason my science fiction/fantasy books are marketed for children: only children are open enough to understand them" (p. 295).

Writers of science fiction for children and young people include many well known names in the general field of science fiction. Robert Heinlein, Lester Del Ray, Andre Norton, Ray Bradbury, Isaac Asimov, and Arthur C. Clarke are some of the better-known writers who have written books on both the adult and juvenile levels. Other popular authors of science fiction for children and young people include Madeleine L'Engle, John Christopher, Peter Dickinson, Sylvia Engdahl, Alice Lightner, Monica Hughes, Jerome Beatty, Patricia Wrightson, and Eleanor Cameron.

ELEMENT OF LITERATURE: FOCUS ON THEME

One definition of theme, according to Stan Malless and Jeff McQuain in *The Elements of English*, is "the point of a story" (p. 24). They stress that the theme is not the plot. Readers usually agree on the plot of a story but may not agree on the theme. There may be more than one theme that may or may not be stated. The reader should discover the theme(s) while reading the story or through discussion with others who have read the story.

Rebecca Lukens states that theme in literature is "the idea that holds the story together" and is the "significant truth" (p. 111). She notes that the theme usually remains with the reader after the plot is forgotten. Sylvan Barnet, in *A Short Guide to Writing about Literature*, says that theme is the underlying idea that helps the reader to see what the plot is really about.

Donna Norton emphasizes in *Through the Eyes of a Child* that the theme "ties the plot, characterization, and setting together in a meaningful whole" (p. 95). Zena Sutherland and May Hill Arbuthnot, in the seventh edition of *Children and Books*, explain theme as the central core or often the message of the book. "It gives readers a vision, through fiction, of the author's perception of human experience" (p. 48).

Themes in literature are either explicit or implicit. The explicit themes are those that are stated by the author clearly and openly in the story. In *Mind-Call*, by Wilanne Belden, a theme of struggle for self-control against mind control or visualization is expressed explicitly when the author states that Tallie accepted and conquered her past and would never accept other visualizations as her own. The implicit themes are those that are implied or shown through dialogue, characters, or actions. In *A Wrinkle in Time*, by Madeleine L'Engle, the theme of evil and darkness is expressed implicitly in the descriptions, actions, and meanings of "It."

Themes vary in different genres. In realistic fiction, themes may reflect real problems of growing up and personal development, as in Judy Blume's *Are You There God? It's Me, Margaret* or in Jerry Spinelli's *Space Station Seventh Grade*. The theme of establishing good relationships between children and adults is depicted in Katherine Paterson's *The Great Gilly Hopkins*. The theme of self-reliance and ability to handle problems is demonstrated in Cynthia Voigt's *Homecoming*. Themes in fantasy literature often express fundamental issues of life, universal truths, imagination and wonder, and good or evil. J. R. R. Tolkien develops the theme between good and evil in *The Hobbit*. Ursula Le Guin portrays the universal theme of overcoming personal problems and obtaining maturity and freedom in *The Tombs of Atuan*. In historical fiction, themes include the futility of war, search for a better life, independence, loyalty and honor, righting injustices, human greed, and freedom. A number of these themes, as well as one of friendship and working together, are depicted in Elizabeth George Speare's *The Sign of the Beaver*. The themes of war, hatred, and persecution are expressed in Johanna Reiss's *The Upstairs Room*. In adventure stories, themes of conflict dominate the genre. These include conflicts of person-against-person, person-against-nature, and person-against-self. The conflict with and survival against nature is reflected in Gary Paulsen's *Hatchet* and in Jean George's *Julie of the Wolves*. In animal stories the themes vary from human interaction with animals, love and devotion, protection of animals, close relationships among animals and humans, loyalty, overcoming obstacles, survival, and responsibility. Friendship, loyalty, and loss are all themes expressed in E. B. White's *Charlotte's Web*. The theme of taming, keeping, and parting with a wild animal pet is presented in Marjorie Kinnan Rawlings's *The Yearling* and Jean George's *Cry of the Crow*.

Themes are a very important part of literature for children and young people whether they are implicit, explicit, multiple, primary, or secondary. Themes give meaning and texture to literature while enlarging and expanding the reader's world of understanding, discovery, and delight.

There are 175 theme entries in *The Science Fiction Encyclopedia*, edited by Peter Nichols. This comprehensive list includes the familiar themes of aliens, automation, ecology, fantastic voyages, invasion, life on other worlds, the moon, robots, rockets, space flight, spaceships, time travel, and Utopias. Also included are the less familiar themes of absurdist science fiction, cyborgs, eschatology, hive-minds, optimism and pessimism, space opera, sword and sorcery, and weather control.

A historical study of the themes in science fiction reveals the changes in emphasis from the early days to the present. In 1864, Jules Verne wrote *Journey to the Center of the Earth*, which deals with the themes of exploration and wonders of the world. In 1897, H. G. Wells wrote *The War of the Worlds* with the theme of aliens and invasions. In 1938, C. S. Lewis wrote *Out of the Silent Planet* with a theological, intercontinental theme. In 1956, John Christopher wrote *The Death of Grass* with the theme of ecology and upsetting the balance of nature. In 1990, George Ryman wrote an adult science fiction story, *The Child Garden*, dealing with the themes of biological revolution, postelectronic culture, genetic engineering, and interim-learning stages.

The themes in science fiction for children and young people are usually universal themes like good and evil, danger, friendship, loyalty, quests, and heroes and heroines. Other popular themes include adventures of exploration, aliens, spaceships, rockets, and robots. *The Science Fiction Encyclopedia* states that most of the science fiction for juveniles before 1920 was written for boys. This included dime novels, comic books, and series books like Tom Swift and "The Great Marvel Series." The themes were of lost worlds, inventions, and wars. In 1929, Hugh Lofting wrote *Dr. Dolittle in the Moon*, and, in 1946, William Pene Du Bois wrote *The Twenty-One Balloons;* both were enjoyed by many children. Pseudo-science and magic were combined themes in Andre Norton's "Witch World Series." Robert Heinlein's themes of growing into adulthood and assuming moral responsibilities have made him one of the outstanding writers of science fiction for older children. His use of children and young people as protagonists make his books very appealing to young readers. John Christopher and Sylvia Engdahl also use young protagonists. John Christopher's *The White Mountains* promotes the themes of resistance to aliens and the struggle against conformity. Sylvia Engdahl, in *Enchantress from the Stars* and *The Far Side of Evil*, uses the theme of technology combined with intelligence working for just causes to overcome evil.

RECOMMENDED LISTS

Recommended Titles for Teaching the Science Fiction Genre Units

Ursula Le Guin says in her book of essays on science fiction, *The Language of the Night*, that what sets science fiction apart from other fiction is "its use of new metaphors, drawn from certain great dominates of our contemporary life" (p. 159). She states that these metaphors include science, technology, space travel, alternative societies, alternative biology, and the future. The following recommended titles include most of these themes.

Christopher, John. *Dragon Dance.* New York: E. P. Dutton, 1986. RL: Grade 7. IL: Grades 7–10.

Simon and Brad are cousins. Simon is from England and Brad is from America. Together they encounter a white ball of light that is a fireball. This encounter sends them into another world or alternate world. It is a world geographically identical to their own but very different in all other ways. It is in a different time period and is a frightening world. The unusual aspect is that everything exists as if the Roman Empire had retained control until the twentieth century. Brad and Simon are taken captives of Indians and are prized as personal attendants. One Indian woman likes Brad and smothers him with her attention. The Indians come under the control of a slave trader who puts them in a deep trance and takes them to China on a junk. Brad and Simon cannot be hypnotized but travel to China with the Indians. The Chinese are puzzled by Brad and Simon, who learn Chinese and are taken to the Supreme Excellent Lord Yuan Chu at the Imperial Palace. There they meet the Son of Heaven, the boy emperor, who likes Brad and Simon very much. The real ruler is the Dowager Empress. She distrusts Brad and Simon and wants them away from the young Emperor. Brad and Simon go to the Bonzery of Grace, where they are to receive instruction from the priests of Bei-Kun. The laws of Bei-Kun were established by Roger Bacon, who lived in the alternative world in thirteenth-century China. The Bonzery of Grace is a beautiful place with exotic fruits, plants, and courtyards. It is a Shangri-la. Brad meets a beautiful girl in her mid-teens, Li Mei, and is enticed to come under her control. He hears a man's voice telling him that there is nothing to fear and to be at peace. Simon is controlled by a man called Bei-Pen. Simon and Brad are separated and have to fight to keep control of their minds and destinies. They find that things are not as they seem, and they have many surprises.

The theme of mind control is stated both explicitly and implicitly through the characters and their actions. The theme of growing toward manhood and taking control of one's destiny is implicit throughout the story. The concept of mind control, the Bonzery of Grace, and the laws of Bei-Kun are difficult concepts with reading levels of grade 7 and up that require the reader to use higher thinking skills and advanced reading skills.

An alternative book by John Christopher on a lower reading and interest level is *The White Mountains*.

Christopher, John. *The White Mountains*. New York: Macmillan, 1964. RL: Grade 6. IL: Grades 5–10. PB: Macmillan.

Will Parker is very upset about the upcoming capping ceremony on his fourteenth birthday. He will be capped with a steel plate on his skull and will then be controlled by the hated Tripods, who have taken over the earth. It is the twenty-first century. The Tripods are large machine-creatures or robots who use their capping techniques to make all adults obedient and subservient. Will and his friends, Henry and Beanpole, learn that there are some free people who live in the White Mountains. They decide to try to join the free people before they are capped. The Tripods follow the young men and try to prevent their escape. Will and his friends have many adventures and hazards to face on their journey, but at last they successfully reach the White Mountains and freedom.

There are a number of themes in *The White Mountains*. These include the importance of free will, good against evil, and freedom.

Engdahl, Sylvia. *Enchantress from the Stars.* New York: Atheneum, 1971. RL: Grade 7. IL: Grades 7–10. PB: Macmillan.

Elana hides aboard her father's spaceship to accompany him and her boyfriend on a mission to another planet. She is a field agent in training for the anthropological service but has not yet been commissioned. She wants to observe and learn from her father. Elana knows that her chosen field of service will require hard study and hard work and will include some danger. This mission is of special interest because it involves three peoples of different levels of advancement. When they arrive on Andrecia, Elana learns that the mission is to save a people, the Younglings, from extinction. The Younglings live under a feudal system. A rich, new planet has sent an Imperial Exploration Corps to take over the planet and to colonize it. They plan to exterminate the natives, whom they consider humanoid animals. The Imperials begin to clear the area of green trees and grass and to sterilize the ground. They use a machine shaped like a prehistoric beast as a rock chewer. They wear pressure suits and helmets to guard against bacteria. The natives are very frightened by all of this and think that the machine is a dragon. All natives who go to fight the "dragon" are captured and never return to their homes. When one of the spaceship team members, an experienced young lady, is destroyed by the enemy, Elana is enlisted by her father to take part in the mission. She is instructed to be careful not to disclose her identity and to use only native physical weapons. She cannot use all of her powers. She does use her magic powers to help Georyn, a native woodcutter, who is sent by his father to go into the dark forest and destroy the "dragon." The woodcutters believe that Elana is enchanted. She instructs Georyn and helps him to develop faith and belief in himself and his abilities to overthrow the Imperials. Elana makes mistakes, discloses some of her power to Jarel, one of the Imperials, and becomes emotionally involved with Georyn. But the mission is a success and Elana, now wiser and sadder, returns to her planet with her father and boyfriend.

The theme of saving a people from extinction by making the invading colonists leave of their own will is explicitly stated. The theme of conscious control over psychic powers is implicitly shown through the actions of the characters. The theme of the consequences of power is also implicitly stated.

Godfrey, Martyn. *I Spent My Summer Vacation Kidnapped into Space.* New York: Scholastic, 1990. RL: Grade 5. IL: Grades 5–9.

The setting is sometime in the near future. Jared and Reeann, students at Bush Academy in Houston, decide to go offworld in an Academy shuttle to look for bloodstone. They did not want to go on the traditional sixth-grade end-of-the-year trip to Brazil. They are not supposed to fly a shuttle until they get a license at age 13. Their parents work for NASA-O, an organization in charge of sending settlers to Outworlds.

Reeann had planned to go to summer camp on Mars and visit her grandparents on Ganymede, near Jupiter. Jared had planned to spend his vacation at home since he now had his computer online with the Library of UGF. While on Asteroid F6HJ8 looking for bloodstone, Jared and Reeann are kidnapped by humanoid Torkan aliens, who look like ugly koala bears. The Torkans keep threatening to kill Jared and Reeann, but they take them to their planet, Freetal. Jared and Reeann are sold to a circus on Freetal. As a sport and entertainment at the circus, Jared and Reeann are put in a cage with huge, slimy worms. The worms eat their victims. Jared and Reeann must use their human intelligence to overcome the worms and win their release. This test was planned by Gam, a disguised agent of the emperor. Jared and Reeann are sent by the emperor to rescue his young daughter who is being held captive on the planet Weke by the emperor's evil cousin. Jared and Reeann are disguised as pet monkeys. They must again use their human intelligence to outwit the captors on Weke. They finally get to a freeworld, Yugur, where they can return to Earth and their homes in Houston. They laugh when they think that a teacher may ask them to write a story about How I Spent My Summer Vacation.

The themes of the superiority of human intelligence and friendship are explicitly stated several times in the story. Other themes are space travel, spaceships, and future life in outerworlds.

This is a delightful book for reading aloud, reading and studying as a class project, or individual reading.

Heinlein, Robert A. *Citizen of the Galaxy.* New York: Charles Scribner's Sons, 1957, 1985. RL: Grade 7. IL: Grade 7 and up. PB: Ballentine.

Thorby, a young slave, is in the capital of Jubbul and the Nine Worlds, where he is auctioned to Baslim, the Cripple. The time is far in the future when the human race has colonized many planets. Thorby does not remember his own home, planet, or early ancestry. He only remembers being on a large slave spaceship, being mistreated, beaten, and hungry. Baslim sees Thorby as having a great deal of potential. He believes that Thorby might be of unmutated Earth ancestry because of his eyes and the shape of his ears. Baslim is in disguise as a beggar, but he is actually an undercover agent. Baslim knows many languages and teaches Thorby not only to read and speak them, but to think and reason as well. He teaches Thorby that the way to find justice is "to deal fairly with other people and not worry about how they deal with you" (p. 109). Baslim never discloses his business to Thorby, but he gives him messages (in code and under hypnosis) to memorize, with instructions on how to carry them out if Baslim is captured. Thorby calls Baslim "Pop" and does not want his freedom even though it is offered by Baslim. Thorby receives his manumission anyway and registers his freedom at the Royal Archives. A line is tattooed through the serial number on his body. Baslim, the Cripple, is very kind to Thorby and wins his trust and love for life.

When Baslim is captured and killed, Thorby is able to escape and deliver one of his messages to Captain Krausa, the skipper of the *Sisu* ship. Thorby does not understand the message, but the captain does. The message gives instructions to care for Thorby and to help locate his family and restore him to his own people. The skipper accepts Thorby aboard and adopts him out of gratitude to Baslim. He says that debts are always paid. Thorby stays on the *Sisu*, gains ship's rank, and learns the ways of the trade ship. He makes friends with Mata, Jeri, and Fritz and adjusts to his new family and to life aboard the *Sisu*. He is taken to the Guard Cruiser *Hydra* as part of the message from Baslim. Thorby now is able to understand the message and accepts his new assignment because it is what Pop told him to do. Thorby enjoys learning duties of the Guardsmen and the challenges of the new ship. When his identity is finally confirmed, he is taken to lovely Terra, Mother of the Worlds. He learns that he is heir to the famous, wealthy Rudbek Enterprises. He unravels some of the business dealings of his company and continues his fight for justice.

The theme of *Citizen of the Galaxy* is freedom and justice and opposition to slavery. The message is one of lifting the yoke of oppression and breaking the chains of injustice throughout the galaxy no matter what it costs.

This powerful and exciting book is science fiction at its classic best. It can be read by good readers in the seventh and eighth grades, by high school students, and by adults.

L'Engle, Madeleine. *A Wrinkle in Time.* New York: Farrar, Straus & Giroux, 1962. RL: Grade 5. IL: Grades 5–9. PB: Dell.

Meg Murray and her brilliant young brother, Charles Wallace Murray, and Calvin O'Keefe become involved in travel to a strange planet. After Meg's and Charles's father disappears from the earth, an old lady named Mrs. Whatsit visits the Murray household and encourages the travel to another planet by telling them that there *is* such a thing as a tesseract. The parents, who are scientists, had discussed the concept of tesseract. The father had been working on this concept when he disappeared. The children are told that their father is in grave danger and only they can save him; they must be willing to tesser, or travel, in the fifth dimension. The children are eager to do this. Mrs. Who and Mrs. Whatsit tell Meg that if she wants to help her father, she must stake her life on the truth as her father has staked his life on the truth. Mrs. Whatsit gives each child a special gift by strengthening their greatest ability. Meg, Charles Wallace, and Calvin use their gifts to fight against evil and try to rescue Mr. Murray.

The three children go to Camazotz, the location of the Central Intelligence Center, where they become involved in a fierce battle between opposing forces of good and evil. They fight the dark and evil "It" to rescue Mr. Murray. Meg also must use her special gift to free Charles Wallace. All of them tesser back to earth with newfound knowledge of good and evil.

The themes of good and evil, love and hate permeate the book and are expressed in both explicit and implicit ways. "It" is described implicitly as a dark, evil thing.

Norton, Andre, and Dorothy Madlee. *Star Ka'at.* New York: Pocket Books, 1976. RL: Grade 4. IL: Grades 4–6.

Jim is a young orphan who lives with a foster family. He

remains very upset over the death of his parents in a plane crash. He had always wanted a pet but had never had one. When he meets Tiro, a large, handsome black cat, Jim is bewildered by the fact that he seems able to communicate with Tiro. Elly Mae is a young black girl who is very poor. She tries to take care of her sick grandmother by collecting bottles and discarded items to sell. Elly Mae meets Mer, a beautiful, slender, grayish-white cat, and she claims Mer for her own after she gets over her initial fear. Elly Mae can also communicate with Mer. Tiro and Mer are intelligent cats from outer space. They believe that the earth will soon be destroyed by war, and they have come to rescue their kin and take them back aboard a shuttle to their planet in this galaxy. Elly Mae's grandmother dies, and Jim's foster family is planning to move. Neither Elly Mae nor Jim really have a home. When they accidently discover a spaceship and the hordes of cats in it, they are taken aboard the spaceship with the cats. Elly Mae and Jim develop mind-send, thought-send, and mind-kin with Tiro and Mer and are "claimed" by them.

The themes of being alone, friendship, companionship, and trust are implicitly implied through the characters and the actions of the story. The themes of righting wrongs and acceptance of the future are explicitly expressed. "The future would be very different, but he was not afraid anymore, not with the kin about him" (p. 118).

Recommended Titles for Individual or Group Study

Christopher, John. *The City of Gold and Lead.* New York: Macmillan, 1967. RL: Grade 6. IL: Grades 5–9.

This is the second volume in *The White Mountains* trilogy. Will and his friends take part in an athletic contest, and as winners, they go to the city of the Tripods. They win the right and privilege to serve the Masters. Will goes with the purpose of spying on the Tripods.

Christopher, John. *The Pool of Fire.* New York: Macmillan, 1968. RL: Grade 6. IL: Grades 5–9.

This is the third volume in *The White Mountains* trilogy. Will works with the free people to defeat the Tripods through sabotage.

With their new freedom, the people try to set up their own government. Because of quarreling and competition, the people cannot agree. Will is very disappointed but works with a small group interested in world unity.

Danziger, Paula. *This Place Has No Atmosphere.* New York: Delacorte Press, 1986. RL: Grade 5. IL: Grades 5–9. PB: Dell.

Aurora is a teenager living on earth in 2057. Her life at school is filled with robots, computers, mood clothes, Walkperson earrings, viddisks, telekinetic powers, special friends, and Matthew. He is nice, cute, fun, and Aurora's new boyfriend. Everything is looking great until Aurora's family, as part of their job with the government, takes an assignment on the moon. Aurora has a very difficult time adjusting to life on the moon. Her one bright spot is her teacher, Mr. Wilcox, who is also the principal, guidance counselor, and media specialist. Hal, who has lived on the moon for ten years, becomes a special friend. Together they help put on a play, and Aurora begins to adjust to her new life on the moon.

Hoover, H. M. *The Delikon.* New York: Viking, 1977. RL: Grade 6. IL: Grades 5–9.

The Delikon Society from outer space has ruled earth for centuries. The Delikon is an evil group of space creatures. They send their teachers to earth to train children for leadership. The people of earth have no freedom. When Aron and his family cross the boundary laid out by the ruling house, they are in danger. They are caught up in a revolution against the Delikon and manage to escape.

L'Engle, Madeleine. *Wind in the Door.* New York: Farrar, Straus & Giroux, 1973. RL: Grade 7. IL: Grades 5–9. PB: Dell.

Meg Murray, Charles Wallace Murray, and Calvin O'Keefe are involved in a suspenseful drama in galactic space in this companion piece to *A Wrinkle in Time.* Charles Wallace seems near death in the small world of Mitochondrion. Meg uses her special powers to extend her love in helping to save her brother and overcome evil.

Pinkwater, Daniel M. *Fat Men from Space*. New York: Dodd, Mead & Company, 1977. RL: Grade 5. IL: Grades 5–6.

William hears about space people who are invading the earth from a radio broadcast through a filling in his tooth. He boards the spaceship of the junk-food pirates and takes off for adventures filled with fun and food. When the fat men from space take off with all of the junk food, William has to learn to eat health foods.

Picture Storybooks for Teaching Theme

Alexander, Martha. *Marty McGee's Space Lab, No Girls Allowed*. New York: Dial Press, 1981.

Marty McGee has a private, top-secret space lab with a large sign on the door: "No girls allowed." Marty is finishing a space helmet that he thinks will enable him to fly. Rachel, Marty's sister, is told to stay out. But baby sister Jenny goes into the lab and takes the helmet. She puts it on and uses her rattle to make the helmet fly. Marty misses his space helmet and is accusing Rachel of taking it when Jenny flies into the room wearing the helmet. Marty is furious and restates that no girls are allowed in the lab. He then tries to make the helmet fly, but it will not fly for him. He has to ask Jenny what she did to make it fly. The girls are delighted that Marty needs their help and insist that he change his sign to include them as space pilots. To his dismay, Marty finds that he is too heavy to fly in his space helmet. It only seems to work for little girls.

The theme of the book, "no girls allowed," is the age-old theme of the battle of the sexes, especially applied to the field of science and invention. It is explicitly stated through the title, posted on the door, and restated throughout the book. The theme is modified to show that girls are allowed and belong in the scientific world when Marty finds that he needs them.

This small-scale book needs to be passed around the room after reading to allow the students to view the illustrations.

Counsel, June. *But Martin!* Illustrated by Carolyn Dinan. London: Faber & Faber, 1984.

Lee, Lloyd, Billy, and Angela are sad when they must return to school, but finding Martin changes this. Lee has a smooth, golden face and black, silky hair. Lloyd has a round, brown face and black, bouncy hair. Billy has a square, red face and red, spiky hair. Angela has a long, white face and fair, floaty hair. But Martin has a green face and, instead of hair, has two long antennae. Martin is delightful. He joins the group at school and bleeps, floats, vanishes, and enters the room through the wall. He is a whiz and knows everything. He is a great teacher and helps Lee, Lloyd, Billy, and Angela learn mathematics and spelling skills before he returns home via his flying saucer.

The theme in *But Martin!* is implicitly developed to show that differences in color and race are not important and that friendship is possible among all races, including aliens. Although all of the children look different than one another and Martin looks very different than all the rest, they all like each other just as they are.

This is a delightful book with excellent illustrations and is highly recommended for sharing.

Glass, Andrew. *My Brother Tries To Make Me Laugh.* New York: Lothrop, Lee & Shepard, 1984.

Zena and Odeon are space children who travel in a spaceship with their parents toward earth. During the long journey, Odeon tries to entertain his younger sister, Zena, by making funny faces and telling silly stories. He tells her that on earth children ride giraffes to school, let elephants live under their tables to eat all the unwanted vegetables, and live in jumbo jets. On their spaceship, Robot brings their meals and takes turns driving. Everyone helps with the chores of suspending the plates and vacuum-packing the cups. Odeon secretly programs the computer to tell Zena that earthlings are called "Snackers" and that they go to the moon to get cheesy moonrocks to eat on their crackers. Robot then secretly telephones the earthling family they are to visit to tell them Odeon's stories and asks them to pretend that they are true. When Odeon, Zena, and their parents are greeted by the earthling family, they are invited to have a snack of moonrocks and crackers. Odeon is just as surprised as everyone else. He says that he thought he just made up the stories to make his sister laugh. The earthlings then tell about Robot's telephone call and everyone has a good laugh. Odeon and Zena decide that their visit to earth will be fun.

The themes of making new friends, sharing humor and fun,

and caring for family members are stated explicitly throughout the story.

The illustrations are humorous and delightful. They are great for visualizing the themes of science fiction.

TEACHING TIPS: THE SCIENCE FICTION GENRE AND THEME

Teaching the science fiction genre unit can be exciting and challenging for both students and teachers. Many students already enjoy science fiction through film, television, comic books, science fiction magazines, and books. Other students know at least something about the genre and can be challenged to join the journey into science fiction.

Start the unit by showing the videotape or movie of *Star Wars* or *E. T.* Even though students will be very familiar with both, there is something special about sharing an experience with other classmates. Ask students to view with the purpose of discovering something that they missed in previous viewings. Use the film as a springboard to a discussion of the science fiction genre. Supplement the discussion with information from the genre introduction included in this chapter.

Introduce the literary element of the theme of the story by selecting and using science fiction picture storybooks. Suggested titles such as *But Martin!*, by June Counsel, and *My Brother Tries To Make Me Laugh*, by Andrew Glass, have been provided. These may be supplemented or substituted with other available titles. Use *A to Zoo: Subject Access to Children's Picture Books*, by Carolyn and John Lima, to locate additional titles. The subject heading of science fiction is not included, but such headings as space and spaceships, robots, and the moon provide many suggestions. If a number of science fiction picture storybooks are available, they can be used by small groups. Each group can read aloud one book and discuss the theme. They can select one person in the group to share the book and tell the theme to the class. Using the background notes on theme that have been provided, discuss and give examples in a large group activity. Advanced readers can explore science fiction literature through a filmstrip series, *Reading Science Fiction*, which analyzes the themes of robots, aliens, voyages to imaginary worlds, and visions of the future with works by H. G. Wells, Jules

Verne, Arthur Clarke, and Isaac Asimov.

Plan and prepare objectives for the unit according to reading levels, class organization, and amount of time allocated to the unit. As suggested in the introductory chapter, books for class use for this unit need to be selected at an early date so that they can be ordered or put on reserve and made available on schedule. If the entire class is not reading the same book, small groups can be formed. John Christopher's *The White Mountains* trilogy can be used with students on a grade 6 reading level, or his *Fire Ball* trilogy can be used with students on more advanced reading levels. Madeleine L'Engle's trilogy of books about the Murrays can be used with students on reading levels of grade 5. Groups can also be organized by authors or around themes in science fiction literature. With careful selection, older students can enjoy some well-written adult science fiction within their reading levels.

Use the suggested activities that follow to go out of this world with science fiction. It will be worth the trip!

FOCUS ON CRITICAL-THINKING AND COMMUNICATION SKILLS: READING FOR DETAIL AND ANALYSIS

Use science fiction literature to focus students on comprehension skills. By planning and incorporating reading skills into the literature unit, students can relate to themes and adventures in science fiction while increasing their reading skills.

Basic study guides can be prepared for students to use as they read. This would apply especially if the entire class is reading the same title. In *Ideas for Teaching English in the Junior High and Middle School,* edited by Candy Carter and Zora Rashkis, it is suggested that the format of a study guide might include an introduction with questions to be answered before reading, basic questions to be answered during reading, vocabulary questions to enhance vocabulary development, thought questions to be answered after reading, and "going beyond the story" questions for applying the concepts to their own experience.

Include the following reading skills in planning activities for this unit:

1. Read, listen, or view with a purpose

2. Identify and explain cause-and-effect relationships
3. Compare and contrast events in science fiction stories to current-day events
4. Predict the outcome of a science fiction story
5. Use context clues to determine the meaning of new words
6. Identify the characteristics of a science fiction story
7. Search for explicit statements of the primary theme of a science fiction story
8. Search for explicit statements given as part of the narrative as possible messages on the theme from the author
9. Locate or recall implicit statements of the theme or themes of a science fiction story
10. Identify supporting details regarding time and place in a science fiction story

Suggestions for incorporating these skills into the science fiction genre unit are included in the related activities sections.

ACTIVITIES

Activities Related to Teaching the Science Fiction Genre

Gather a wide assortment of visual and supplementary material on science fiction themes to use as interest centers, on bulletin boards, and in display racks. Ask the library media specialist to assist with this collection. Be sure to utilize sources such as NASA, the Air and Space Museum, National Geographic Society, and the Smithsonian Institution.

Use the video series *Star Wars Collection,* available from Critics' Choice Video. The collection includes the trilogy of *Star Wars, The Empire Strikes Back,* and *Return of the Jedi* as well as *From Star Wars to Jedi: The Making of a Saga.* All four videos can be shown to the class or students can be divided into groups to take turns viewing one of the movies. They also could be loaned to students for home use. Ask students to compare and contrast at least two events in the movies with current-day activities.

Let students go to the library media center to locate information and write brief summaries of topics such as space exploration, astronauts, astronomy, the moon, UFOs, and spaceships.

Obtain a cassette tape or record of H. G. Wells's *The War of the Worlds*. Tell the students about the radio dramatization by Orson Welles on October 30, 1938, when listeners thought this was the news story of a real happening. Ask the students to listen to the recording and imagine that they are hearing it today as a radio broadcast. After listening to the recording, let students discuss their reactions. Ask if it sounded real to them and if they found it to be frightening.

Discuss in a large group activity the titles of the science fiction books to be used in the teaching unit. Ask the students to make predictions about the content of the book from the title. After the students have read about one-third of their book, ask them to compare their earlier prediction based on the title with the actual content of the book. Let them now make predictions about the outcome of events in the book.

Inform students that they should determine the time and place of the setting for the story they read. Ask them to make notes identifying supporting details regarding the time and place.

Divide the class into groups and assign one of the planets to each group. Tell the students to locate and make a list of facts about their planet including size, distance from the earth, and environment. Ask them to imagine a spaceship trip in the future to that planet and make a list of their fantasies about their trip and life there. They will have to plan an environment that can overcome the problems of sustaining life on that planet.

Plan with the library media specialist to provide a research activity in the library media center concerning technological changes from 1915 to the present that have had a great impact on the lives of citizens. Tell the students to browse through resources such as encyclopedias and reference books, books of first facts, pictorial histories, time lines, lists of inventors and inventions, and historical surveys. Ask them to make a list of the changes along with available dates. In a large group discussion, list the students' findings on the chalkboard or on a transparency. Then, let the students brainstorm ideas on what new technological changes might be developed in the next 75 years. List these ideas as before. At the conclusion of the science fiction genre unit, look again at the ideas for future changes obtained from the students' brainstorming session. Ask if the science fiction book that they read contained any of their suggestions.

Select an eventful episode from one science fiction book to read to the class. It might be the fight with the slimy worms in Martyn Godfrey's *I Spent My Summer Vacation Kidnapped into Space* or Thorby's decision to investigate his billionaire company's activities in Robert Heinlein's *Citizen of the Galaxy*. Let the students compare what they might have done under the same circumstances with what the characters actually did in the story.

Tell students to use context clues to determine the meaning of new words as they read their science fiction story. Ask them to compile a list of these new words to share in discussion time.

With advanced students, use the computer program *Write a Story!* for Apple computers (from Sunburst Communications). It is the fourth program in the *Magic Slate* series. The program deals with writing a science fiction story about the future. The complete story will contain 22 chapters. It involves developing characters, writing, revising, and proofreading. Different students can write a chapter as an independent study project. This is an involved activity requiring large periods of time and good planning.

Review the characteristics of a science fiction story and ask students to write a paragraph describing the characteristics.

Activities Related to Teaching Theme

Play the theme song from *Star Wars* and let students draw images related to science fiction. Tell the students that they can share their illustrations if they would like, but they are not required to do so.

Ask students to tell in a large group discussion period how they discovered the primary theme of their science fiction story. Let them discuss how the theme differs from the plot.

Instruct the students to search for explicit statements of the primary theme of a science fiction story, either by characters in the story or as a part of the narrative provided by the author.

Ask the students to search for implicit statements or actions that reveal the theme in a science fiction story.

Involve students in a media production expressing one of the themes from a science fiction story. This can be a slide/tape, animated super-8mm movie, video, skit, bulletin board, or mural production.

Propose the question, "If an alien were to walk into your yard, how would you communicate? How would you demonstrate the theme of friendship?" Let volunteers pantomime their ideas.

Divide the students into groups according to the theme of the science fiction story they read, if the entire class did not read the same story. Ask the students to discuss the themes and compare and contrast the similarities and differences.

Discuss the theme of the picture storybook *But Martin!* if it is available. Ask how the theme applies to young people in the United States today and if it could apply to the future with aliens.

Additional Activities

Plan a science fiction-related field trip to space centers, art galleries, planetariums, or museums in your area.

Prepare an annotated bibliography of science fiction books in the school library media center by asking students who read individual science fiction stories to contribute an annotation. Remind the students to use good bibliographic form. Give the annotations to the library media specialist for use in the library media center.

Encourage students to continue reading additional science fiction stories for pleasure.

NONPRINT RESOURCES

Audiocassettes

The Word for the World is Forest by Ursula Le Guin. Book of the Road. Tale of interplanetary colonization and extraterrestrials.

Computer Programs

Write a Story! Program four of the *Magic Slate* series. Sunburst Communications.

Filmstrips

Reading Science Fiction. Random House Media. Titles include *Voyages to Imaginary Worlds; Heroes, Robots, and Aliens; Tomorrow's Discoveries Today.*

Science Fiction Literature for Children series. Pied Piper Productions. Includes *City of Gold and Lead*, by John Christopher, and *A Wrinkle in Time* by Madeleine L' Engle.

Videotapes

E. T. the Extra-Terrestrial. MCA.
Star Wars Collection: Star Wars, The Empire Strikes Back, and Return of the Jedi. Fox.

References

Barnet, Sylvan. *A Short Guide to Writing about Literature.* New York: Little, Brown & Company, 1986.
Carter, Candy, and Zora Rashkis, eds. *Ideas for Teaching English in the Junior High and Middle School.* Urbana, IL: National Council of Teachers of English, 1980.
Cullinan, Bernice E., ed. *Children's Literature in the Reading Program.* Newark, DE: International Reading Association, 1987.
Donelson, Kenneth L., and Alleen P. Nilsen. *Literature for Today's Young Adults.* Glenview, IL: Scott, Foresman and Company, 1980.
Gunn, James. *Alternate Worlds.* Englewood Cliffs, NJ: Prentice-Hall, 1975.
Le Guin, Ursula. *The Language of the Night.* New York: G. P. Putnam's Sons, 1979.
Lima, Carolyn, and John Lima. *A to Zoo: Subject Access to Children's Picture Books.* 3d ed. New York: R. R. Bowker, 1989.
Lukens, Rebecca. *A Critical Handbook of Children's Literature.* 3d ed. Glenview, IL: Scott, Foresman and Company, 1986.
Malless, Stan, and Jeff McQuain. *The Elements of English.* New York: Madison Books, 1988.
Nichols, Peter, ed. *The Science Fiction Encyclopedia.* Garden City, NY: Doubleday, 1979.
Norton, Donna. *Through the Eyes of a Child: An Introduction to Children's Literature.* 2d ed. Columbus, OH: Merrill Publishing Company, 1987.
Paulin, Mary Ann. *Creative Uses of Children's Literature.* Hamden, CT: Shoestring Press, 1982.
Sutherland, Zena, and May Hill Arbuthnot. *Children and Books.* 7th ed. Glenview, IL: Scott, Foresman and Company, 1986.

6

Realistic Fiction

"'Is it true?' the child asks. 'Is the story true?' . . . And my answer for you is the same answer that I give the child who asks. 'I hope so. I meant for it to be true. I tried hard to make it so.'"
Katherine Paterson
Gates of Excellence: On Reading and Writing Books for Children

INTRODUCTION

The realistic fiction genre is the body of literature that portrays real-life situations. The story is possible, set in modern times, with events that could occur. Everything in the story, from the characters to the plot, could happen to people today. The plot is an accurate portrayal of the events of the contemporary world. The setting is recognizable, whether it is at home, at school, at an outdoor rock concert, at a pizza parlor, or at a shopping mall. The spirit of the times is captured in scenes that reflect everyday life. The characters are understandable, and their behavior and speech are true to their age and experience. They respond to the situations with believable behavior, whether right or wrong.

Realistic fiction encompasses many types of fiction. In the broadest sense this includes stories of adventure, animals, friendship and romance, humor, mystery, and sports. Only friendship, romance, and sports books are included as a part of realistic fiction for the purposes of this book. Adventure, animal, humor, and mystery stories are treated as separate genres. Terms encountered in discussing realistic fiction books include relevant books, problem novels, and everyday occurrences. Problem novels portray situations that children and young people face: poverty, discrimination, peer pressure, family troubles, divorce, separation, stepparents, health, accidents, death, drugs, gender, social position, retarded sibling, conflicts, and school difficulties. They raise tough questions that do not have easy answers.

In some contemporary realistic fiction with accurate pictures of the events taking place, the harsher side of life is depicted in unhappy endings or left open-ended. The unhappy endings, if based on realistic happenings, show the author's dedication and courage not to twist the truth. But as in real life, there are many realistic stories that do have happy endings. In his article entitled "The New Realism," Robert Burch gives his opinion about writing for young people: "I think that when it comes to realism in their stories, honesty is what we owe them."

For the purposes of this book, realistic fiction stories are limited to twentieth-century stories about plausible contemporary life. The main characters are usually children or young people. Stories are about family life, school, vacations, work experience, problems, conflicts, and/or social issues.

Realistic fiction extends the horizons of children and young people, helping them to gain insight about what life might hold for them. It broadens their interests, allows them to see themselves and others, introduces them to many new adventures, and shows them different ways of dealing with problems or conflicts. According to Constantine Georgiou in *Children and Their Literature,* realistic stories have a perennial appeal to children because "most children are confronted with similar delights and pains" (p. 361).

Important criteria for realistic fiction include a good story with universal themes, honesty and accuracy, recognizable characters, and portrayal of real-life situations.

Questions to ask when selecting realistic fiction stories include:

1. Are the stories built around positive ideals?
2. Are the themes realistic to the life of a child or young adult?
3. Is the action appropriate to a realistic story?
4. Is the action consistent to real life?
5. Does the plot lead to better understanding of self?

6. Do characters seem real? Do they talk and act as real people?
7. Do characters reflect basic needs of security and acceptance?
8. Is the language true-to-life while retaining a measure of beauty and imagination?
9. Is the book overly sensational?
10. Does the book have lasting value?

Authors of realistic fiction that are popular with children and young people include Judy Blume, Paula Danziger, Lois Lowry, Eve Bunting, Richard Peck, Virginia Hamilton, Robert Peck, Katherine Paterson, Mildred Taylor, Betsy Byars, Beverly Cleary, Lois Lenski, Bette Greene, Keith Robertson, S. E. Hinton, and E.L. Konigsburg.

ELEMENT OF LITERATURE: FOCUS ON CHARACTERIZATION

Characterization is considered one of the most important elements in realistic fiction stories. In good realistic fiction, characters are recognizable, they have a personality, and they respond to actions in a way consistent with what the readers expect. They have emotional and social qualities that distinguish them from other people. Their thoughts and actions are believable. Their appearance, dress, speech, and manners relate to the contemporary world. They reveal their true selves in their actions and deeds. The significance of characterization is underscored by Robert Burch in "Fiction and Realism," where he states that realistic stories should be "fleshed out" with believable characters about whom the reader can care.

Characterization in fantasy and science fiction shows inventiveness and individuality and is consistent while moving from one world to another. Characters remain convincing and true to their nature.

The development of characters is shown through summaries, action, description, and dialogue. In *A Fine White Dust,* by Cynthia Rylant, the main character is developed through a combination of action, description, and dialogue. A secondary character, Jim the preacher man, is described and developed through summaries and thoughts. Through dialogue in Lois Lowry's *Rabble Starkey,* Rabble and Sweet Ho help develop the other characters. Readers can identify with the development of characters who are shown as human beings with human traits, who have problems and make mistakes. This development often progresses to show a character changed or transformed from the person shown at the beginning of the story. This is especially true in the case of the protagonist. Knowing the cause that results in the change helps readers to identify with the character. Readers often see this potential for change during the course of the book.

Readers learn about the central characters as they read and observe how the characters look, dress, think, feel, and react, as well as what they do and say. They follow the central character's involvement in making decisions and planning actions. They relate especially to a central character who is about their age. Knowing the age of the main character is a great help in discovering and understanding that character.

The central character is fully developed and becomes a real person to the reader. Sometimes the character is admirable, endearing, likable, and fun to know. At other times the character is caustic, proud, and haughty. Events in the story may alter old traits and replace them with new and, hopefully, more likable traits. The protagonist holds the center of attention but draws attention to the supporting cast.

Rebecca Lukens identifies characters as round, flat, dynamic, or static in *A Critical Handbook of Children's Literature,* Third Edition. The round characters are the central or primary characters. The flat characters have subordinate roles and are less important or secondary characters. They do help carry the conflict or action and support the roles of the central characters. Minor and background characters are developed only enough to fill in needed information or action.

In realistic fiction for children and young adults, good characterization is indispensable. The characters are vividly revealed as recognizable, contemporary human beings. There may be a hero, heroine, associates, friends, enemies, and even a villain. The villain is involved in the conflict or problem that has to be overcome by the hero or heroine with the help of their associates or friends. The plot, theme, or central idea of the story is believable to the readers and is in harmony with the characterizations. Central characters are introduced early in the story so that young readers can easily identify with them. Depending upon the point of view, the narrator may be the central character telling the story in first person. The thoughts and feelings of the protagonist are embedded in the actions. If the story is told in third person, the narrator may reflect the views of many of the characters or those of the author. The object is to show the relationship of the characters to the story in such a way as to involve the readers in the story and hold their attention.

An example of skillfully drawn characters in realistic fiction is Cynthia Rylant's *A Fine White Dust*. The central character is Peter Cassidy, who is 13 years old. He likes the summertime when he has time off from school; the free time gives him plenty of opportunity to think. He likes riding his bike, eating chili dogs, and being with his best friend, Rufus. Together they go to the volunteer firehouse to eat a bag of pork rinds and split a coke. Pete loves going to church and has loved it ever since he was a small boy. By the time he was in the fifth grade, he had a profound religious faith. Rufus does not share Pete's religious fervor; in fact, he is a confirmed atheist. Pete's parents do not attend church or share his faith either. This causes many problems between Pete and his parents and many arguments. He is worried about the spiritual condition of his parents. Yet, he resists learning about his parents' reasons, or "secrets," as he calls them. Pete has a longing inside for more than church on Sunday. An itinerant preacher who holds a revival deeply touches Pete and fills a void in his life. Pete becomes so attached to the preacher that he is willing to give up his family and his friend to go with the preacher and to fulfill a mission or quest. When he decides to leave home, Pete thinks about the things he loves, and he decides to take reminders of them with him. These things include pictures of his family, a ceramic cross, an award he won for being the best speller, and his clothes. He finds out that life can be hard when the preacher leaves without him. Pete has some black days of despair and expresses anger, hurt, and disillusionment. Through the healing experience, Pete's anger turns into a greater awareness of God, himself, his family, and his friendship with Rufus.

A very important character is James Carson, the itinerant preacher. He is a young drifter, talented, tall and good-looking, with light blue eyes and a face that glows. He has a way with words and a voice that makes people sway with its rhythm. Sweat pours off him as he preaches; he controls the people who sob, faint, and hug each other as they respond to the preaching. He is consumed by his religious power over the people. He is worn out by preaching. He awakens and fosters a profound religious fervor in Pete, who becomes totally enamored with the preacher. He builds a friendship with Pete and listens, really listens, to what Pete has to say. He confides in Pete about his wild early days, his call to preaching, and his rewards from preaching. He stirs Pete up when he says he sees him as a preacher, and he asks Pete to go with him to help save people. When he leaves town, he forgets Pete and takes a young girl with him instead.

A secondary character is Rufus, a true friend of Pete. He is honest and practical, confident but not cocky. He is solid to count on, solid like a rock. He is a confirmed atheist but tolerant of Peter's strong belief. He warns Pete about the preacher and tells Pete that the preacher has him "crazy in the head." Rufus follows Pete to the place where he is to meet the preacher and hides in the bushes. He is angry with Pete but still stands by him. He waits there many hours and gently takes Pete home when the preacher does not show up. Rufus waits through Pete's dark days to renew and rekindle the friendship.

Background characters include the parents of Pete. His mother feels a strong love for her son but is reluctant to show her emotions. She is quiet, subservient to her husband, and works unobtrusively around the house and in the garden. She follows her husband's lead in family matters. On one occasion she attends the revival service, sitting in the back, but she never discusses this with Pete. She gently nurses Pete back to health from his dark despair. Pete's father provides for the family and is a homebody. He likes to stay at home, eat a good dinner, and relax. He does not go to church but prefers to stay home and read the paper. When Pete confronts his father with a plea that he and Pete's mother attend church, the father argues with Pete. He tells Pete that there is more to it than Pete can see, things that Pete might not understand. The father assures Pete that he can go to church as much as he wants, but he also tells him "our souls are not yours to save."

Cynthia Rylant has created characters that are real, believable, and immensely interesting. Peter, the central character, is sensitive, devout, and vulnerable. His thoughts and actions are consistent to his beliefs. His faith is tested, but it endures. He grows as a person as he overcomes his anger and as he realizes the importance of friendship and family ties. Jim, the preacher man, is shown to be dedicated to the call to preach and teach, even though he is confused about his mission. His power and control over people are vividly described. His human feelings of loneliness and his misguided religious service are the human qualities that distinguish him and lead him to abuse his power and to betray the trust of Peter. Rufus, a secondary character, is true to his nature and proves his loyalty and friendship. Peter's parents are background characters who are not fully developed or explained. They serve to provide the religious conflict in Peter's life. Their lack of understanding of Peter motivates him to seek other outlets for his religious beliefs and practices.

A Fine White Dust is an excellent illustration of character development. It is included in the recommended titles for realistic fiction teaching units and is highly recommended for individual reading.

Katherine Paterson, a master of characterization, has created another unforgettable character in her book *Park's Quest*. The main character is Parkington Waddell Broughton V. He lives in a world of make-believe, fantasy, quests, and adventures. His school librarian gives him books that he likes about dragons, castles, and tales of King Arthur. He reveals his own thoughts in terms of his fantasy world. Since he hides this side of his life from his mother, he comments that his "true identity must remain concealed from this ungrateful wench" (p. 6). His father, who was killed in the Vietnam War, saw Park when he was three or four months old and said he looked just like a "porky pig." His mother calls him Pork rather than Park. She never talks about his father and Park never dares to dream about his father. Perhaps he has been afraid before, but now he wants to know the man whose name he carries. He wonders if his grandfather Parkington Waddell Broughton III might still be alive. He has one picture of his father that he found while flipping through a book. His father's face was thin and strong. He was a bomber pilot. The picture was in a book of poems and is dated "6/23/70." Park wonders if this is the date his parents were married. Park decides to read the books on the bookshelf that his mother, Randy, never touches. He feels that the books can become a living link to finding out about his father because books tell you something about the person who owned them. Park reads his father's books during the months of November through February. He recalls that his mother had taken him on a winter day to Bethany Beach, Delaware, driving the entire distance without speaking a word to him. She had taken his hand and headed for the oceanfront, where she stood and looked out at the angry white foam of the waves. She never spoke until they were almost back in Washington, when they pulled into a McDonald's. Her face was white and hard and her hand shook as she lifted her cup. Ever since that day, Park has seen his mother differently. She is a pretty blonde: thin as a magazine model, blonde hair curling about her face, eyes of clear blue, skin pale and smooth. Sometimes Park gets a glimpse of something hidden deep inside her—something that frightens him. But she is a good mother who does not hit him and rarely yells. She protects him and calls from work to check on him. She is usually fun to be with. But behind her bantering is a coldness, this darkness, this heart of darkness that he cannot fathom. It has to do with his father, he is sure of that now. Park visits the Vietnam Memorial without his mother knowing it and finds his father's name. When he tells his mother about the visit, he reveals his intense desire to know all about his father. His mother finally makes arrangements for Park to visit his father's family in Virginia. Park has many surprises awaiting him. He finds out that his grandfather has had a second stroke and is upset about his coming; the talkative housekeeper, Mrs. Davenport, is incompetent and lazy; his uncle Frank lives in another house on the farm, runs the farm, and is married to a Vietnamese woman; his parents were divorced before his father's death; and the little Vietnamese spitfire of a girl who is such a terror to him is a very important missing piece in the puzzle of his life. He shows growth and maturity when he is able to share empathy and love for his grandfather and Thanh and when he confronts his mother via phone to discuss the family secrets.

Thanh is a secondary character of great importance to the story. She is 11 years old and came with her mother to America from Vietnam. She has long, stringy, sweaty hair under her jaunty red cap. She is caustic, teasing, proud, and haughty. Park thinks of her as a "sassy little foreign squirt." Mrs. Davenport describes her like one of the barn's kittens—"all claws and teeth"—until you get to know her. Thanh's broken English and defiant attitude magnify the problem. She resents Park for coming into her territory. She is afraid that Frank, her new father, will not want her when his own baby is born, especially if the baby is a boy. When Park shoots and injures a crow, all of Thanh's anger surfaces because she thinks he is a murderer. In nursing the bird back to health, Park and Thanh come to terms with each other, bring some joy into the grandfather's life, and piece together the story of their relationship. "'We bruzzuh. You, me?' She looked down at him. 'Crazy thing I ever hear.' . . . 'And we have same old grandfahzuh?'"

Park's mother, Frank, Mrs. Davenport, and grandfather are secondary supporting characters who play subordinate roles. They help carry the action and conflict.

This is an excellent story for class study because of its strong characterization and multilayered plot.

RECOMMENDED LISTS

Recommended Titles for Teaching the Realistic Fiction Genre Unit

Brooks, Bruce. *The Moves Make the Man*. New York: Harper & Row, 1984. RL: Grade 7. IL: Grades 7–10. PB: Harper. Cornerstone.

Jerome Fox, a thirteen-year-old black basketball player, tells the story of the friendship that develops between himself and Bix, a white friend. Jerome is the first black student in a newly integrated junior high school in the 1950s, and even his talents as a basketball player are not enough to win his acceptance by the coach and some of the basketball players. He has a very understanding and capable mother who is concerned about her son spending so much time alone on a nearby basketball court. Jerome is responsive to family needs but spends all of his spare time completely immersed in basketball. He practices and practices, making all the moves from reverse spin to triple jump. Bix comes from a wealthy family, but he has many family problems. His mother is ill and is sent to a mental institution, and his stepfather is antagonistic toward him. Bix loves baseball but is encouraged by Jerome to learn basketball. Jerome becomes the teacher as night after night they meet to shoot baskets. Bix, however, refuses to use fake moves. Jerome insists that the fake moves are part of the game. Bix says they are not for him. "If the game is worth playing it is worth playing straight, clean." When Bix challenges his stepfather to a basketball shooting contest and wins, he wins the right to visit his mother in the mental institution. The visit brings tragic results. Jerome tries to help his friend, but many problems remain. Reflecting on the situation, Jerome muses, "There are no moves you truly make alone."

The author develops strong characterization by using basketball terminology and contrasting attitudes of the two protagonists. By using first-person narration, the author conveys the deep feelings, motives, and attitudes of Jerome. Bix is described and known through the eyes and feelings of Jerome.

The basketball theme of this book makes it popular with readers; however, it is not an easy book to read because of its subtlety, contrasting attitudes, and double meanings. The author avoids simple answers and obvious resolutions. It is recommended for use with highly able readers in the seventh grade and able readers in grade 8 and up.

Fox, Paula. *One-Eyed Cat.* New York: Bradbury Press, 1984. RL: Grade 6. IL: Grades 5–9. PB: Dell. Cornerstone.

Ned Wallis lives with his minister father and his mother who is ill. His Uncle Hilary gives him an air rifle for his eleventh birthday, but his parents say that he must wait until he is older before using it. His father puts it in the attic for safekeeping. Ned knows that his father trusts him to obey, but he cannot resist the temptation to fire the gun. He slips it out of the attic and fires it once at a shadow against the barn. He believes that he sees a slight movement from one of the windows in the house and worries that he has been seen. He begins to feel guilty but is not accused by his family. Later he sees a one-eyed, grey cat, and his neighbor comments that someone probably used the cat as target practice. Ned is convinced that he is the guilty person. He tries to help his neighbor take care of the cat and tells lies that deepen into more lies in his effort to save the cat. He is consumed by guilt until he confesses to the critically ill neighbor. He works very hard to save the cat from starvation and cold during the winter months. He finally confesses to his mother as they observe the one-eyed cat with kittens. His mother confesses to him her own feelings of unworthiness regarding an incident years before.

The outstanding character portrayal of Ned by the author focuses on his actions, feelings, and thoughts during this traumatic experience. Readers experience the conflict, dishonoring of trust, temptation, fear, guilt, self-realization, confession, relief, and satisfying conclusion. The readers meet an unforgettable character and understand his motives, way of life, and family relationships.

This is an excellent choice for class study, either as a read-aloud or as individual reading. It is an outstanding example of characterization of the protagonist.

Konigsburg, E. L. *From the Mixed-Up Files of Mrs. Basil E. Frankweiler.* New York: Atheneum, 1967. RL: Grade 6. IL: Grades 4–8. PB: Dell. Cornerstone.

Claudie Kincaid, who is 11 years old, and her brother, Jamie, run away from home and establish residence in New York's Metropolitan Museum of Art. They have an adventurous daily life that includes breakfast at the automat, worrying about clean underwear and washing clothes, standing on the toilet seat in the restrooms to avoid being caught, eating pretzels and chestnuts, and playing Lady Claudia and Sir James. Claudia has the executive ability of a corporation president and carefully plans every move. Claudia and Jamie become involved in establishing the authenticity of a small statue of an angel, a recent museum acquisition attributed to Michelangelo. They go to the public library and use their research skills to learn about the Renaissance and Michelangelo. They finally go to the grand estate of the eccentric Mrs. Frankweiler to solve the mystery.

The characterizations by the author are convincing and lifelike, firmly rooted in reality, and presented in contemporary terms. The children remain true to their natures and thus are accepted by readers.

An activity related to this book in the following teaching tips suggests a comparison of *From the Mixed-Up Files of Mrs. Basil E. Frankweiler* with *Secrets of the Shopping Mall* by Richard Peck. *Secrets of the Shopping Mall* involves young people living in a shopping mall.

Lowry, Lois. *Rabble Starkey.* New York: Houghton Mifflin, 1987. RL: Grade 6. IL: Grades 5–9. PB: Dell.

Sweet Hosanna, known as Sweet Ho, got married when she

was 13 and at 14 had a daughter, Parable Ann, known as Rabble. Her husband left her, and Sweet Ho took her daughter home to her mother in the mountains of West Virginia. When her mother died, Sweet Ho took Rabble to live in a two-room apartment above a garage. She now works for the Bigelow family, whose little baby is Gunther, and whose daughter Veronica is 12 years old, the same age as Rabble. The father, Phil, is loving and kind, but the mother has emotional problems and must be hospitalized after a traumatic experience with the baby. Sweet Ho and Rabble move into the guest bedroom of the Bigelows, and Sweet Ho takes care of the family. Rabble loves it there and experiences the kind of family life she has always wanted. She writes a story about her home and expresses the importance of feelings. She and Veronica become best friends and go to a boy-and-girl party in new dresses that Phil buys for them. Phil helps Sweet Ho to return to school. When the mother returns home, Sweet Ho and Rabble move on so that Sweet Ho can attend college. Rabble is sorry to leave but is comforted by the fact that home is a feeling she has experienced.

Both Rabble and Sweet Ho are primary characters who are developed through dialogue and action. Rabble is a typical preteen with a variety of problems and concerns about growing up, friendship, and need for family ties. She is realistically portrayed. Sweet Ho is admirable, likable, and determined to provide a good home for her daughter and to succeed in preparing herself for the future. Veronica and Phil are secondary characters who support the main characters through their actions and dialogue. The baby and the mother are background characters who play a part in the story but are not well developed.

Miles, Betty. *Maudie and Me and the Dirty Book*. New York: Alfred A. Knopf, 1980. RL: Grade 5. IL: Grades 5–7.   PB: Knopf.

Kate Harris worries about making friends and whether certain people like her. When she enters Revere Middle School, her elementary school class is no longer together but is mixed in with three other elementary feeder schools. Kate is suddenly with many strangers. It is confusing because everyone is trying to form new groups and cliques and wondering where to sit in class, in the cafeteria, and in the auditorium. Her old friends are already making new friends and sometimes Kate feels left out. When her English teacher, Ms. Plotkin, introduces a special interschool reading project, Kate volunteers. So does Maudie Schmidt, a girl whom Kate considers different, funny-looking, and fat. Kate does not want to be stuck with Maudie, but she resigns herself to the fact that the two of them will be working together on the reading project. They are to go to an elementary school and work with students in the first grade by reading aloud to them, helping them with their own reading, and sometimes writing stories for them. By sharing their interest in books and reading, they hope to influence first-grade students in reading also.

When Kate reads aloud from the book *Birthday Dog* to the first-grade class, she is startled when the students start asking questions on mating. The discussion becomes very frank with students using explicit sexual terms. This starts an angry controversy when parents complain about the illustration of the mother dog giving birth and the discussion about mating. Parents, administrators, teachers, librarians, students, citizens, and the press become involved in a censorship issue discussing whether the book is "educational" or "smut." Kate gets unexpected support from one of the "cutest" boys in her class. The school board holds a meeting to decide whether the interschool project should continue. At the meeting, Kate defends the book and the project by stating that kids have a right to learn things. She asks that the project be continued so that little kids can be helped to learn to read. The controversy strengthens the friendship of Kate and Maudie as they share laughter and tears, confidences, experiences, problems, and support for each other. Their circle of friendship is extended to include some boys in their class who also oppose censorship.

The two main characters are well developed and believable. They are depicted as typical middle school students who are worried about homerooms, schedules, being in cliques, where to sit at lunch, passing notes, and making friends. They talk about getting crushes on boys and attending parties. The parents, teachers, and friends are secondary characters who influence the actions of the story. The administrators, librarian, citizens, and press are background characters.

This is recommended for individual reading rather than as a read-aloud. Since both sides of censorship are well presented, it provides a springboard for a large group discussion on censorship.

Nixon, Joan Lowry. *And Maggie Makes Three.* New York: Harcourt Brace Jovanovich, 1986. RL: Grade 6. IL: Grades 6–10.

Maggie, 12 years old, goes to live with her grandmother since her father travels most of the time and her mother is dead. Her father is a famous film director who recently married a twenty-year-old starlet. Maggie has difficulty adjusting to school life. She makes enemies with two boys who vow to get even with her. Her new friend, Lisa, makes school and home life more enjoyable. Maggie's interest in drama brings conflict when she and Lisa both want the same part in a high school play in which middle school students were invited to participate. Maggie is excited when she is selected to perform in the *Sound of Music* since her mother played the leading role years ago. Maggie invites her father and his wife to the performance and is very disappointed when they do not attend. Alex, an outstanding high school drama student, adds a flavor of romance that brings both happiness and sorrow. When Maggie performs in the "Middle School Review," her father and his wife attend the performance. The two boys who vowed revenge drench Maggie with a bucket of water before she goes on stage. The audience, her family, and her friends enjoy the ensuing antics and song.

Paterson, Katherine. *Park's Quest.* New York: E. P. Dutton, 1988. RL: Grade 6. IL: Grades 6–9.

See information under Element of Literature: Focus on Characterization.

Peck, Richard. *Representing Super Doll.* New York: Viking, 1974. RL: Grade 7. IL: Grades 7–10. PB: Dell.

Verna, an Indiana farmgirl, has too much of the town girl in her to stomach killing chickens. Her mama's vision stops in the small town of Mount Yeomas, but Verna's vision goes beyond. Verna is a sophomore in high school. She works her way up the school social ladder from a farmgirl to a member of a prestigious club. Her mother wants the other girls to know that even though they live on a farm, they know some of the social graces. She invites the girls to dinner and has a beautiful tablesetting and an elegant meal. Verna is very proud and tells her mom that everything was perfect. Everyone is impressed. Verna's older brother comes home from college and meets all of Verna's friends. Her brother tells her that she is better looking than any of them and that she will have her day. One member of the club, Darlene, is very beautiful but not academically bright. Darlene is a natural blonde with all the physical attributes of a beauty queen. Her mother keeps entering her in beauty contests. Darlene's mother is described as living on "anticipation and alimony." When Darlene wins a beauty contest and a trip to New York City, Verna is asked to accompany her. This gives Verna an opportunity to meet Sheri, her brother's girlfriend, who is an airline stewardess. Darlene and Verna attend interviews and parties. Verna takes time out to visit Sheri and to see some of New York City with someone she meets. Darlene is tense and resents Verna not being with her every moment. She accuses Verna of being jealous. Before the taping of the television program "Spot the Frauds," Verna is asked to substitute for one of the contestants. The audience has to pick out the real beauty queen from among the contestants. Darlene's answers in the interview are very poor, and Verna is picked as the real beauty queen. Darlene begins to change when she tells Verna that her mother has made her life miserable with the constant reminder that she could become Miss America. She is determined to try to live her own life. Verna begins to see herself in a new light also, but not as a beauty queen.

The author's characterization of Verna and Darlene is well developed. They are portrayed as recognizable, contemporary human beings. The plot of the story is believable to the readers and is in harmony with the characterizations. The thoughts and feelings of the protagonist, Verna, are embedded in the actions. The characterization of Darlene leads to self-discovery and personal growth. The mothers, Verna's brother, and his girlfriend are secondary characters who help carry the story and support the central characters. The friends of Verna and Darlene are not well defined and serve as minor or background characters.

Rylant, Cynthia. *A Fine White Dust.* New York: Macmillan, 1986.
    RL: Grade 5. IL: Grades 5–9.

See information under Element of Literature: Focus on Characterization.

Wersba, Barbara. *Crazy Vanilla*. New York: Harper & Row, 1986. RL: Grade 7. IL: Grades 8–10.

Tyler Woodruff is 14 years old and wants to become a wildlife photographer. He loves to spend time in the family house in the Hamptons to take photographs. His family is wealthy and they have homes in New York City, Florida, and the Hamptons. His father is a stockbroker and his mother is an alcoholic. His family life is disrupted when Cameron, Tyler's brother, declares that he is a homosexual. Cameron's subsequent estrangement from the family is especially difficult for Tyler, who has always been close to him. Tyler loses himself in his photography and wants to buy an expensive lens that his father will not buy for him. He decides to enter an ice cream-naming contest in a local ice cream parlor in hopes of winning money to buy the lens. He is sure that his name, "Crazy Vanilla," will win, but he is disappointed. He is upset one day when another person is at his favorite photography spot taking pictures. He discovers that the person is the little redheaded waitress from the ice cream parlor. Her name is Mitzi. She is an excellent photographer and teaches Tyler some new techniques. They become friends. Mitzi has a difficult home life also. Her mother is very unsettled and never stays in one place very long. She is eccentric and has never grown out of the "flower child" or "hippie" stage. Cameron comes for a visit with his friend, Vincent, a very successful designer. He is somewhat accepted by Tyler's father because of his business success. Tyler decides that he likes Vincent and begins to reestablish his friendship with his brother. Mitzi helps Tyler to build his own self-esteem, stand up to his father, and establish a better relationship with his mother. When Mitzi tells Tyler that she and her mother are moving, he is very unhappy. Mitzi declares that she will keep in touch with him and she does telephone him.

The main character, Tyler, is well developed and convincing. He tells his own story in such a way as to involve the readers in his thoughts, feelings, and perceptions. Mitzi, the secondary character, is interesting, believable, and important to the action and resolution of some of the problems. Readers are involved in the emotions of both Tyler and Mitzi. Tyler's parents, Cameron, Vincent, and Mitzi's mother are minor characters who provide the background and conflict in the story.

This book is recommended for individual reading by more mature students in grade 8 and up.

Recommended Titles for Individual or Group Study

Craven, Margaret. *I Heard the Owl Call My Name.* New York: Doubleday, 1973. RL: 8. IL: Grades 8–10. PB: Dell.

Mark Brian, a young Anglican priest, is assigned to serve a parish of Kwakiutl Indians on a seacoast in the wilds of British Columbia. Learning of his fatal illness, Mark absorbs enough of the meaning of life from the tribe of vanishing Indians to face death without fear.

Dygard, Thomas. *Halfback Tough.* New York: William Morrow, 1986. RL: Grade 5. IL: Grades 7–10. PB: Penguin.

Joe's personality problems threaten his chances to succeed on the football field. His practice of violating the rules and looking down on everyone else does not go over well with the coach or other players. With determination, hard work, and help from others, Joe obtains the necessary ingredients in winning the respect of others.

Kerr, M. E. *Gentlehands.* New York: Harper & Row, 1978. RL: Grade 7. IL: Grades 8–10. PB: Bantam.

Buddy meets and falls in love with a girl from a wealthy family. He is very proud of his refined and cultured grandfather and feels that his girlfriend's parents will be impressed with him. Buddy is devastated when he discovers that his grandfather is suspected of being a Nazi war criminal.

Kerr, M. E. *The Son of Someone Famous.* New York: Harper & Row, 1974. RL: Grade 7. IL: Grades 7–10.

Sixteen-year-old Adam, son of a famous father, thinks of himself as nothing. He tries to escape living under a spotlight by assuming a pseudonym while he is living with his grandfather in a small Vermont town. To add to Adam's plight, his grandfather has a drinking problem. Adam gets to know Brenda Belle Blossom, the town tomboy. They form an alliance which he calls "Nothing Power" and she calls "Going Steady."

MacLachlan, Patricia. *Cassie Binegar.* New York: Harper & Row, 1982. RL: Grade 5. IL: Grades 5–7. PB: Harper.

Cassie Binegar (rhymes with vinegar) is upset because her family moves to an old house with cottages on a beach. Her father and brothers are fishermen. Her relatives come for a visit and stay in the cottages. Cassie wishes that her family were more "normal" instead of going barefoot or wearing feathers. She also needs space of her own and has special hiding places. Cassie becomes friends with Margaret Mary, a girl her age, who moves in nearby. Margaret Mary's house and family are always neat and in order. Cassie learns that not everything on the outside is the same as the inside. Her Gran comes and helps Cassie to accept herself.

Paterson, Katherine. *Come Sing, Jimmy Jo.* New York: E. P. Dutton, 1985. RL: Grade 5. IL: Grades 5–9. PB: Avon.

James Johnson, an eleven-year-old, comes from a family of professional singers and string-pickers. He only sings for his grandmother, with whom he lives while his family is away performing. The manager of the group overhears James singing and wants him to appear with the group on a television show. James is given the name of Jimmy Jo and reaches celebrity status. There is family infighting when Jimmy Jo's popularity upstages the group. He has to come to terms with his gift, his classmates at school, his two fathers, and his family. His grandmother and friends help him with the choices.

Voigt, Cynthia. *Dicey's Song.* New York: Atheneum, 1981. RL: Grade 5. IL: Grades 5–8. PB: Fawcett.

Dicey leads her three siblings to a new home with their grandmother in Maryland after they are abandoned by their mother. The journey is a difficult one, as Dicey first takes her brothers and sister to a great aunt's house. When they find that the aunt is dead and that the local authorities want to place them in foster homes, Dicey is determined to find their maternal grandmother and to win a home with her.

Voigt, Cynthia. *Tell Me If Lovers Are Losers.* New York: Atheneum, 1982. RL: Grade 7. IL: Grades 7–10. PB: Macmillan.

Ann, Niki, and Hildy are first-year college roommates at Stanford College for Women. They have very different socioeconomic backgrounds and temperament. They have a difficult time finding common ground until they are on the same volleyball team. They learn the meaning of team-play, and this helps bring about their maturing as individuals. They work out their differences and become friends. When tragedy strikes, the friendship that they feel plays a big part in their acceptance of loss and grief.

Yep, Lawrence. *Child of the Owl.* New York: Harper & Row, 1977. RL: Grade 6. IL: Grades 5–8. PB: Harper.

Twelve-year-old Casey lives in San Francisco. She learns about her Chinese heritage from her grandmother and by attending Chinese classes. She loves the legend of the Owl Story and the carved jade pendant. She struggles with understanding herself and her problem father, Barney.

Picture Storybooks for Teaching Realistic Fiction

Picture storybook characters in realistic fiction are portrayed as real people in recognizable settings. By learning about the characters in picture storybooks, students can quickly grasp the concepts of characterization and observe character development. The characters in many picture storybooks have a mixture of human qualities. Their actions match the pattern of their childhood behavior. They are solid, believable characters.

Bauer, Caroline Feller. *My Mom Travels a Lot.* Illustrated by Nancy Winslow Parker. New York: Frederick Warne, 1981.

This is another picture storybook that succinctly illustrates realistic characters in a realistic family situation. The pros and cons of a family coping with a working mother who travels to distant places are conveyed with humor, pathos, and understanding in words and pictures. The story is told in the first person by the mother's little girl, who says that the good things about her mother's travels are that they get to go to the airport, they get long-distance telephone calls and postcards, they get presents, and they eat out often. The little girl doesn't always have to make her bed, and she gets to stay up late sometimes. The bad things about her mother's travels are that she misses her mother's good-night kiss, the times when she isn't home for things like the daughter's school play, or when the puppies were born. Dad can't find her boots when it is raining, and she can't remember to water the flowers. But mostly the daughter and her dad miss Mom. The best thing, both daughter and her dad agree, is that Mom always comes home.

The little girl is the central character. She is portrayed as a typical child, sleeping with her big dog and her teddy bear and eating cookies on the floor. She forgets to water the plants because she is so busy playing soccer. She lets the puppies have the run of the house, and she reads late at night sprawled out on the couch with her dog. Her books, cookies, and cup are on the floor. She climbs a tree and thinks about how much she misses her mom. It makes sense that she decorates her dog's box with postcards after the puppies are born and that she eats out in a fancy restaurant with her dad. She shows the strong attachment that most children feel for their mothers when she is so happy about her mom's coming home. She snuggles close to her mom as the family looks at a map to find the places where her mom has been. Dad and Mom, Susie, and the puppies are secondary characters who play an important part in the action, but they are not as fully developed or explained as is the young daughter.

Blos, Joan. *The Grandpa Days*. Illustrated by Emily Arnold McCully. New York: Simon & Schuster, 1989.

In this picture storybook, two characters are contrasted in a loving, happy way. Philip is a young boy who spends a week with his grandpa. He brings his clothes in a small suitcase. He learns that his grandpa built his mother a treehouse when she was a little girl. He sees the plans for the treehouse. The plans inspire him to draw plans for something he would like his grandpa to build for him. He listens to his grandpa's explanations. He learns all about woodworking tools and how to use each one. He keeps drawing plans that are too difficult. He learns about the supplies on hand and the tools that can be used. He thinks about what he has learned and finally draws plans that he and his grandpa can use. He works very hard helping his grandpa with the building. He is very excited when it snows and his mother comes. He gets to show her his new sled and to ride it first. Grandpa is an older man who remembers the joy of building something special for his daughter when she was young. Out of sentiment he kept the treehouse plans and now happily shows them to his grandson. Grandpa wears glasses when he reads. He reads the newspaper and falls asleep in his chair. He eats a snack. He keeps all of his tools and working areas neat. He is patient with Philip and lets Philip learn on his own rather than telling him what to do. He demonstrates the use of his tools and lets Philip practice using them. He teaches Philip the names of the trees from which his wood came. He works with Philip and guides him in using the tools as together they build a sled. He dresses warmly and goes out in the snow with his daughter and Philip to take turns trying out the new sled.

Philip is portrayed as a happy little boy who enjoys being with his grandpa. When he draws plans for building something with his grandpa, he begins by drawing a rocketship. Later he draws a racing car. He learns the difference between childish wishes and practical ideas. He thinks and thinks about the available resources and makes a decision based on what he has learned. He works hard to accomplish his goal and is very pleased with the results. Grandpa is described in word and picture as a gentle, loving man. He is happy to have Philip spend a week with him. He wants to teach Philip how to use his tools and to respect and admire the art of woodworking. Grandpa lets Philip make his own decisions without forcing his opinions on him. He takes the time and patience to let Philip use the tools and learn by doing. When the work is finished, he is ready to join his daughter and Philip in play. Both Philip and Grandpa are central characters who are well developed and true to life. They enjoy mutual respect and admiration. Grandpa lets Philip grow and experience the satisfaction of accomplishing a goal. Philip's mother is an important background character. She is alluded to by Grandpa when he talks about her as his little girl. She arrives at the end of the week to applaud the finished product and to take part in the celebration.

Bunting, Eve. *The Wall*. Illustrated by Ronald Himler. New York: Clarion, 1990.

The Wall, by Eve Bunting, is a very touching picture storybook realistically depicting the story of a little boy and his father who come to Washington, D.C. to the Vietnam Veterans Memorial. They are looking on the wall for the name of the boy's grandfather, who was killed in the Vietnam War. The little boy is the narrator. He describes the black, shiny surface as a mirror wall. He registers his impressions and thoughts as he and his dad search for the name. As his dad searches for the name, the son observes the other people who have come to the wall. A man in a wheelchair who doesn't have any legs smiles and says "Hi, son." An old man and woman, as old as his grandmother, are hugging and crying. A man and his grandson walk by. The boy asks if they can go to the river now. The grandpa tells his grandson to button his jacket because it is cold. A bunch of girls in school uniforms are carrying little American flags. They make a lot of noise and ask a lot of questions. One of them asks if the wall is for the dead soldiers. The teacher explains, "The names are the names of the dead. But the wall is for all of us." They plant their flags in front of the wall as they leave. The young boy sees the teddy bear, pictures, and flowers that have been left in front of the wall. His dad runs his fingers over the rows of etched names under 1967, the year the boy's grandpa died. His dad finds the name and explains that his father was just his age when he was killed. He rubs his fingers over and over the name as if he wants to wipe it away. He lifts his son so that he can touch the name. He makes a rubbing on paper to take home with them. He stands very still with his head bent for a long time in front of the wall. He takes out a school picture of his son and puts it on the ground below the name. The son exclaims that his grandpa won't know who he is. His dad replies that he thinks Grandpa will know. He tells the boy that the wall is a place of honor and that he is proud that the boy's grandpa is included. The boy replies that he is proud too, but he would rather have Grandpa here telling him to button his jacket because it is cold.

The main characters are the father and his son. Each is depicted in a realistic manner. The son carefully observes everything around him, feels the significance of the place and events, and is moved by them. Even though he did not know his grandpa, he senses the cruelty of war and the loss of loved ones. He watches the boy and his grandpa who walk by and wishes that he had his grandpa to take him to the river and tell him to button his coat. The reader gets the feeling that the memory of this day will always be etched in the mind of the little boy. The boy's dad is shown as a caring, loving person who has traveled a long way to show honor, respect, and loyalty to his own father. He wants his son to share this special time and learn the significance of the names on the wall. He shows his deep emotions and sorrow when he finds the name and traces it. His quiet, prayerful attitude blots out the surrounding noise. He wants to be sure that his son knows that it is an honor for Grandpa's name to be here. The presence of the grandpa is strongly felt, even though he is only a background character. His name, George Munoz, is etched in nice, even letters. His service to his country is recognized since he gave his life in the Vietnam War in 1967. Other background characters who visit the wall are seen only briefly, but their actions add to the boy's impressions of the wall.

Keats, Ezra Jack. *The Snowy Day*. New York: Viking, 1962.

Ezra Jack Keats creates a special character in *The Snowy Day*. Peter is an engaging little black American boy. His excitement in waking up to find the ground covered with snow is conveyed in word and picture. He dresses for the weather and runs outside to play. He makes tracks in the snow and reacts with good humor that he is not old enough to take part in a snowball fight. Instead he makes a snowman and makes the form of angels in the snow. He pretends he is mountain climbing as he climbs up a big hill. He slides down. He picks up some snow and puts it in his pocket. He goes home and tells his mother all about his adventures. She is very interested in what he has to say. He thinks and thinks about the good time that he had. When he checks his pocket for the snow, he is very sad to discover that it is no longer there. He sleeps and dreams that the sun melted all the snow. He awakens to find new snow falling. He calls a friend and they go out together in the deep, deep snow.

Peter is depicted as a typical little boy who plays, pretends, and desires to hold on to the fun with the snow by putting some in his pocket. His surprise and disappointment that the snow is gone are models of childhood behavior. Sharing his adventures, thinking about the good times, and worrying about the snow melting are universal childhood traits. His joy in seeing new snow falling and his desire to play in the snow with a friend reflect his and other small children's happy outlook and excitement.

He is a well-rounded character, developed in a straightforward manner.

TEACHING TIPS: THE REALISTIC FICTION GENRE AND CHARACTERIZATION

Realistic fiction is a popular genre among children and young people. Many of the students will have favorite authors or will be "addicted" to certain types of realistic fiction. New horizons can be opened to students as they "sample, taste, chew, and digest" new realistic stories. Activities of reading, discussing, viewing, acting, and portraying characters can stimulate them to read and enjoy additional books in this genre. Help students to progress from the familiar popular authors to lesser-known, but highly capable, authors of realistic fiction like Vera and Bill Cleaver, Mary Stewart, Rosemary Wells, and M. E. Kerr.

Plan the unit along with the activities in time for careful selection of materials, for reserve books, or for special orders. Realistic fiction books are readily available in hardback, paperback, Perma-Bound, and large-print editions. Plan fun activities and enjoy them along with the students. Be sure to include some of the delightful books that are popular, short, and easy to read. These include stories for younger or less able readers: Judy Blume's *Are You There God? It's Me, Margaret;* Betsy Byar's *The Summer of the Swans;* Beverly Cleary's *Ramona Quimby, Age 8;* Louise Fitzhugh's *Harriet the Spy;* Sheila Greenwald's *Give Us a Great Big Smile, Rosy Cole;* and Sydney Taylor's *All-of-a-Kind Family.*

Remember that the literary element for emphasis with realistic fiction is characterization and that the critical-thinking and communication skill emphasis is on oral communication. The activities and ideas for teaching reflect this emphasis. All books selected for teaching in this unit have strong central characters. Suggested activities include reading aloud, monologues, dramatic skits, booktalking, oral reports, and storytelling.

Begin this unit by asking students to name unforgettable characters from books that they especially remember, identify with, like, or dislike. Their responses may include Max, Charlotte, Paddington, Dorothy, Cinderella, Harriet, Henry, Homer Price, Pippi Longstocking, Winnie-the-Pooh, Robin Hood, Tom Sawyer, Anne of Green Gables, Alice, Laura, Bilbo, Pied Piper, Snoopy, The Wicked Witch, Tin Woodman, or Ramona. Let them describe, identify, recall an incident, or give reasons for likes or dislikes. An activity matching characters with books may be done orally. Since students also like to hear teachers discuss characters and books that they remember from their childhood, tell them about your unforgettable characters. Many of them may be the familiar ones already listed or unusual ones like Hitty from *Hitty, Her First Hundred Years*, Big Tiger and Christian from the book of the same name, or Margaret Lechow from *The Ark*. An excellent sourcebook is Margery Fisher's *Who's Who in Children's Books: A Treasury of the Familiar Characters of Childhood*. As an extra credit homework assignment, ask students to find out from parents, grandparents, relatives, or an older adult the names of book characters that they especially remember. Allow students class time to orally report on their findings.

Select several realistic fiction books to show to the class. Include some books that will be used for the reading/teaching unit. Read the titles to students and ask how many of them have read any of these books. Ask those who have not read them if they can guess what the books are about just by hearing the titles. Ask them what type or genre the books fall into. Review the term *genre* if needed. Tell them that for the next several weeks they will be reading and discussing realistic fiction. Let them discuss what realistic fiction means to them. Give them a definition and examples. Use the information provided in the genre introduction at the beginning of this chapter.

Ask the students to guess what literary element will be emphasized during this unit on realistic fiction. If necessary, remind them of the discussion on unforgettable characters. Explain to them that this study will emphasize characterization. Ask for a volunteer to pantomime or improvise the characterization of a typical "realistic ten-to-fourteen-year-old character." If there are no volunteers, tell the students that you will invite a "guest" to perform a character sketch at a later class meeting. Invite a teacher, administrator, parent, or drama group from a high school to present the characterizations.

To teach characterization, use picture storybooks. Use the examples already cited with detailed annotations or choose other representative titles. The following books have examples of questions and presentation ideas that may be adapted to other picture storybooks. Read *My Mom Travels a Lot*, by Caroline Bauer, and show the pictures by Nancy Parker. Ask the students to describe the main character. Let them tell about the activities of the little girl, the bad habits she has, her mannerisms, and her likes and dislikes. Ask the students to tell who the supporting characters are. Let them discuss the difference between the central character and the supporting characters. Show them examples of pictures and words that help to determine the differences.

In *The Grandpa Days*, by Joan Blos, both Philip and Grandpa are central characters. Read the book and show the illustrations by Emily McCully. Divide the class into two groups. Appoint a group leader and recorder for each group. Tell the students that you are going to read the book and show them the pictures again. Tell them that group one will listen and look for information on Philip, while group two will listen and look for information on Grandpa. After rereading the book, allow the groups to meet, discuss the character, and record their findings. Ask each group leader to report orally to the class. Explain that there is one background character and ask students to identify that person.

Use *The Snowy Day*, by Jack Ezra Keats, to discuss how Peter classifies as a realistic character. Read the book and show the illustrations. If students live in a climate where there is snow, let them tell how they react to a snowy day. If they have not seen or experienced a snowy day, let them describe what they think such a day would be like. Ask them to compare the reactions and activities of someone their age with the actions and activities of Peter.

For a change of pace before students start reading their realistic fiction books, select a videotape, filmstrip, or movie from the library media center's collection to reinforce what the students have learned about realistic fiction and characterization. Let the students enjoy the media presentation without requiring feedback or an assignment. Suggestions include *The Great Gilly Hopkins* (sound filmstrip or enhanced video), *The Outsiders* (sound filmstrip), *The Pigman* (sound filmstrip), and *Scorpions* (live-action video), available from American School Publishers.

Select realistic fiction books for class study from the many available titles in the library media center or order paperback copies. Suggestions for reading/study by the entire class include: Lois Lowry's *Rabble Starkey;* Katherine Paterson's *Park's Quest;* Paula Fox's *One-Eyed Cat;* and Betty Miles's *Maudie and Me and the Dirty Book*. Small groups reading the same title can be organized around reading levels or students' interests. To assist students with selection of individual titles, invite the children's or young adult specialist from the public library to the classroom to give a booktalk on realistic fiction stories, or ask the school library media specialist to prepare an annotated bibliography for use by students. Annotated lists are also included in this chapter.

Many activities related to teaching realistic fiction, characterization, and oral communications follow the introduction to oral communication skills.

FOCUS ON CRITICAL-THINKING AND COMMUNICATION SKILLS: ORAL COMMUNICATIONS

Students need to learn and practice the skills of oral communication. Teach these skills and provide training and practice by combining oral communication activities with the realistic fiction literature unit. These skills include preparing and giving narrative and expository oral presentations and responding to oral performances. Students will:

1. Organize data for speaking
2. Prepare and present a speech
3. Utilize beginning, middle, and ending statements
4. Use supporting details and conclusions
5. Use effective transitions
6. Analyze their own speaking techniques
7. Identify and correct speech problems
8. Give oral directions
9. Practice spontaneous oral expression
10. Show evidence of vocabulary development
11. Include expressions of attitude, moods, and emotions
12. Understand purpose and methods of appeal
13. Perform creative dramatics: pantomime, role-playing, puppets, original scripts

14. Use visual aids
15. Learn to interact with other speakers
16. Use appropriate language to express thoughts orally
17. Practice oral reading, emphasizing pitch, stress, and juncture
18. Demonstrate good listening skills
19. Respond to verbal and nonverbal communications
20. Respond with courtesy and enthusiasm to oral performances of literature and drama

By incorporating these skills into lessons and activities derived from realistic fiction books, students will enjoy themselves and gain valuable experience in oral expression. For instance, if students read M. E. Kerr's *Gentlehands,* they might have a debate on the pros and cons of punishing Nazi war criminals. They would use many oral communication skills while gathering and organizing data for supporting evidence, opposing arguments, disproving statements, and rebuttal. If they read some of Katherine Paterson's realistic fiction stories, such as *Bridge to Terabithia; Come Sing, Jimmy Jo; The Great Gilly Hopkins;* or *Jacob Have I Loved,* they might decide to have a telephone interview with Mrs. Paterson. This would entail reading and rereading sections of her books, making notes, writing down questions, and learning background information on Mrs. Paterson. Sources of information include biographical reference books in the library media center, filmstrips from the Miller-Brody *Meet the Newbery Author* series, or the live-action video *The Author's Eye: Katherine Paterson* from American School Publishers. Students may use their oral communication skills by brainstorming, summarizing, sharing ideas, discussing information, recalling facts, and deciding on the interview questions and procedures. They can have "mock" practice sessions with different students playing the role of the author. They will have an opportunity to use their best oral language skills during the telephone interview.

ACTIVITIES

Activities Related to Teaching the Realistic Fiction Genre

These activities relate to the teaching of realistic fiction without the emphasis on characterization, which will follow in the next section. These activities do include practice in many oral communication skills.

Review with students good practices for oral reading. Emphasize appropriate tone of voice and volume. Include pitch, stress, and juncture. Demonstrate these procedures by reading aloud. Choose a realistic fiction book like Lois Lowry's *Rabble Starkey*. Read several pages from the beginning of the book. If time permits, include a professionally recorded realistic story like *The TV Kid*, by Betsy Byars, which is a listening cassette from American School Publishers. If desired, use a segment from *The Secret Garden*, written by Frances Hodgson Burnett and read by Flo Gibson, from Audio Book Contractors. Ask students to pick out an interesting segment from the realistic fiction book they are reading. Tell them to practice reading this portion at home. Arrange with the library media specialist to set up a "studio" or area for individual use by students to record on video or cassette tape. Schedule the taping sessions to coincide with independent reading time. Tell the students that only they will view or hear the recording. Ask them to critically analyze their speaking techniques when they review and listen to their recording. Hold a conference to discuss the students' analysis. Encourage them to practice reading aloud to correct their speech problems. If the students need professional help, refer them to a staff member who can provide this help. Schedule brief oral reading times for all students during a class session.

To help students interact with other students and use appropriate language to express thoughts orally, organize students to form discussion groups on topics from realistic fiction books. These topics can include divorce, adoption, foster homes, diseases, death, drugs, jealousy, and siblings with disabilities. Or select four realistic fiction "problem novels" and obtain multiple copies of each book. Divide the class into groups by reading levels and assign one title to each group. For example, for books on death, use *Bridge to Terabithia* by Katherine Paterson; *A Taste of Blackberries* by Doris Smith; *A Summer to Die* by Lois Lowry; or *I Heard the Owl Call My Name* by Margaret Craven. For books on foster children, use *The Pinballs*, by Betsy Byars, or *The Great Gilly Hopkins* by Katherine Paterson. For books on retarded siblings, use *What About Me?*, by Colby Rodowsky, or *Summer of the Swans* by Betsy Byars. For books dealing with divorce or one-parent families, use *Rabble Starkey* by Lois Lowry; *The Son of Someone Famous* by M. E. Kerr; or *Divorce*

Express by Paula Danziger. Tell each group as they read the book to think about the problem presented, how the problem affected the main character, and if the problem was resolved or unresolved. Ask them to discuss these ideas in their small groups. Let them choose one person from the group to represent them on a panel discussion group. Allow the four people on the panel discussion group to show their book, give the title and author, and state the problem and the solutions given in the book. After each person gives this background information, allow the students on the panel to discuss the pros and cons of the solutions and to discuss other ways that the problem could be handled.

Let students react with spontaneous oral expressions as they tell about the ending of the realistic fiction story they read. If they were disappointed by the ending, ask them how they would change it.

Help them to gain perspective on the ending by eliciting different points of view from other students.

Activities Related to Teaching Characterization

As students read realistic fiction stories, they can add to their storehouse of "unforgettable characters." Some of these characters will be extentions or mirrors of themselves while others will be patterns of idols or heroes. In some instances the characters will provide a negative image, one that students do not want to emulate. In any case, characters are such an important part of realistic fiction stories that the study of characterization provides many opportunities for interesting and informative activities. Many of these activities will involve oral communication skills.

If students read individual titles, they can participate in a number of activities relating to characterization. Books that lend themselves to these types of activities are *Queenie Peavy* by Robert Burch; *M. C. Higgins, the Great* by Virginia Hamilton; *Dear Lovey Heart, I Am Desperate* by Ellen Conford; *Where the Lilies Bloom* by Vera and Bill Cleaver; *Dinky Hocker Shoots Smack* by M. E. Kerr; *I Am the Cheese* by Robert Cormier; and *One Fat Summer* by Robert Lipstye. Let the students write a biographical sketch of a character and present it orally to the class. Ask them to dress as the character and present a monologue or do a pantomime of actions representative of the character. Have the students take the identity of a character and write diary entries to read to the class. Assist students in writing a character analysis to present orally with the use of transparencies. Remind the students to follow the guidelines that were taught concerning organizing data; utilizing beginning, middle, and ending statements; using supporting details; and using effective transitions. Ask them to read passages from the book to show the development of the character or to record these passages on a cassette player to play for the class.

If small groups of students read one title, use some of the following suggestions for activities related to teaching characterization. Books that are appropriate for these activities are *Cassie Binegar* by Patricia MacLachlan; *Cider Days* by Mary Stolz; *M. C. Higgins, the Great* by Virginia Hamilton; *All Together Now* by Sue Ellen Bridgers; *Rabble Starkey* by Lois Lowry; *Get on Out of Here, Philip Hall* by Bette Greene; *Maggie Forever* by Joan Lowry Nixon; *Does This School Have Capital Punishment?* by Nat Hentoff; *Durango Street* by Frank Bonham; *Representing Super Doll* by Richard Peck; *The Outsiders* by S. E. Hinton; *Dicey's Song* by Cynthia Voigt; *Pigman* by Paul Zindel; *Winning Kicker* by Thomas Dygard; and *Maudie and Me and the Dirty Book* by Betty Miles.

Let each group write and perform a skit that uses most of the characters of the book. Ask the students to make and wear large signs with the names of the characters and outline in red the names of central characters.

With students working in groups, ask them to write an advertisement for their book featuring the central characters. Combine all of the advertisements into a booklet and give a copy to each student. Be sure to put several copies in the library media center. Plan for the best advertisements to be read over the school's intercom during Book Week or National Library Week.

Another suggestion is to let each group select a passage from their book to read to the class by assigning dialogue spoken by central characters to different students and assigning a narrator to read the other parts.

If the entire class reads the same book, plan enjoyable activities involving characterization for all students. For example, if the class reads S. E. Hinton's *The Outsiders,* ask students in a large group session to give the names of the characters, including the supporting characters. List the names on a piece of paper. Cut out each name and place it in a small box. Divide the class into groups. Let someone from each group pick one of the names. Ask each group to carefully go through the book to locate details about their character. After compiling the information, allow the students to present the character to the class by a skit, monologue, news bulletin, "A Day in the Life of _____" (for example, Ponyboy), a videotaped characterization, or an audio recording with sound effects, presenting a biographical sketch of the character. If the students have seen the television series "The Outsiders," ask them to compare and contrast the characters as portrayed in the televised version to the book version. For a change-of-pace activity, ask students to search through *The Outsiders* to find out what fads were popular with the characters as presented in the book. Let them go to the library media center to locate and compare information on the period of the 1960s, such as the music, hairstyles, fads, clothing, dating, sports, and slang terms. Or have a fashion show and let students dress as one of the characters, pantomime traits of the character, and ask other students to guess the name of that character.

If students read *Park's Quest*, by Katherine Paterson, begin the discussion of the book by reading the picture storybook *The Wall* by Eve Bunting. Information on the book is in the section on Picture Storybooks. Ask students to compare the little boy in the picture storybook with Park. Have students write their impressions of the central characters, Park and Thanh. Let them read these aloud in class. Discuss the different reactions of the students. Ask students to write a brief description of each character in the book. Using the computer program *Crossword Magic*, let each student make a crossword puzzle entitled "Characters in Park's Quest" with the descriptions of the characters as clues and the names of the characters as answers. To help students better understand Park's mother and father, let them search for descriptive words and phrases. Ask students how Park was able to learn a great deal about his father. Let students make a list of his father's books that Park read. Allow more able readers to read aloud and discuss the fantasy world of Park. They may want to read the story of Percivale or other knights of Arthur's Round Table and contrast the quests. Ask for volunteers to work on a character sketch of Thanh. Let them present the information to the class in a series of transparencies, on posters, or in a skit. To close the study of the characters in *Park's Quest*, give the students an opportunity to express their reaction to the characters, what they would do in the place of the central characters, how the characters grow or change, and whether or not they feel that the characters are depicted as real people.

If the class reads Joan L. Nixon's *And Maggie Makes Three,* include activities on characterizations especially related to dramatics. Students can visualize the characters and grasp their individual characteristics, speech, and mannerisms when the book is read aloud. Encourage students to perform impromptu improvisations, pantomime, role-playing, and skits featuring all of the central characters. Ask the students to brainstorm group-project ideas. If possible, take students on a field trip to see a live performance of a contemporary realistic drama at a local high school or college. Remind students to respond with courtesy and enthusiasm to the performance.

If the class is divided into two groups, have one group read *From the Mixed-Up Files of Mrs. Basil E. Frankweiler,* by E. L. Konigsburg, while the other group reads *Secrets of the Shopping Mall* by Richard Peck. Let students present the characteristics of the central characters. Ask each group to determine the character who has the most businesslike approach to finding food and a place to sleep, which character has the most innovative ideas, and which character has the most influence in bringing the adventure to a close.

Additional Activities

Computer programs blend technology with literature to provide a number of interesting activities for students. A very comprehensive program is *The Electronic Bookshelf.* It is a reading motivation and management program that, according to their catalog, "encourages students to read favorably-reviewed and highly recommended children's and young adult literature for pleasure and/or credit." Series II corresponds with the reading and interest of students in grades 5–9. A 1990 addition to the program is *The Electronic Bookshelf Program Disks, Battle of the Books* with question sets to coordinate with the book quizzes. Use available computers and other computer programs to enhance the literature program. If a computer lab is available, students can work independently; if a single classroom computer is available or a computer is available in the library media center, students can take turns during silent reading sessions. Some programs are adaptable for use by the whole class on a large monitor connected to one computer. *BookBrain,* distributed by Oryx Press, is available for Apple II computers for grades 4–6 and 7–9. Students searching for realistic fiction titles can use the subject guide, author or title guide, or Book Detective section "Kids Like Me" to read annotations to assist them with the selection. *BookWhiz,* distributed by Educational Testing Service for grades 6–9, includes brief and expanded annotations for books. The books are listed under eight genres with subgroups. The library media specialist can add or delete titles to adapt the selections to the holdings of the library media center for both of these computer programs. They are especially helpful when students need to locate a book to read for a unit such as realistic fiction.

Puppetry is a fun activity that may be used by individuals, small groups, or an entire class. It may be used to highlight characters, to show scenes, or to tell the story. Students may make rod puppets, bag puppets, papier-mâché puppets, shadow puppets, or finger puppets utilizing bags, paper plates, socks, cardboard, rods, and gloves. A formal method of presentation requires the use of a script, which may be written by students and memorized or read during the performance. An informal method of presentation utilizes spontaneous lines, actions, and staging. Mary Ann Paulin's *Creative Uses of Children's Literature* includes the steps to follow in planning, creating, and performing puppet shows. Students might enjoy planning and producing a puppet show for elementary students using one of the picture storybooks included in this chapter. This would be a good time to involve the library media specialist, the art teacher, and the music teacher.

NONPRINT RESOURCES

Audiocassettes

The Secret Garden by Frances Hodgson Burnett. Audio Book Contractors, 1987.
The TV Kid by Betsy Byars. Random House Media.

Computer Programs

BookBrain, Grades 4–6. Apple. Version 3.0. Phoenix, AZ: Oryx Press, 1990.

BookBrain, Grades 7–9. Apple. Version 1.1. Phoenix, AZ: Oryx Press, 1990.
BookWhiz, Grades 6–9. Apple, IBM. Princeton, NJ: Educational Testing Service, 1987.
Crossword Magic. Mindscape Apple II family, IBM, Macintosh.
The Electronic Bookshelf Program Disks, Battle of the Books, Title Disks: Series II, Grades 5–9. Apple IIe, IIgs, IIc+ in 5 1/4" disk format. Frankfort, Indiana: The Electronic Bookshelf, 1990.

Filmstrips

The Great Gilly Hopkins by Katherine Paterson. Random House Media.
Meet the Newbery Author—Katherine Paterson. Miller-Brody Productions.
The Outsiders by S. E. Hinton. Random House Media.
The Pigman by Paul Zindel. Random House Media.

Videotapes

The Author's Eye: Katherine Paterson. Random House Media. (live-action video)
The Planet of Junior Brown. Random House Media. (enhanced video)
Scorpions by Walter Dean Myers. Random House Media. (live-action video)

References

The Best of The Web 1976–1982, edited by Charlotte Huck and Janet Hickman. Ohio State University, 1982.
Burch, Robert. "The New Realism." In *Children and Literature: Views and Reviews,* by Virginia Haviland. New York: Lothrop, Lee & Shepard, 1973.
Fisher, Margery. *Who's Who in Children's Books: A Treasury of the Familiar Characters of Childhood.* New York: Holt, Rinehart and Winston, 1975.
Georgiou, Constantine. *Children and Their Literature.* Englewood Cliffs, NJ: Prentice-Hall, 1969.
Kalb, Virginia. "Curriculum Connections: Literature." *School Library Media Quarterly* (Spring 1990): 175–176.

Lukens, Rebecca. *A Critical Handbook of Children's Literature.* Glenview, IL: Scott, Foresman and Company, 1981.

Norton, Donna. *Through the Eyes of a Child: An Introduction to Children's Literature.* 2d ed. Columbus, OH: Merrill Publishing Company, 1987.

Paterson, Katherine. *Gates of Excellence: On Reading and Writing Books for Children.* New York: Nelson, 1981.

Paulin, Mary Ann. *Creative Uses of Children's Literature.* Hamden, CT: Shoestring Press, 1982.

7

Historical Fiction

"The prime object of writing an historical novel is an exercise of the heart rather than the head. It is an exploration of the imagination, a discovery of other people living at other times and faced with other problems than our own. In other words, it is an extension of the author's human sympathies."
Hester Burton
"The Writing of Historical Novels"

INTRODUCTION

Historical fiction as a genre is more clear-cut and more easily distinguishable from other genres because of the similarities and common set of characteristics in most historical fiction books for children and young adults. These characteristics include a good story, an accurate historical setting, a re-creation of the past, and events that occurred or could possibly have occurred. The plot deals with universal themes basic to human nature: loyalty, revenge, love, hate, good, evil, ambition, life, death, quests, and honorable causes. The characters are well developed and portray the impact of the period upon their lives. Often the central character or protagonist is a young person who is involved in a cause related to that period who faces problems, challenges, or opportunities similar to those faced by today's young people.

The best historical fiction is well researched, contains genuine historical information, and combines an interesting story with an accurate description of what it was like to be living during the period. Historical facts are skillfully interwoven into the story so that the story rings true and is plausible and believable. Authentic descriptions of clothing, food, transportation, entertainment, customs, language, manners and details of everyday life are included to provide the color and flavor of the times. In historical fiction for young children, the events are usually presented in chronological order. For older children events are sometimes presented as flashbacks.

The main purpose of historical fiction is to entertain and foster the joy of reading. However, when children and young adults read good historical fiction, they develop a sense of history and a way of looking at the past.

As Constantine Georgiou states in *Children and Their Literature*, "Fine historical stories invite readers to live an adventure in the past vicariously. Young readers can thus witness historical events, meet historical characters, recapture the flavor of an era, and enter a new world whose experiences can deepen and broaden" (p. 304).

ELEMENT OF LITERATURE: FOCUS ON SETTING

Setting involves time and place. Time can be any time, such as the present: the setting for realistic stories; the past: the setting for historical fiction; or the future: the setting for science fiction stories. *Switcharound,* by Lois Lowry, is set in the present; *Across Five Aprils,* by Irene Hunt, is set in the past; *The White Mountains,* by John Christopher, is set in the future. Time can be a specific historical period such as the War of 1812, or it can be specified years such as 1830–1832 depicted in *A Gathering of Days* by Joan Blos. It can be a general period of time such as the Viking period, the seventeenth century, or the Stone Age, which is the setting for Harry Behn's *Faraway Lurs.* Time can encompass a person's lifetime, a few months, or a few days as in Diana Jones's *Eight Days of Lukeby,* or just 24 hours as in *Against Time!* by Roderic Jeffries. Place can be a geographical location such as ancient Tenochtitlan, the mountains of Tibet, the Great Wall of China, or Richmond, Virginia. It can be 107 Maple Street from *The House on Maple Street,* by Bonnie Pryor, or the Tower of London. Place can be a room like the one in *The Upstairs Room* by Johanna Reis; a 1950 Gold Cadillac, the setting for Mildred Taylor's *The Gold Cadillac;* a slave ship, the *Moonlight,* as described in *The Slave Dancer* by Paula Fox;

or an imaginary kingdom like the one created by Leslie and Jess in *A Bridge to Terabithia* by Katherine Paterson.

As in motion pictures and the theatre, setting includes all the physical surroundings, furniture, buildings, and properties. Physical details are described to enable the reader to sense by seeing, smelling, feeling, or tasting what is happening in the story. Setting also includes the environment and the external conditions affecting the story. These may include manners, customs, and the general way of life in which the story's action is taking place. Setting helps to create a mood or atmosphere and establish the emotional, social, and moral climate. Setting can serve as a *backdrop* for the story if it is relatively unimportant to the development of the plot, theme, or characterization. Many realistic stories, such as Judy Blume's *Blubber,* Paula Danziger's *The Cat Ate My Gymsuit,* or Lois Lowry's *Anastasia Krupnik,* use the setting as a backdrop. However, in such stories as Gary Paulsen's *Hatchet* or Jean George's *Julie of the Wolves,* the setting is an integral part of the story and is essential to it. The readers will rely upon the details of the setting to help them understand the conflict in the stories.

The setting in realistic stories, adventure, mystery, sports, humor, and animal stories may range from familiar local places to distant lands. Descriptions of places and concepts of time are related to those of contemporary life. These elements capture the spirit of the story if they are convincingly real and true-to-life.

The setting in fantasy or science fiction stories, whether real or imaginary, is sharpened by detailed description and attention to minute details. The setting may reveal a magical, fantastic, or technological world that still gives an air of reality to the story. The sense of time, period, and place support the action of the story.

The best historical fiction almost always requires that the setting be an integral part of the story. Based on serious research, the details are interwoven into the narrative to give authenticity to the characters and plot. The past is re-created. The setting is described in vivid details so that the readers can imagine or envision the setting in their own minds. When the culture and daily life of a people are depicted in fully realized characters, the readers can sense what it felt like to be living in that place during that period of time.

In the tape series *Prelude: Children's Book Council Mini-Seminars on Using Books Creatively,* Jean Fritz says that historical fiction should be judged as both history and literature, but its value is in the ability to transport children into a past that is believable, useful, and interesting to them.

One way of studying the setting in a historical fiction story is to read a book by one of the well-known historical fiction writers, make a list of criteria for setting, and summarize or use excerpts from the book that meet the criteria. For example, British author Rosemary Sutcliff is one of the outstanding creators of historical fiction. Her books cover many periods of history, including the Bronze Age, Roman-British Worlds, Anglo-Saxon England, Norman England, the Middle Ages, and fifteenth- and sixteenth-century England. Her characters are strong, interesting, sensitive, and convincing heroes and heroines with human emotions and conflicts. They are people with whom children can identify. They are portrayed as real people in a superb reconstruction of period and time.

Knight's Fee is a well researched book by Rosemary Sutcliff. It is a sensitive and convincing story of a young boy who ultimately becomes a knight. After reading *Knight's Fee,* the following criteria were selected for studying its setting:

1. Awareness and understanding of the period
2. Authenticity
3. Ancient rituals
4. Sense of passage of time
5. Glimpses of life
6. Attention to minor details
7. Unity of elements
8. General environment incorporated in background
9. Issues of period are clear
10. Convincing and believable characters

Following is a summary taken from *Knight's Fee* that illustrates the criteria for setting. *Knight's Fee* is set in Norman England in the year 1080. The orphan Randal lived in the kennels and was treated as one of the dogs: whipped with oxhide whips and purged with buckthorn in the spring. The Arundel knights wore the new fashionable long sleeves and trailing skirts with their tunics. The eyes of Hugh Goch, Lord of Arundel, were cold and inhuman, like a bird of prey. Within the castle walls a town had grown up, with barracks, mews, stables, kennels, granaries, storehouses, baking sheds, and armories. The smoke of the torches held by squires in the great hall permeated the scene. Herluin, the Minstrel, composed a song about a great lord who spent his rage on one small boy. All of his life Randal remembered every detail of the scene: the magpie-chequer of the chessboard and the silence of the pieces as Hugh Goch and Herluin moved kings and queens and knights in a game to decide Randal's fate. The game was compared to the political situation when King Red William had fought against Duke Robert. It was checkmate for the Lord of Arundel, and the brat Randal belonged to Herluin. Randal felt betrayed when he was given to Sir Everard. Riding behind his new master on Valiant, Sir Everard's horse, Randal saw a straggle of deep-thatched huts, hawthorn and old fruit trees, and a low hall with its byres and barns around it. The place was called Dean; it was to be Randal's home. And Randal sensed that it was home. He was to become a varlet and later a squire to Bevis, Sir Everard's grandson. The friendship and camaraderie grew between Bevis and Randal and was sealed when Bevis cut his beautiful red amber in two and gave one half to Randal, who vowed to carry it with him always. There was much learning to do with wax tablets, light weapons, and waiting tables. The brawling life of the manor was filled with the rich, greasy smell of the kitchen and the sour smell in the great hall. They ate barley cakes with bramble syrup and little dried apples. On fast day no meat was served with the thick fish soup, eel pies, kale, dark barley bread, and baked pears. All Soul's Eve and May Day were celebrated as they had been since before the memory of man. They attended Mass on Sundays and saints' days. In the evenings they played chess or listened to a reading from *The Lives of the Saints*. The news of recent happenings was brought to the manor by visitors who told of the Crusade nearing the gates of Jerusalem, the death of Hugh Goch in Wales, the seige of Nicaea, the battle of Dorylaeum, and of Duke Robert. Sir Everard had held the Dean for many years for a fee, called a knight's fee, that he paid to Baron de Braose. Barons received their hold from the king; lesser folk received theirs from barons. When Randal was 15, he became a squire to Bevis. With the death of King Red William, his brother Henry became the new king. His marriage to a lady of Scotland helped fuse Norman and Saxon to make one England years later. War gear, besides mail, was leather jacks, daggers, war-bows, and arrows. Randal never forgot the scene as Bevis knelt on the eve of knighthood in the small church lit by candlelight for a night's vigil at the altar with his drawn sword before him. "It seemed that the business of being made a knight was one of the lonely things of life, like being born or dying." Bevis's and Randal's eyes met with the brightness shared between them. Randal took a sprig of rosemary given to him by the red-haired girl and put it in the leather bag with the piece of red amber. As squire to Bevis, Randal rode behind his knight in battle and took up his banner when Bevis was mortally wounded. Randal asked Bevis to give him knighthood from his hand if he judged Randal to be worthy. Randal took his half of the red amber and exchanged it for Bevis's half. He slipped his half into the bag inside of the loose hauberk "over Bevis' quiet heart."

Another way to study setting in historical fiction is to read a historical fiction story, then search through the story for examples of:

1. Geographical places (cities, towns, rivers, islands)
2. Names of special places significant to the story (Red Fox Tavern, Adam's Dry Good Store, Tom's Bakery, Lakeland Park)
3. Famous people (George Washington, Queen Elizabeth I, Hitler)
4. Groups or types of people significant to the story (soldiers, teachers, explorers, tradesmen)
5. Food (hush puppies, raw fish, watermelons)
6. Clothing (chain-mail, calico dress, sack cloth)
7. Items of special significance to the period of time (oil lamps, feather beds, hornbooks)
8. Colorful language (spicy scent of newly gathered apples)
9. Actions significant to the period of time (tea was dumped in Boston Harbor)
10. Transportation (stagecoach, canoe, clipper ships)

An example to read is *Sarah Bishop,* by Scott O'Dell, which is set in the American Revolution period from 1775 to 1783. The story is based on a true account of the life of Sarah Bishop. Sarah was born in England, came to the colonies with her family shortly before the American Revolution, and settled on Long Island. After the battle for Brooklyn Heights and while New York City was still burning, she fled into the wilderness of Westchester County. There she lived on Long Pond, known to the Indians as Waccabue. Captain Cunningham, British Provost, who "starved the living and fed the dead" and who played an important part in Sarah's life, was tried in England after the war on charges of forgery, convicted, and sent to the gallows.

The following are examples of setting in *Sarah Bishop*:

1. Geographical places: Long Island, New York City, Boston, Halifax, Ridgeford Village, Hempstead, Staten Island, New York Bay, Brookland Fort, North River Ridgeford, White Plains
2. Names of special places significant to the story: Purdy's Mill, Lion and Lamb Tavern, *Scorpion* (British prison ship in Wallabout Bay), Lambert Prison, Morton and Son's Store, Quaker Meeting House, Mott's Corner, Red Lion, Lambert and Sons Sugar Merchants, Trinity Church, Connecticut Ferry, Golden Arrow Tavern, wig-making shop
3. Famous people: General George Washington, King George, John Adams, Admiral Richard Howe, Major Sterling, Captain Cunningham
4. Groups or types of people significant to the story: Skinners, gangs of patriots who went about burning people's property who were loyal to King George; Tories; Hessians, professional soldiers or mercenaries who came from Germany; Master Wentworth, who taught reading and writing; rebels; runaway slaves; Indians; Quakers
5. Food: Succotash and Indian pudding, fish cakes, fish chowder, Roxbury Russets (apples), eggs and ham and corncakes, Indian maize, rye and cornmeal and white flour, mugs of tea, rum punch, acorns to make flour, wintergreen tea, smoked fish, trout, deer, molasses, salt, honey, squibs, tarts
6. Clothing: Chemise, wigs, snowshoes, leather strings, lace trim on men's shirts, deerskin jacket, King George's crown and long jeweled robe
7. Items of special significance to the period of time: Lamps, muslin sack, grandfather clock, pamphlet "Common Sense" by Thomas Paine, musket, bay mare,

carryall, candles, shillings, Continental paper money, Brown Betty musket, gourds, deer tallow, jackknife, ax, Bible, canoe, animal traps, knitting
8. Colorful language or customs: Long hair worn in a club tied with a leather string, brewing tea from black birch leaves and bark, selling hair to a wig maker, a cuff on the ear
9. Actions significant to the period: Witch-hunting, burying money and silverware in ground, trapping, quoting scripture, carrying a Bible, selling furs, superstitions, tarred and feathered
10. Transportation: Horseback, dugout canoe, ships, walking

RECOMMENDED LISTS

Recommended Titles for Teaching the Historical Fiction Genre Unit

Clapp, Patricia. *I'm Deborah Sampson: A Soldier in the War of the Revolution.* New York: Lothrop, Lee & Shepard, 1977. RL: Grade 7. IL: Grades 8–11.

This story is based on a true account of Deborah Sampson Gannett who enlists in the Continental Army on May 20, 1782, under the name of Robert Shurtlieff, and serves until she is honorably discharged in October 1783. After being given to a cousin when she is five years old, she is bound to a family for eight years. The Thomas family has ten sons. Deborah is very happy with them and is treated as a member of the family. Eight of the Thomas men join the army soon after the start of the Revolutionary War. Deborah and Robert, who stays at home to help on the farm, fall in love. When Robbie also goes to war and is killed, Deborah feels that she must take Robbie's place in the fight for independence. Her army service is filled with the shock of being surrounded by males, adventure, excitement, and humor. Because of the mature theme of the book, it is suggested for use by older readers from grade 8 and up.

The story is set in the mid-1760s in Plympton, Boston, Concord, New Hampshire, Village of Middleborough, Lexington, Philadelphia, Yorktown, and Baltimore. Students attended school during the winter and carried hot baked potatoes to warm their hands on the way to school and to eat cold at lunch. They read plays of Shakespeare and the journal of the pilgrims at Plymouth in school. Students practiced penmanship by copying from the Bible. In the home there was a cricket stool by the hearth and copper pots and kettles. They used strong soap and cold water for bathing. Deborah got drunk at Sprout's Tavern after enlisting in the Continental Army and receiving a bounty. A soldier's clothes included a blue coat, white waistcoat, breeches, half boots, cap, knapsack, French musket, and haversack. Enemies were the redcoats, smallpox, and fevers. Outhouses served as toilets. Transportation was by horseback, boat, and Conestoga wagon. An important happening was the publication of the Declaration of Independence. A special gift was hand-made shirts. Important people mentioned include King George, General Gage, Samuel Adams, John Hancock, Paul Revere, General George Washington, and General Horatio Gates.

Forbes, Esther. *Johnny Tremain*. Boston: Houghton Mifflin, 1943. RL: Grade 6. IL: Grades 5–9. PB: Dell. Cornerstone.

Johnny, a proud and arrogant lad of 14, is apprenticed to a silversmith until an unfortunate accident cripples his hand. He becomes a courier for the *Boston Observer* and a messenger for the Sons of Liberty. Johnny and Rab forge a deep friendship; later they take part in the Boston Tea Party. Johnny develops into a heroic youth as one of the Revolutionaries.

The setting is Boston in 1773–1775. Important towns are Cambridge, Lexington, and Charlestown. Life in the Lapham household reflects the importance of religion and the Bible. The silversmith shop is interesting, with its anvils, annealing furnace, and crucibles. Places in Boston of significance to the story are Dock Square, Faneuil Hall, Town House, Long Wharf, Hancock's Wharf, Beacon Hill, and Christ's Church. Horses and coaches are the general mode of transportation. Interesting foods are coarse bread, spicy pudding, suckling pig, chocolate, coffee, squabs, tarts, and ale. The printing shop of the *Boston Observer* plays a role in the story and presents the political and personal issues of the day. There is constant friction between the Whigs and Tories. A medal is engraved with the Tree of Liberty. Men wear leather breeches and course shirts. The Nineteenth of April and Lexington on the Village Green become household terms. Some important people mentioned are Governor Hutchinson, Sam and John Adams, Paul Revere, Josiah Quincy, James Otis, John Hancock, and General Gage.

Fox, Paula. *The Slave Dancer*. New York: Bradbury Press, 1973. RL: Grade 7. IL: Grades 7–10. PB: Dell. Cornerstone.

Jessie Bollier, 13 years old, is press-ganged from his home in New Orleans to become a fife player on the slave ship *Moonlight*. Jessie has a difficult time adjusting to the rigors of shipboard life. In his search for friendship and trust, he learns that words do not always match actions. When the slaves are brought on board, Jessie recoils into a rage of hatred. When he recognizes that he also is a captive, he empathizes with the slaves and feels their horror, cruel treatment, and despair. He matures during the voyage and vows to learn a trade beneficial to mankind.

The story is set in New Orleans, in the Atlantic Ocean aboard the *Moonlight*, and at the Bight of Benin. The rigors of shipboard life and duties are presented and include chained naked men, women, and children; stench of the hold; excrement buckets; music of the fife; shuffling feet of the slaves; horror of sickness and death; a beating in the golden light of a radiant sunset; heroic attributes; and course food. Jessie learns a new vocabulary and a feeling of whiteness. The evils of the slave trade permeate the story. Jessie learns a healing trade.

Fritz, Jean. *Homesick: My Own Story*. New York: G. P. Putnam's Sons, 1982. RL: Grade 5. IL: Grades 5–7. Cornerstone.

The story is a memoir of Jean Fritz's childhood in China where her parents were American missionaries. Because of the civil unrest in China, the family returns to America. Jean's adjustment to life in both China and America is told with humor and understanding.

The setting is Hankow, China, on the Yangtze River. It takes place in the 1920s during a turbulent period of civil unrest, Communist uprisings, Russian advisers, and changes in leadership. Important people of the period are Sun Yat-sen, Yuan Shih-k'ai, Chiang Kai-shek, Mao Tse-tung, and Charles Lindbergh. Jean's family voyages to America on board the ship *President Taft* from Shanghai to San Francisco. They travel across the country by car to Washington, Pennsylvania. Songs of the period are "Five Foot Two, Eyes of Blue," and "Gimme a Little Kiss, Will Ya Huh?" Styles include silk stockings, women with bobbed hair, and belts worn around the hips. Movies of the time are *The Phantom of the Opera*, with Lon Chaney, and *Rin-Tin-Tin*. The important dance is The Charleston.

Hunt, Irene. *Across Five Aprils*. Chicago: Follett, 1964. RL: Grade 7. IL: Grades 6–9. PB: Ace.

Jethro is nine years old when the Civil War begins. He lives with his large family on a farm in southern Illinois. Over a period of five Aprils, Jeth works on the farm when his brothers join the army. The family is loyal to the Union, but one brother joins the Confederate Army. This causes many problems for the family. Jeth is a bright young man who searches for knowledge, understanding, and self-improvement. He is encouraged by his teacher, Shad, and a newspaper editor. Details of the war are gleaned through newspaper articles, an atlas, and personal letters. When his cousin becomes a deserter, Jeth writes a letter to President Lincoln asking for a pardon.

The story is set in Hidalgo, Illinois, in April 1861; Newton, Illinois; Jasper County, Illinois; and Ft. Sumter, South Carolina. Important battles are Bull Run, Shiloh, Chickamauga, Antietam, Chancellorsville, Pea Ridge, and Gettysburg. Rivers mentioned are the Mississippi, Rappahannock, Tennessee, and Cumberland. The family lives in a small pioneer's cabin with a hedgerow of lilacs, picket fence, and hard-packed clay roads. The planting of potatoes and crops is described. Sacks of corn and tobacco are exchanged at the store for coffee, sugar, an ax handle, nails, calico, and thread. The family uses a coal-oil lamp. Transportation is by horse, buggy, wagon, and railroad car. Typhoid fever is feared. Southern Illinois drawl and backwoods diction include: reckon, git, fur, hev, yore, furriner, kin, and tol'able. There is much talk about the Union Army, Confederates, abolitionists, slavery, cracker-barrel heroes, and the pain of divided loyalties. Readers realize that today's newspaper accounts will fill the pages of history tomorrow. Families fill picnic baskets and drive in wagons to hear war oratory.

Significant events include the assassination of President Lincoln. "The Battle Hymn of the Republic" is an inspiring song of the period. Important people are Generals Fremont, McClellan, Grant, Buckner, Bragg, Sherman, and Lee. Leaders are Secretary of State Seward, Jefferson Davis, and President Abraham Lincoln.

O'Dell, Scott. *Sarah Bishop*. Boston: Houghton Mifflin, 1980. RL: Grade 5. IL: Grades 7–10. PB: Scholastic.

See information under Element of Literature: Focus on Setting.

Paterson, Katherine. *The Master Puppeteer*. New York: Thomas Y. Crowell, 1976. RL: Grade 5. IL: Grades 5–8. PB: Avon.

Jiro, a thirteen-year-old boy, is apprenticed to Yoshida, master of the puppet theater. Growing up in eighteenth-century Japan in a time of famine and a period of great unrest and turmoil, Jiro is faced with many problems. Jiro is the son of a puppet maker, Hanji. Because of the famine, he leaves his parents and becomes an apprentice. His mother is angry even though she cannot feed her son. Jiro is concerned about his apprenticeship because he feels he has no talent. Jiro is told by Yoshida that "I am your concern. I am the master puppeteer." Jiro is befriended by Okada, a blind reciter who knows every word of every play by heart. Kinshi, the master's son, has a great respect for his father as a puppeteer but not as a father because of his harsh treatment. Kinshi is the senior boy and helps all the apprentices, including Jiro. Jiro learns the unusual ways of doing things at the theater, like having to steal scripts and jostling as an operator's way of saying thanks. Jiro returns home one New Year's Day to find that his mother has been beaten and robbed of her small packet of food given to her by a priest. Going back, Jiro is attacked but is mysteriously saved by his master, Yoshida. Saburo is a bandit with a thousand disguises to hide his identity. He robs the rich to feed the poor. He hosts a command performance of a puppet play at the theater called *The Thief of Tokaido* and invites the poor people to attend. They have a great time watching the outwitting of the dull authorities and the betrayal of Joman, the main character. At the end of the performance the audience is reminded of the betrayal, a message to help protect Saburo. Jiro becomes an accomplished puppeteer. He is surprised to learn the identity of Saburo. The satisfying conclusion includes increased recognition of Jiro's abilities, a reunion with his family, and acceptance of Kinshi by his father. Conflicting values, family ties, and devotion to the theater all combine to make this an appealing and suspenseful story. It also provides an intriguing introduction to the masterful art of Japanese puppetry.

The story is set in the eighteenth century in Osaka, Japan. Food for the poor was very scarce, often only root tea and soup. Bandits, rovers, and street gangs stole food. At the theater, food was more plentiful and included cabbage, rice, vegetables, tea, bean soup, bean cakes, rolls, and sometimes sake. Men's dress included trousers, tunic, sash, loincloth, and wooden clogs. Kumuso monks wore traditional basketlike hats. Families used public baths for a small fee. Plays performed at the puppet theater included *The Battle of Coxinga*. Yoshida had the male lead for this play, although he regarded himself as a specialist of the female puppet. The stage set for this play was very elaborate. Puppeteers wore hoods to operate the puppets by hand, stick, and string. There were some one-man puppets, but most of the puppets required more than one operator; of these, the foot operator was one of the most important. At the end of the performance, the reader raised the script and bowed for the final time.

Recommended Titles for Individual or Group Study

Clapp, Patricia. *Constance: A Story of Early Plymouth*. New York: Lothrop, Lee & Shepard, 1968. RL: Grade 7. IL: Grades 7–10. PB: Penguin.

Constance, 14 years old, is not happy about being on the *Mayflower* in November of 1620. She wants to be back in London. Her father is enthusiastic and eager to begin a new life in the New World. Constance keeps a journal describing the early years of constant hunger, sickness, death, few clothes, fear of Indians, and living conditions. Later, the Indian Sanoset and his daughter become friends with Constance and the white settlers. Constance accepts her new life and has problems choosing a husband.

Reiss, Johanna. *The Upstairs Room*. New York: Thomas Y. Crowell, 1972. RL: Grade 5. IL: Grades 6–9. PB: Harper.

This is a fictionalized story of the author's experiences with Nazi Germany and the Holocaust. Annie finds it difficult to understand why Hitler hates the Jews and why the Jews are treated so harshly. She and her sister are sheltered by a Dutch farming family. In spite of the danger to all, the family protects the girls from the Nazi soldiers.

Speare, Elizabeth George. *The Bronze Bow*. Boston: Houghton Mifflin, 1961. RL: Grade 6. IL: Grades 7–9.

Daniel bar Jarmin joins a guerilla band to fight the Roman conquerors who crucified his father. His blinding hatred causes his sister to suffer and almost costs him his beloved Thacia. When he meets Jesus, he learns that hatred is his enemy, not the Romans. He changes as he substitutes love for hate.

Speare, Elizabeth George. *The Witch of Blackbird Pond*. Boston: Houghton Mifflin, 1958. RL: Grade 5. IL: Grades 5–9. Cornerstone.

Against a backdrop of Puritan New England, young Kit Tyler faces the unyielding hardships of the period with the spirit and determination of one who loves life and good times. When Kit befriends Hannah Tupper, who is suspected of being the witch of Blackbird Pond, Kit is accused of being a witch. She is arrested, imprisoned, and put on trial. She is finally exonerated with the help of friends.

Sutcliff, Rosemary. *The Eagle of the Ninth*. New York: Henry Z. Walck, 1954. RL: Grade 8. IL: Grades 7–9. Windrush.

The story is about Marcus Aquila, a young Roman soldier who is wounded in battle. His quest becomes a great adventure as he searches for his father's lost legion in the wilderness of Britain. The Ninth Legion carries the eagle standard.

Sutcliff, Rosemary. *The Shining Company.* New York: Farrar, Straus & Giroux, 1990. RL: Grade 8. IL: Grades 7–10.

Set in Britain in A.D. 600, this story is based on the poem "The Gododdin." Prosper meets Prince Gorthyn, who admires his daring in trying to save a white hart. Prosper asks to serve the prince and is called two years later to join a war-host summoned by the king to fight the invading Saxons. The company comes to be known as The Shining Company. Prosper experiences the preparations and battles, challenges and treachery, and glory and agony of war. A map of Britain in A.D. 600, a guide to pronunciation, and an author's note add to the understanding of the story.

This is a challenging book and is recommended for highly able readers.

Taylor, Mildred. *Roll of Thunder, Hear My Cry.* New York: Dial Press, 1976. RL: Grade 5. IL: Grades 5–9. PB: Bantam. Cornerstone.

Life in the 1930s is difficult in a southern Mississippi town for black families like the Logan family. Cassie and her younger brother become involved in a controversy at school when they refuse to accept worn-out, discarded books containing racial slurs from white schools. They experience harassment, fear, humiliation, and grief. The loving environment, education, and independence of the family help to uphold their spirits and dignity.

Wilder, Laura Ingalls. *Little House in the Big Woods.* New York: Harper & Row, 1953. RL: Grade 5. IL: Grades 4–8. Cornerstone.

Laura, Mary, Carrie, and Grace are the daughters of the Ingalls family. They live in a log cabin in the Wisconsin forest. The physical details of pioneer life include making lead bullets by the fire, smoking deer meat, and cooking good meals with limited resources. Some happy moments include listening to Pa tell stories, playing with paper dolls made by Ma, and listening to Pa play and sing with his fiddle. Ma tries her best to make a home for the family.

Yep, Laurence. *Dragonwings.* New York: Harper & Row, 1975. RL: Grade 6. IL: Grades 6–9. Cornerstone.

Moon Shadow leaves his mother in China to join his father in

San Francisco. He and his father move to a stable behind Miss Whitlaw's boardinghouse. He learns to read and write English. He develops a friendship with the Whitlaws and teaches them about China. He experiences the Great San Francisco Earthquake of 1906. Moon Shadow joins in his father's dream to build a flying machine. When the flying machine is built, Chinese friends lend their support by pulling "Dragonwings" up the hill, although they consider it to be a folly. "Dragonwings" makes a short but successful flight.

Picture Storybooks for Teaching Setting

Hall, Donald. *Ox-Cart Man*. Illustrated by Barbara Cooney. New York: Viking, 1979.

The day-to-day life of a farming family is shown through the changing of the seasons and the rituals of work, selling, and buying. It presents a sense of time and place and purpose.

The setting is New England in the nineteenth century. This book presents a vivid scene of autumn, with the ox-cart man filling his cart with items his family made or grew all year.

From the wool he sheared, his wife spun yarn and wove a shawl, and his daughter knitted mittens. His son carved birch brooms with a kitchen knife. He packed candles, shingles, goose feathers, maple sugar, potatoes, honey, turnips, and cabbages. He traveled ten days over hills, past farms and villages, until he came to Portsmouth and Portsmouth Market. Here he sold his goods, his ox-cart, and his ox. He bought an iron kettle, embroidery needle, Barlow knife, and wintergreen peppermint candies. He walked home, arriving in the cold, winter sunset. The family worked during the winter months, and in the spring they planted their crops. The cycle continues.

Winter, Jeanette. *Follow the Drinking Gourd*. New York: Alfred A. Knopf, 1988.

By following directions in a song, "The Drinking Gourd," runaway slaves could journey north along the underground railway to freedom in Canada. An old sailor named Peg Leg Joe taught the slaves the song, assisted them with signs along the way, and met them near their journey's end. The song combines American folk tradition and history into the setting for the story.

The setting is portrayed in bright, graphic illustrations that depict the plantation and cotton fields of the South, trees with moss, cabins with fireplaces, and roosters in the yard. Slaves are shown working for their cruel masters and being sold at the auction block. The words of "The Drinking Gourd" tell the slaves to wait until spring when "the sun comes back, and the first quail calls." Then they are to follow the "drinking gourd," or the Big Dipper, which points to the North Star. Under cover of darkness, they go northward with help from the Underground Railway until they come to the river's end, the Ohio River. Finally, with the help of Peg Leg Joe, they reach freedom.

TEACHING TIPS: THE HISTORICAL FICTION GENRE AND SETTING

Historical fiction may be brought to life for the students as they read, discuss, participate in activities, and evaluate this genre. Place the emphasis on involving the students in the sense of "you are there" as they feel, taste, smell, and envision the scenes of the story. Help them get the feeling that history is alive and well and enjoyable. Give them opportunities to read, listen, view, write, and take part in many different types of activities related to historical fiction. To accomplish this will take a lot of planning, reading, preparation, and day-to-day involvement, but the rewards and satisfaction will be worth the effort. Because of the length of the lessons and activities, it is suggested that the classroom teacher, reading teacher, or language arts teacher has the main responsibility for teaching the unit, assisted by the library media specialist.

Plan the unit in advance to allow time for purchase of books or for books to be placed on reserve in the library media center. Draw upon the special skills, knowledge, or talents of associates throughout the teaching of this unit. These may include storytelling, reading aloud, booktalks, cooking, photography, design and construction, and skills development.

Begin the unit by preparing and placing a large, attractive timeline around the room. Use the computer program *TimeLiner*, by Tom Snyder Productions, if available. Bernard Green's *The Timetables of History: A Horizontal Linkage of People and Events* is a good resource book. Be sure to include the dates of important historical events and dates from historical novels that will be used in the unit. Ask students to recall what happened on these dates. Allow time for students to become involved in the activity. Have on hand several reference sources and ask volunteers to search for answers. Ask students if there is one particular period of history or historical event that they would like to have witnessed. Introduce them to historical fiction that will transport them into the past. Use the genre introduction in this chapter and additional sources listed under the references. Select one of your favorite books of historical fiction or use one of the books listed in the historical fiction bibliography. Give a booktalk and read an exciting excerpt from the book. Be sure to describe the setting and the period of history. Point out the date on the timeline. Tell the students that they will be reading and discussing historical fiction books for the next few weeks.

To introduce the literary element of setting, use this chapter's Element of Literature: Focus on Setting. As you mention titles of books and describe the setting as provided in the background information, let students point to the date of the setting on the timeline. Ask students if they remember any picture storybooks or children's books in which the setting played an important part. Tell them that you would like to share some examples with them. Read *Ox-Cart Man* and show them the illustrations as you read each page. Ask the students to describe the setting. Use the notes provided as a guide. Be sure to show the students the title page with the name of the illustrator. Do the same thing with *Follow the Drinking Gourd* or show the videotape of the book. The videotape, published by American School Publishers in 1990, is an iconographic video with electronic effects, using the original art. An additional title of special interest is Paul Goble's *Death of the Iron Horse,* which depicts an Indian triumph when the Cheyenne Indians use their tomahawks and knives to tear up the iron road of the iron horse. Emphasize the criteria for setting in historical stories.

To help students understand setting, conduct the following class exercise. From a random selection of historical fiction books, give each student one book. If there are multiple copies of one title, group those students having the same book title together. Ask the students to browse through the book and locate information on the setting. Tell them to make a list of a few of the supporting details of the setting using the examples they learned from the Focus on Setting section. When the class is brought back into one large group, ask students to share the information they have gathered. Ask them to give the author and title and to point out the period of history on the timeline.

Select historical fiction books for class study based on the reading levels and interests of the students and the availability of materials. If students are on closely related reading levels, one title can be selected for study by the entire class. Examples are Irene Hunt's *Across Five Aprils* or Esther Forbes's *Johnny Tremain*. Of course, this will depend on the availability of multiple copies of one title. If students are on several different reading levels, they can be grouped by reading levels with a different title selected for each small group or with individual titles for each student. Students may also select a historical fiction book of special interest to them from the library media center. A booktalk by the library media specialist will assist students with their selection. If the students are on a reading level of grade 5 or below, the fictionalized biographies by Jean Fritz and *The American Girls Collection* would be both entertaining and informative. These books are appropriate for teaching setting. The books by Jean Fritz are available in paperback from Coward, McCann & Geoghegan and include *Can't You Make Them Behave, King George?*; *Where was Patrick Henry on the 29th of May?*; *Will You Sign Here, John Hancock?*; *What's the Big Idea, Ben Franklin?*; *Why Don't You Get a Horse, Sam Adams?*; and *And Then What Happened, Paul Revere?*. *The American Girls Collection* is a series of historical fiction books about three girls. The first series is about a pioneer girl in the 1850s; the second series is about a girl living near New York City in 1904; the third series is about a girl during World War II. The books are easy to read and attractive. They are available in paperback and in audiocassettes. They are recommended for the seven-to-twelve-year-old reader and may be used in grades 5 and 6. A supplementary "Portfolio of Pastimes" features a cookbook, paper dolls, a diary, plays, and games. They are available from the Pleasant Company.

Many of the historical fiction titles are available in paperback editions and in large-print editions by Cornerstone or Windrush. These are designated in the annotated bibliography of historical fiction books.

Choosing the titles for an entire class, for small groups, or for individuals can be done in several ways. The selections can be books by one author of historical fiction, such as books by Rosemary Sutcliff. She has written over 30 historical fiction books for children.

Many of the titles of her books published in the 1960s and 1970s are now out-of-print in the United States, but they may be found in school library media centers and public libraries. Other selections can be books from one historical period, such as the colonial period of the United States with books like *Constance,* by Patricia Clapp, or *The Witch of Blackbird Pond* by Elizabeth George Speare. They can be books with settings in other countries, such as *The Sign of the Chrysanthemum,* by Katherine Paterson, which is set in Japan, or *The Upstairs Room,* by Johanna Reiss, which is set in Holland during World War II. They can also tie in with the period of history that the students are studying in social studies classes.

Discussions and activities related to the teaching of historical fiction will focus on the literary element, setting, and on the critical-thinking and communication skill, writing. Many examples or ideas for activities follow the next section.

FOCUS ON CRITICAL-THINKING AND COMMUNICATION SKILLS: WRITING SKILLS

In this information age, the ability to communicate facts, information, concepts, and ideas is of the utmost importance. Writing skills must be developed and practiced. The best way to teach these skills is to integrate them into the curriculum. Using literature and meaningful activities, students can be motivated and challenged to increase their writing competency. Writing assignments include exercises in descriptive and narrative writing skills. Emphasis is placed on writing good paragraphs rather than reports. Topics include writing descriptive settings, narrowing the topic, putting events in sequence, distinguishing fact from opinion, using reasons to support opinions, comparing and contrasting, summarizing, choosing words that express the senses, and using reference books as aids to writing.

ACTIVITIES

Activities Related to Teaching the Historical Fiction Genre

Activities related to the teaching of historical fiction include reading, viewing videotapes and filmstrips, listening to recorded narratives and music, drawing illustrations or cartoons, cooking special foods, building miniatures or sets, constructing dioramas, and producing original media. Production ideas include videotapes, radio skits, hand-drawn slides, transparencies, and photography.

Before students begin reading a selected historical fiction book, involve them in a meaningful activity. If the entire class is reading one book, such as *Johnny Tremain,* or if the class is reading from one period of history, such as the Revolutionary War period, this would be a good time to introduce them to that period. With *Johnny Tremain* as an example, use the sound filmstrips from the series *Colonial Life.* Set up stations in the classroom or the library media center. Divide students into groups. Each group rotates to all stations, viewing one filmstrip at each station.

    Station 1. The People
    Station 2. Food and Health
    Station 3. Colonial Costume
    Station 4. Houses
    Station 5. Freedom

Plan a research activity to help students understand the geographical locations for the setting. Reserve reference sources to assist the students. Duplicate an outline map of Massachusetts and one of Boston. Ask students to place the following cities and towns on the map of Massachusetts: Boston, Lexington, Cambridge, and Charlestown. On the map of Boston, ask students to locate Hancock's Wharf, Town House, North Square, Christ's Church, Liberty Tree, and Long Wharf.

If the books selected cover one period of history, such as the Civil War, use the same procedure by selecting filmstrips, videotapes, and geographical reference sources and set up stations for each category. Suggested audiovisual materials are included in the bibliography at the end of this chapter.

If students are reading individual titles of historical fiction books, plan a class activity to emphasize people, articles, and objects of importance to different periods of history. Ask students to take the list of items and place them under the correct heading. Tell them that it is just a fun activity and it is permissible for them to guess. Suggested headings and lists are included but may be adapted to reflect the historical periods of the titles being used by the class.

Sample headings are: Ancient Egypt, Age of Exploration, Colonial Life, and Westward Movement. Sample lists for these headings are: Queen Isabella, Religious Zeal, King Tut, Bonnets, Cleopatra, Gold Rush, Nile River, Pioneers, Colonial Enterprises, Hieroglyphics, Witchcraft, Sphinx, Wigs, Williamsburg, Nefertiti, Lewis and Clark, Trade Routes, Temples and Treasure, Christopher Columbus, Jamestown, Pyramids, Oregon Trail, Conestoga Wagon, Trailblazers, Wagon Trains, Apothecary Shop, and Ferdinand Magellan. A completed sample with answers follows.

Ancient Egypt	Age of Exploration	Colonial Life	Westward Movement
King Tut	Trade Routes	Jamestown	Lewis and Clark
Sphinx	Christopher Columbus	Williamsburg	Trailblazers
Nile River	Colonial Enterprises	Bonnets	Wagon Trains
Hieroglyphics	Temples and Treasure	Wigs	Pioneers
Cleopatra	Queen Isabella	Witchcraft	Oregon Trail
Pyramids	Ferdinand Magellan	Apothecary Shop	Gold Rush
Nefertiti	Religious Zeal		Conestoga Wagon

Depending on the organization of the class, ability levels, and motivation of the students, plan the reading periods accordingly. In most cases, students read silently during class time and at home. Sometimes oral reading of the entire book by the teacher or library media specialist is appropriate. But the important thing to remember is that this is a reading experience and not a viewing of a videotape or movie at this time. Examples of using videotapes or recordings as supplements are included as activities.

After students begin reading a historical fiction book, give them an opportunity to share what they have learned about the setting in a large group discussion. Ask if any of the students feel that they need more information to better understand the historical period depicted in their book. Allow these students time during class session to go to the library media center to locate needed information.

During the reading of the historical fiction book, plan activities that will not interfere with the enjoyment and pleasure of reading. Encourage understanding by being available for conference. Help students to think critically about what they are reading. Open up a class session for discussion if students indicate a need to talk with others about their books. Have a "show-and-tell" day. Ask students to select a description of the setting, whether of time, place, or atmosphere, in the book that they are reading. Tell them to bring an object that is a symbol of this description. This may be a map, picture, a piece of clothing, food, music, drawing, or numerous other objects. Let the student read the description from the book, limiting the selection to one paragraph, and show the item to the class. Give them an example:

Blos, Joan. *A Gathering of Days*. Read the paragraph in which Catherine describes the remaining store of apples, cabbages, potatoes, and parsnips in her journal entry of Tuesday, April 5, 1831 (p. 61). Bring in a potato with sprouts or a slightly shriveled apple. Discuss parsnips and recipes for cooking them and the need for storage of food items during the winter months.

If the entire class is reading the same historical fiction book, appropriate activities include vocabulary development, questions on sections of the book, small group discussions, and large group discussions. To vary the pace, read aloud interesting descriptions of setting or the influence of the setting on a character. Make several copies of a small segment of the text and highlight the dialogue portion to be read by different students. Assign to a narrator the portions not included as dialogue.

Activities Related to Teaching Setting

All activities in this section relate in some way to the setting in historical fiction books. Most activities include written assignments to promote communication skills.

After students complete the reading of their historical fiction book, review the importance of setting. Emphasize that setting in historical fiction books must be seen in relation to the other literary elements. Often the plot, theme, point of view, and characterization develop from the environment, the physical surroundings or geography, and the political or social events of the period.

As a review, use an additional example of setting as time and place from a children's book. An excellent example is Tony Johnston's *Yonder*, illustrated by Lloyd Bloom. This narrative poem expresses the passing of time through nature's change of seasons and through one familiy's history from youth to old age. It is available in an iconographic videotape from American School Publishers. The poem has been set to music. Show the illustrations and read the text or show the videotape. Let students explain the setting.

Questions that bring out the relationship of the setting to the action or conflict in the story help students to better understand the importance of setting. The following questions and statements serve as guidelines for adaption to the abilities of the students and to the objectives of the teacher. Choose writing assignments from them.

1. Describe the geographical environment of the story.
2. Explain the protagonists' attitude toward the environment.
3. What is the author's attitude toward the setting? Is it friendly, hostile, realistic, or impersonal?
4. Compare the home life of the main character with the home life of someone you know. Include physical surroundings, leisure activities, chores, food, and dress.
5. Describe how the author uses details of the senses to convey touch, sight, smell, and taste.
6. In the development of the story, how much time is involved? Describe the passing of time using examples from the story.
7. Is the author successful in describing the political or social conditions of the period? Why or why not?
8. Are details vital to the story explained in concrete terms?
9. Does the setting give a sense of time, period, place, and emotional climate to the story?
10. Are details provided to give glimpses of daily life? Give examples.
11. Is the setting sharp and clear?
12. Does the setting support the action of the story without interfering with the human interest of the story?
13. Are authentic details of time, place, and social order included? Make a list of these. Check reference sources in the library media center to verify authenticity.
14. Describe colorful costumes, activities of daily life, and social customs.

15. Does the story promote an understanding of the period?
16. Is the period of time shown in chronological order? List a sequence of events that lead up to a significant time in the life of the main character.
17. Are minor details faithful to the historical period? Give examples.
18. Compare and contrast customs of that period of history with customs of today. Include some of the following: food, clothing, education, books, music, celebrations of holidays, religious activities, travel, games, sports, and occupations.
19. What environment had the most effect on the outcome of the story? Was it physical, social, economic, or political? Support your choice with facts.
20. What scene do you remember the most from the story? Describe the scene.
21. Was there one object that the main character valued highly or one object that you found very interesting? Describe the object and the effect it had on the story.
22. Summarize the setting in one paragraph.
23. Make a timeline showing the passing of time in the story.
24. Were there any words or phrases used by the characters that demonstrate a different language pattern than that used today? Give examples.
25. Analyze a political or social situation described in the story. Distinguish between fact or opinion. Write a summary of your conclusions.

Give students basic guidelines for the writing activities. Include some of the following ideas and suggestions.

Steps in Writing a Good Paragraph

Use a word processor to compose, revise, and make the final copy, if available.

1. Make a list of points or ideas that you want to express in your writing.
2. Decide on your central idea.
3. Look through your list of points to find those that support your central thought.

4. Visualize what you want to say.
5. Write a good topic sentence.
6. Use simple words and combinations of words. Use action verbs.
7. Communicate the feeling that you want to express.
8. Read the paragraph critically. Read it aloud.
9. Revise your paragraph.
10. Write final copy in good handwriting, by typing, or on a word processor.

Additional Activities

Ask students to make a diorama of the setting for their historical fiction story. Display the dioramas with a copy of the book in the library media center.

Work with the library media specialist to teach students how to make hand-drawn slides and how to prepare a storyboard. Let students write their storyboard script with emphasis on the setting of the historical fiction book that they read. After they complete the slides, students can tape the accompanying script.

Show students a sample diary or journal like *A Gathering of Days* by Joan Blos. Ask the students to write several entries for a diary or journal about a journey or a visit to a place made by the main character.

If all the students read the same historical fiction book, let them plan and make a large display model of the setting: a farm in Illinois, a castle in Britain, a log cabin in the wilderness, a slave ship on the Atlantic Ocean, a plantation in the South, a model of early Boston, a battleground of the Civil War, or a Chinese junk on the Yangtze River. Work with the art teacher and industrial arts teacher throughout the planning and construction periods. In the planning stage, ask students to prepare written descriptions of geographic features and objects to be included in the display.

Ask students to write a good paragraph describing the time and place of the setting of the historical fiction book that they read.

If small groups of students read the same book, let them plan a dramatization of "a day in the life of" the main character and videotape the skits or perform them for the class.

Let students find recipes of foods eaten during the period of history of their historical fiction book. Ask them to prepare one sample dish or bring one item of food to class. If there is a home economics class, this activity can be coordinated with the teacher. Share foods with the students. Ask each student to tell the name of the book, the author, and something about the food item.

Using the resources in the library media center, ask students to find illustrations of the dress for the period of history covered by their historical fiction books. Costume books, historical reference sources, encyclopedias, and nonfiction books covering different periods of history are excellent sources. Have students draw illustrations, photograph them, or make transparencies of illustrations.

Work with the music teacher to locate music or recordings of music from different periods of history. Play selections to the class and let them identify the period of history.

Help students write a script for a radio broadcast advertisement of a historical fiction book that emphasizes the setting of the book.

Show a videotape based on one historical fiction book. If the students have read the book, let them compare and contrast the setting in the videotape with the description in the book or in their "mind's eye."

Let students listen to recorded selections about the setting of a book of historical fiction.

Review card catalog subject headings for historical fiction books using the format available in the library media center, whether standard catalog, microfiche, or computerized. Help students understand and use the entire heading to locate additional historical fiction titles. For example: United States—History—Revolution, 1775–1783—Fiction.

Make a bibliography of titles of historical fiction books related to the period of time in the book read by the student.

Let students use a computer program like *The Children's Writing and Publishing Center,* from the Learning Company, to write and illustrate an imaginative setting for a specific historical period.

Use the computer program *TimeLiner,* by Tom Snyder Productions, to create timelines of varying lengths. Several sample historical timelines are included that can be edited or merged with students' ideas. Timelines are printed in banner format.

Allow students to use a computer program to select additional historical fiction books. *BookWhiz* contains lists of books that may be modified to reflect the holdings of the library media center. The *Electronic Bookshelf, Series II* also contains many historical fiction book titles for grades 5–9.

Enlist students in preparing a time capsule of items important to them in school. Get permission to bury the capsule on school property under the planting of a tree. Get assistance from the science teacher. The tree planting might be on Earth Day or Arbor Day.

NONPRINT RESOURCES

Audiocassettes

Dragonwings by Laurence Yep. Miller-Brody Productions.
Prelude: Children's Book Council Mini-Seminars on Using Books Creatively. Series 3. New York: Children's Book Council, 1977.
The Witch of Blackbird Pond by Elizabeth George Speare. Listening Library.

Computer Programs

BookWhiz. Educational Testing Service.
The Children's Writing and Publishing Center. Learning Company.
The Electronic Bookshelf, Series II. Electronic Bookshelf.
TimeLiner. Tom Snyder Productions.

Filmstrips

The American Revolution. Random House Media.
The Civil War. National Geographic Society.
Colonial Life. Educational Dimensions.
Ox-Cart Man by Donald Hall. Random House Media.
Roll of Thunder, Hear My Cry by Mildred Taylor. Random House Media.
Sign of the Beaver by Elizabeth George Speare. Miller-Brody Productions.

Videotapes

Across Five Aprils by Irene Hunt. Random House Media. (enhanced video)

Follow the Drinking Gourd by Jeanette Winter. Random House Media. (iconographic video)
Sarah, Plain and Tall by Patricia MacLachlan. Random House Media. (enhanced video)
The Upstairs Room by Johanna Reiss. Random House Media. (enhanced video)
The Witch of Blackbird Pond by Elizabeth George Speare. Children's Television International.

References

Bodart, Joni. *Booktalk! Two: Booktalk for All Ages and Audiences.* 2d ed. New York: The H. W. Wilson Company, 1985.
Burton, Hester. "The Writing of Historical Novels." In *Children and Literature: Views and Reviews,* edited by Virginia Haviland. New York: Lothrop, Lee & Shepard, 1973.
Georgiou, Constantine. *Children and Their Literature.* Englewood Cliffs, NJ: Prentice–Hall, 1969.
Green, Bernard. *The Timetables of History: A Horizontal Linkage of People and Events.* New York: Simon & Schuster, 1975.
Halsted, Judith Wynn. *Guiding Gifted Readers: From Preschool to High School.* Columbus, OH: Ohio Psychology Publishing Company, 1988.
Haviland, Virginia, ed. *Children and Literature: Views and Reviews.* New York: Lothrop, Lee & Shepard, 1973.
Hogrefe, Pearl. *The Process of Creative Writing.* 3d ed. New York: Harper & Row, 1963.
Johnson, Edna, Evelyn Sickels, and Frances Sayers. *Anthology of Children's Literature.* 4th ed. Boston: Houghton Mifflin, 1970.
Landsberg, Michele. *Reading for the Love of It.* New York: Prentice-Hall, 1987.
Lukens, Rebecca. *A Critical Handbook of Children's Literature.* 3d ed. Glenview, IL: Scott, Foresman and Company, 1986.
Norton, Donna. *Through the Eyes of a Child: An Introduction to Children's Literature.* 2d ed., Columbus, OH: Merrill Publishing Company, 1987.
Reader's Digest Success With Words: A Guide to the American Language. Pleasantville, NY: The Reader's Digest Association, 1983.
Sutherland, Zena, and May Hill Arbuthnot. *Children and Books.* 7th ed. Glenview, IL: Scott, Foresman and Company, 1986.

8

Animal

*"I'm going out to fetch the little calf
That's standing by the mother. It's so young
It totters when she licks it with her tongue.
I shan't be gone long.—You come too."*
     Robert Frost
     "The Pasture"

INTRODUCTION

The animal genre is very appealing to people of all ages. Robert Frost's invitation, "You come too," is eagerly accepted by many people. Young children are fond of Beatrix Potter's *The Tale of Peter Rabbit*, Michael Bond's *A Bear Called Paddington*, Gabrielle Vincent's *Ernest and Celestine's Picnic*, and Arnold Lobel's *Frog and Toad Are Friends*. Older children like *Charlotte's Web* by E. B. White; *Mrs. Frisby and the Rats of NIMH* by Robert O'Brien; and *King of the Wind* by Marguerite Henry. Young adults identify with Sheila Burnford's *The Incredible Journey* and Jean George's *Cry of the Crow*. Among the animal stories popular with adults are *Watership Down* by Richard Adams; *Never Cry Wolf* by Farley Mowat; and "The Bear" by William Faulkner.

Owning and caring for pets helps stimulate interest in animals. Older children and adults who are pet owners are knowledgeable observers of animal traits, and they are keenly aware of animal behavior. They respond to the physical, social, and emotional needs of their pets. They watch carefully for any conflicts that might disrupt the security of a pet's life. Pet owners of all ages build a sense of loyalty and devotion to their animal friends. This warm relationship often causes sorrow when a pet is lost, injured, or dies. Credible stories of relationships between humans and pets are of special interest to pet owners.

Pets are no longer only dogs, cats, birds, fish, horses, and reptiles. There is a growing popularity for pigs as pets. Their owners claim, and research supports, that pigs are smart, can be housetrained, and are free from fleas. Other animals adopted as pets include goats, sheep, owls, raccoons, skunks, monkeys, and chimpanzees. Wild animals are often adopted as pets, especially if they are young, abandoned, or injured. Stories about wild animals and birds as pets illustrate the perilous balance between animals and humans and the problems that can arise. Such stories include Marjorie Kinnan Rawling's *The Yearling*, about a pet deer; John and Jean George's *Meph, the Pet Skunk;* Lucy Boston's *Stranger at Green Knowe*, about an escaped zoo gorilla; Farley Mowat's *Owls in the Family;* Sterling North's *Rascal*, about a raccoon; Jean George's *Cry of the Crow;* Walt Morey's *Gentle Ben*, about a bear; and Allan Eckert's *Incident at Hawk's Hill,* about a badger.

Fictional stories about animals can be grouped according to the treatment and characteristics given to the animals. They behave like animals; they behave like animals except they can talk; they behave like humans. Alan Purves and Dianne Monson list a continuum of animal story types in *Experiencing Children's Literature*. This list includes animals as animals with the focus on humans or animals, animals with the power of speech who interact with humans, animals who mingle with humans, and animals as humans.

In the realistic fiction genre, animals behave like animals. They are portrayed consistently and objectively. They are not given the power of speech or humanized. Characteristics and behavior of animals are realistically described. Some of the stories are based on true incidents or on the author's experiences with pets or wildlife. Incidents can be humorous, mysterious, adventurous, or sad. Conflicts are often animal against animal, animal against humans, or animals against society. The conflict can occur when an animal is mistreated, injured, or forced to change environments. Themes of love, responsibility, protection, human interaction, loyalty, and death are stressed in many realistic fiction stories. Outstanding examples of animal stories in this genre are Sheila Burnford's *The Incredible Journey,* Theodore Taylor's *The Trouble with Tuck,*

Sterling North's *Rascal,* and Jim Kjelgaard's *Big Red.*

In the fantasy genre, animals are depicted in a wide range of types. In Kenneth Graham's *The Wind in the Willows,* animals behave as people with the power of speech. They dress and act like people by eating at hotels, going on picnics, having automobile accidents, getting involved with the law, and taking country walks. Margaret Blount, in *Animal Land: The Creatures of Children's Fiction,* states that when adults read *The Wind in the Willows* they realize that "the animals are Olympians, middle-aged men living in what must be early retirement, earning nothing, paying for nothing, doing nothing as becomes animals, yet very much involved with the real world" (p. 148). Of course, when children read the book they see the charming and lovable characters of Badger, Mole, Rat, and Toad and enjoy their humorous and fascinating adventures and are forever enriched by the experience. In Beatrix Potter's stories about Peter Rabbit, animals interact with humans, talk like people, but still retain animal qualities and live in the animal world. In folklore and myths, animals have magical powers and gifts of prophecy to grant wishes or to cast out spells. Their appearance is often strange, grotesque, or unusual. They can be harmful, frightening, dangerous, beautiful, or helpful creatures. Paul Goble's *The Gift of the Sacred Dog* describes what happened when the boy prayed to the Great Spirit for help: "The clouds parted. Someone came riding toward the boy on the back of a beautiful animal. There was thunder in its nostrils and lightning in its legs; its eyes shone like stars and hair on its neck and tail trailed like clouds" (unpaged). In "The Three Billy Goats Gruff," talking animals with exaggerated human characteristics provide humor and lessons for the reader. Toy versions of animals that talk and communicate with humans provide magical adventures for the young. In Michael Bond's Paddington Bear stories, Paddington joins the human world when he lives with the Brown family and gets into one amusing adventure after the other.

Criteria for evaluating animal stories depends on whether or not the story is realistic fiction or fantasy. In realistic fiction, animals should be portrayed with objective interest. Authentic characteristics and traits as well as how animals really live, their relationships to humans and other animals, or their relationship to the environment should be shown. They should not be humanized or sentimentalized; the problem of anthropomorphism should be avoided.

Stories should be based on research and facts. Marguerite Henry's *King of the Wind* is an outstanding example of realistic fiction following these criteria in the animal genre. In fantasy fiction, animals should be depicted as believable; it is where the impossible becomes possible. Stories should permit the reader to enter the world of "what-ifs." Stories should contain characters that are credible and consistent, themes that are universal and affirm human values, settings that provide detailed information and are an integral part of the story, and plots that are original and exciting.

Animal stories for children and young people foster growth and understanding as they attribute human traits to animals. Children see themselves in the actions of animals whose needs and feelings are similar to theirs. These recognizable traits bring humor and delight as children listen to the stories or read the stories themselves. Stories provide a close observation of animal life, encourage a sense of kinship, promote loyalty, teach sex casually, instill responsibility, and encourage a desire to nurture and protect. According to Bernice Cullinan in *Literature and the Child*, children's affinity with animals and pets and their care helps them to "recognize another's needs—the first step toward compassion" (p. 440). Animal stories foster this compassion when animals and humans help each other out of dangerous predicaments, build bonds and bridges, and protect and love each other.

ELEMENT OF LITERATURE: FOCUS ON POINT OF VIEW

Point of view is the literary term used to describe the way the author presents the actions of the story. It can also describe the author's personal attitude toward the subject. It is largely determined by the person who tells the story. Sometimes it is the "I" of the story. In Scott O'Dell's *Island of the Blue Dolphins,* the story is told from the point of view of Karana: "I will tell you about my island." In Herman Melville's *Moby Dick,* the story is told from the point of view of Ishmael, the only survivor of the crew. Point of view is the vantage point or perspective from which a story is told. It is the technical aspect of fiction. Rebecca Lukens, in *A Critical Handbook of Children's Literature,* defines point of view as seeing "events through the eyes and mind of one character" (p. 128). To the reader, the point of view depends upon who sees and tells the action. The point of view is an integral part of a story and influences the rest of the story.

The author has a wide range of choices in selecting the point of view from which to tell the story. The first-person "I" may tell the story as he or she experiences, observes, or understands it by sharing thoughts and feelings toward the events. This person is often called the first-person narrator. This type of point of view is limited because the narrator can only tell his or her thoughts or perceptions and cannot include actions that would be unknown or out of his or her realm of experience. The first-person narrative form often used by authors is told in the past tense as a reminiscence, diary, or flashback. This allows the author more freedom to control time and space. An example of this type of animal story is *Where the Red Fern Grows* by Wilson Rawls. The story is told in the first person by Billy, who is now grown. When he sees an old hound dog in a dogfight, he comes to the rescue. This stirs memories. "How wonderful the memories were. Piece by piece the story unfolded." He reminisces about the time he was ten years old and tells the story of his two dogs, Old Dan and Little Ann.

In the third-person point of view, the story is told by someone outside of the story who refers to all of the characters by name or as "he," "she," or "they." An example of a third-person point of view is Paul Goble's *The Gift of the Sacred Dog*. An outside narrator tells the story and refers to the boy, his parents, and the rider. The omniscient or "all-knowing" point of view gives the author the vantage point of writing from the third person while presenting the thoughts and feelings of all the characters. Time and place are not restricted. An excellent example of the omniscient point of view is E. B. White's *Charlotte's Web*. The author shows his reader his realistic world and his imaginative world, comments on the behavior of his characters, and shows the thoughts and feelings of the characters in the past, present, and future. In a limited omniscient point of view, the author tells the story in third person through a central character and concentrates on what the character sees, hears, or thinks. An example of this type of animal story is Lynn Hall's *Danza!* Paulo discovers his love for horses and his heritage when he visits the United States from Puerto Rico. Paulo's thoughts and feelings are portrayed when he goes to live on his grandfather's ranch and cares for Danza, a Paso Fino stallion. The author is not limited to telling the entire story from one point of view but may mix first person with third person or combinations of both.

Sometimes the first-person narrator alternates between different people. A picture storybook that illustrates this principle is Roger Duvoisin's *See What I Am*. The primary colors boast of their importance as they are portrayed as a yellow tiger, a bluejay, a cardinal, a brown horse, and so forth. Each color says "Look at me ... I am yellow ... I am blue." Max the kitten reveals the colors on each page and shows his real colors, a combination of all of the colors.

In animal stories, the point of view may be from an animal. *Socks*, by Beverly Cleary, is told from the point of view of the cat; *Rabbit Hill*, by Robert Lawson, is told from the point of view the rabbits; and *Hurry Home, Candy*, by Meindert De Jong, is told from the point of view of a dog.

One of the objects of fiction is to involve the reader in the story itself. The point of view that the author uses in telling the story often helps to involve the readers. It helps the reader accept the story. Point of view assists the reader in experiencing the joys and sorrows, successes and failures, courage and fears of the protagonist, and the resulting actions or experiences.

RECOMMENDED LISTS

Recommended Titles for Teaching the Animal Genre Unit

Burnford, Sheila. *The Incredible Journey*. Boston: Little, Brown & Company, 1960. RL: Grade 7. IL: Grades 6–12.

The three animals are an unforgettable trio. The old, white English bullterrier, Bodger, has a battered body and is a mixture of fighter and devoted family pet. The young, large red-gold Labrador retriever, Luath, has a powerful build and is a trained hunter and leader. The Siamese cat, Tao, has a long slim body, long monkeylike paws, and is obedient and trained to return to a whistle. The three animals belong to a professor, Jim Hunter, whose home is about 250 miles away. He is invited to give lectures in England for nine months. John Longridge, a colleague and friend, offers to keep the pets until the family returns from England. About a month before the family is to return, John Longridge leaves for a vacation at his mountain cabin. He leaves the trio of pets in the care of a housekeeper, but the animals have other ideas. The Labrador has never stopped pining for his master and is determined to return to his home somewhere to the west. He leads the trio across the Canadian wilderness in the Indian summer days and nights. They always go westward. The old dog often grows weary, and all of them are hungry. The cat helps supply food, catching everything from a partridge to mice. The trio fights a bear and her cub. The old dog and the cat are sheltered for awhile by some friendly Indians. The Lab grows restless and barks for the two to come and follow him. The Lab, having been trained to retrieve without harming, finds it difficult to get enough food. A swift river becomes a formidable foe for the trio when a beaver dam breaks. The two dogs manage to get across the river, but the cat is swept away. The cat is rescued by a little Finnish girl who lives in a cabin. He is nursed back to health, but he is now temporarily deaf. When he regains his hearing in about four days, he sets out to find his companions. The Lab and bullterrier get in a fight with a collie. The fight restores the morale of the old dog. The cat picks up the trail of the dogs and, after encounters with animals and humans, rejoins them. The trio is very contented but hungry for food, affection, and human companionship. A mountain family, the Mackenzies, supply all of the trio's needs and treat their wounds as well. Rested and fed, the three begin the last 50 miles of their journey. John Longridge is dismayed to find the dogs missing when he returns home. Finally he senses that the Lab has taken the other two animals to their home across Canada to be there when the family returns from England. By telephone, Indian guides, and foresters, the trio is traced across the country from sightings along the way. The Hunter family is joined by Longridge at their summer cottage. Happily, they are soon joined by Tao, Bodger, and Luath.

The Incredible Journey is told from an omniscient point of view in the third person. The narrator tells the story from without. The animals retain their animal characteristics; they are not given human thoughts. They are realistic and believable. This is one of the classic animal stories of all times. It lends itself to reading aloud, reading independently, reading in groups, and rereading.

Cleary, Beverly. *Socks.* New York: Dell, 1973. RL: Grade 5. IL: Grades 4–6. PB: Dell.

Socks, a tabby kitten with white paws, is put into a mailbox by his owners when a noisy, fussy family of children try to buy him. Later he is sold for 50 cents to Mr. and Mrs. Bricker. They live in an old house with a nice yard. Socks becomes a member of the family and reacts with affection to his owners but keeps his firm determination about getting his own way. Things begin to change when the Brickers have a baby. The baby gets most of the attention, and Socks is jealous and angry. He gets into a lot of mischief trying to get attention. He is unhappy when he gets put on a diet and an exercise program. He likes the babysitter, who comes with her own survival kit and knows just how to give Socks the attention he craves. Nana, the grandmother, does not like cats, and Socks knows this. He crawls into her suitcase and tries to sleep on her nice clothes; he mangles her wig that was on a Styrofoam head. He wants to let her know that he belongs here and she does not. When Socks bites Mrs. Bricker, he is banished from the house and moved to the garage. When he is injured in a fight, the Brickers give him the attention and care he longs for. He develops an interest in the baby, Charles William, and the two of them become playmates.

The story is told in third person from the point of view of Socks. The cat retains animal characteristics and cannot talk. The reader is told Socks's innermost thoughts and feelings. He thinks that owners must be disciplined; he encourages Mrs. Bricker to follow him to the refrigerator; he is filled with fear, curiosity, and jealousy; he clearly implies, "I have found a friend. This is where I belong." The format and large print make this book more suitable to grades 5 and 6.

Eckert, Allan. *Incident at Hawk's Hill.* Boston: Little, Brown & Company, 1971. RL: Grade 7. IL: Grades 7–9. PB: Bantam.

The MacDonald family lives on a farm in the wilderness of Canada in the 1870s. They have four children between the ages of 6 and 16. Ben, the youngest, is very small for his age and very shy. His love for all animals and his ability to communicate with them is misunderstood even by his father. A crude neighbor becomes interested in Ben's ability to communicate with animals when his vicious dog stops at the point of attacking Ben. The neighbor,

George Burton, spreads rumors about this strange child. Ben is warned about the dangerous badgers but cannot resist watching, learning, and communicating with a large badger he encounters one day. When Ben's father tells him of the danger and says that he hopes the badgers will be caught in Burton's trap, Ben retreats back into his own world. He examines a dead badger that Burton brings to show his family. When Ben is lost in a storm, he finds shelter in the den of a badger. All the pups in the mother badger's third litter have died. The mother badger had been caught in a trap set by Burton, and the pups had starved. Ben begins making the sounds he learned in his other meeting with a badger and succeeds in communicating with the badger. He is "adopted" by the mother badger and is fed, protected, and sheltered by her. A deep affection develops between them, and Ben becomes more Badgerlike as the weeks go by. After a terrible fight with Burton's dog, Ben's physical condition begins to deteriorate. John, his brother, discovers Ben, but Ben and the badger both fight for their freedom. John is finally able to get Ben home, where he receives a rousing welcome. The badger follows Ben, and disaster strikes again when Burton comes to visit.

The point of view in *Incident at Hawk's Hill* changes back and forth from Ben, the MacDonald family, and the badger. It is told in the third person, with limited omniscience. It is a powerful, realistic, brutal, and even savage story. It also contains a moral or religious message. The impact of the story will remain for a long time for those who choose to use it. It is recommended for mature readers or for reading aloud to grade 7 and up.

Henry, Marguerite. *Misty of Chincoteague.* Chicago: Rand McNally, 1947. RL: Grade 6. IL: Grades 5–8.

Paul and Maureen live with their grandparents while their parents are in China. Grandpa runs a pony farm in Chincoteague, Virginia. Paul and Maureen love the ponies but hate to have them sold. They dream of the day when they will own their own pony and be able to keep it. They love to go to Assateague Island with their grandfather to see the wild ponies. One day they get a glimpse of the Phantom, a beautiful wild pony. For several years the Phantom has eluded being captured and sold during the annual Pony Penning Day. Paul and Maureen vow to own her. They get all types of odd jobs to raise money. On Pony Penning Day, Paul is allowed to ride with the roundup men on Assateague to bring ponies to Chincoteague for an auction sale to raise money for the volunteer fire department. Paul is fortunate to spot a pony in the brush and mist; its tail is mingled with copper and silver. He is surprised to learn that it is the Phantom with her tiny colt. Paul follows them to Tom's Point, where the ponies swim across the channel to Chincoteague. The colt has difficulty making the trip, and Paul jumps in the water to give her assistance. He calls the colt Misty. Paul and Maureen are sure that they will be able to buy the Phantom and Misty and are heartbroken to learn that they are already sold. They had dreams of racing the Phantom against Black Comet next year. When the man who bought Phantom and Misty learns that his son has won a sorrel colt in a raffle, he allows Paul and Maureen to buy the Phantom and Misty. Misty accepts humans and adjusts to them. The Phantom slowly follows the colt's lead. She is trained for racing and wins the race against Black Comet. The Phantom is then given her freedom and returns to her isle of wild things.

Misty of Chincoteague is told from the omniscient point of view. The narrator is outside the story and has the freedom to present information about the legend surrounding the mystery of the wild ponies on Assateague, the feelings of both the humans and the horses, the background information on Pony Penning Day, and the daily experiences of the characters. The story is based on real happenings and is well researched and factual. It is an excellent story for reading aloud or reading and studying with the entire class.

Lawson, Robert. *Rabbit Hill.* New York: Viking, 1944. RL: Grade 7. IL: Grades 3–7. PB: Penguin.

Little Georgie and his rabbit family show concern when they learn that new Folks are moving into the Big House. His mother worries about all the possible dangers but hopes that the new tenants will have a good garden since the last Folks were shiftless and not planting Folks. Little Georgie's father, a southern gentleman, adopts an optimistic attitude and conveys this through his eloquent speech. All of the other animals are excited about the new Folks coming and speculate what kind of Folk they will be. Little Georgie is sent on a trip to bring Uncle Analdas for a visit. He is instructed about all the dangers and given a briefing on all the dogs along the route. He composes a song about the new Folks coming and carelessly allows himself to get chased by Old Hound. He has to jump across Deadman's Brook to escape. On their trip back home, Uncle Analdas tells Little Georgie stories about the adventures of Grandad and Granmamy and their ancestors who lived during the bad times of the Revolutionary War. He tells Little Georgie that there is some sense in the tedious song he sings about new Folks coming, because "There's Good Times, Georgie, an' there's Bad Times, but they go. An' there's good Folks an' there's bad Folks, an' they go too—but there's always new Folks comin'" (p. 54). The animals throughout the area take up the song, and it spreads to Mr. Daley at the Corner Store. The new Folks move in and measure up to the high standards of the animals. They put up a sign that says "Please Drive Carefully on Account of Small Animals." The workmen around the house are dismayed when the new Folk refuse to mend a wall or get rid of mole holes in the yard because of their love for the beautiful animals. They are accused of reading books too much. When Georgie gets injured by a car, he is taken care of at the new Folk's house. The animals become concerned about him, especially when they see a large crate near the garden. This turns out to be a statue of St. Francis of Assisi with little animals all around his feet. The animals are in Good Times as they eat, preserve, and pack away provisions for the winter. A posted sign reads, "There is enough for all." The animals agree and patrol the grounds for wandering marauders.

Rabbit Hill is told in third person from the animals' point of view. It is a consistent point of view with believable characters. The animals retain many of their animal characteristics. They have the power of speech but do not communicate through language with the humans.

This delightful story, with its sensitive illustrations, can be enjoyed on many levels. It can be read to children, read by some children from grades 5 up, and read or reread by adults. A more recent book, *Watership Down,* by Richard Adams, continues the tradition of good animal fantasy.

Rawls, Wilson. *Where the Red Fern Grows.* New York: Doubleday, 1973. RL: Grade 8. IL: Grades 6–10. PB: Bantam. Cornerstone.

As a grown man, Billy leaves his office one day and witnesses a fight between several dogs. An old hound is greatly outnumbered until Billy steps in and rescues him. When Billy returns home, he takes down two gleaming cups from the mantel and begins to reminisce about his boyhood days in the Ozarks. The memories are wonderful. He tells the story about his puppy love when he was ten years old. This love was the real kind for a four-footed, wiggly-tailed animal. It was during the Depression and money was scarce. When his father tells him that he can get him a collie, Billy insists that he must have hounds: coon dogs. And he wants two of them. Billy reads an ad for coon puppies in a magazine. They cost $25 apiece. That is a fortune to Billy. He tells his grandfather about his plan. Billy then sets out to earn some money and saves every penny in his bank made from a can. He catches crawfish to sell to the fishermen along with vegetables, and he traps animals for their furs. After one year he has saved $27.46, and in another year he has his $50. He is now 13 years old. He asks his grandfather to order the pups. The pups arrive in a town about 30 miles away. Unable to wait for their delivery, Billy walks across the mountains to get them. It is his first visit to a town, and he is amazed at all the sights he sees. He buys gifts for his family, is teased and called a hillbilly, and has his first bottle of soda pop. When he returns home with his beloved pups, the training and fun begins. His grandpa gives him some advice on how to get a coonskin so the pups can become hunters. Old Dan and Little Ann become his constant companions through trouble and bad times and through the joys of hunting in the great outdoors. Billy's training leads to their winning two cups, a gold one and a silver one. The dogs, protecting Billy, get in a fight with a savage mountain lion and both of them die. They are buried in the mountains where the red fern grows.

Where the Red Fern Grows is an autobiographical story. It is told in first person from Billy's point of view. By telling the story as a reminiscence, time and space are controlled by the narrator, allowing him more freedom in telling the story. This is a moving and exciting adventure story of faith, loyalty, and devotion. It is recommended for reading aloud or for individual study as a class project.

There are many other well-known and popular animal stories suitable for class study. Many students will already be familiar with them. Just in case they have not read them or had them read aloud, consider the following:

Farley, Walter. *The Black Stallion*
Graham, Kenneth. *The Wind in the Willows*
Sewell, Anna. *Black Beauty*
White, E. B. *Charlotte's Web*

Recommended Titles for Individual or Group Study

Diggs, Lucy. *Everyday Friends.* New York: Atheneum, 1986. RL: Grade 5. IL: Grades 5–8. PB: Troll.

Marcy is a daydreamer. It is hard for her to stick to one thing like her older sister stuck to ballet. Marcy feels left out as the new school year begins. Her best friend has a new friend and new interests. Marcy meets Natasha Jones, a new student who is an accomplished horse rider and jumper. Natasha's mother is an artist and accomplished horsewoman who teaches riding. Marcy wants to give up her piano lessons and replace them with horseback riding lessons. Marcy and Natasha have some good times together, but they also have some misunderstandings. Their friendship blooms when they think of the upcoming summer and the horse shows they can attend together.

Hall, Lynn. *Ride a Wild Dream.* Chicago: Follett, 1969. RL: Grade 5. IL: Grades 5–8. PB: Avon.

On Jon's twelfth birthday, his Dad gives him a card that promises him one gilt sow and all the money he earns from her to do with as he likes. Jon is overjoyed because he knows that now he can buy a horse. He finds his dream horse—a copper-bright palomino—and names the horse Sun God. He loves the rides and taking care of Sun God. Jon has difficulty managing Sun God and has some wild rides and narrow escapes. One of his brothers tells him to get rid of the horse before he gets killed, but Jon will not listen. An accident finally brings Jon to make a difficult decision.

Henry, Marguerite. *King of the Wind.* Skokie, IL: Rand McNally, 1948, 1976. RL: Grade 6. IL: Grades 5–7.

A golden stallion from Morocco, Sham, was renamed the Godolphin Arabian. His speed and stamina are still legendary in the world of horse racing. Agba, the horseboy, loved Sham and was delighted to be chosen to accompany Sham to France as a gift for the boy king. But it took many years and many owners for the horse to have a chance to prove himself. His sons Lath, Cade, and Regulus proved his worth, as did his later descendants.

London, Jack. *The Call of the Wild*. New York: Macmillan, 1970 (orig. 1903). RL: Grade 6. IL: Grades 5–10. PB: Viking.

Buck is a loyal pet who is stolen from his home in California to become a rugged working dog during the Alaskan Gold Rush in the Klondike. He retains his spirit through mistreatment and beatings. He is finally purchased by a kind man and remains loyal to him until his death. Buck's desire to roam with the wolf pack is then realized.

Morey, Walt. *Gentle Ben*. New York: E. P. Dutton, 1965. RL: Grade 6. IL: Grades 6–9. PB: Camelot.

A brown bear cub becomes the pet of Mark, a thirteen-year-old boy. Mark names his pet Ben. A very special relationship of trust and love develops between the two. There are some people who are opposed to Mark keeping a bear as a pet. Mark takes on the challenges and keeps his pet as long as he can.

North, Sterling. *Rascal*. New York: E. P. Dutton, 1963. RL: Grade 7. IL: Grades 6–9. PB: Avon.

Sterling has lived alone with his father since his mother's death. The two of them love the outdoors and wildlife. When Sterling finds a baby raccoon, he adopts it and raises it as a pet, a companion, and a friend. The raccoon is named Rascal because he often gets into mischief. Problems arise when a housekeeper is hired at the insistence of Sterling's older sisters. Sterling now must decide what to do with Rascal since the raccoon can no longer have the freedom he once had to roam the house.

Peck, Robert. *A Day No Pigs Would Die*. New York: Alfred A. Knopf, 1972. RL: Grade 7. IL: Grades 7–9. PB: Dell. Cornerstone.

Robert is raised in the Shaker Way on the family's Vermont

farm. His father is a hog butcher by trade. Robert is given a pig by a neighbor whom he helps. Robert is very proud of his pig and very fond of her. He raises her as a pet. He also learns how to run the family farm and learns about animal breeding. Robert does not understand his father's stern ways until he learns that his father is ill and does not have long to live. His father tells Robert that his pet pig must be killed since she cannot produce a litter.

Steinbeck, John. *The Red Pony.* New York: Viking, 1933. RL: Grade 5. IL: Grades 7 up. PB: Bantam.

Jody's breath was short and his throat was dry as he looked at the little red pony colt. Haltingly he asked, "Mine?" He had longed for his own pony and now he had Galiban. He and Billy Buck trained the colt, who seemed to be laughing at Jody every time he kicked him or stomped on Jody's feet. Jody and Galiban grew to love each other and enjoyed their rides into the brush. They came back smelling of sweet sage. The colt became ill and broke away from his stall to run toward the mountains where he died. Jody was heartbroken. Later his father asked Jody if he would work for another horse. He was told to be patient and to wait for Nellie to have a colt. The cost of the colt was high; it cost the mare's life. Jody matured and became a special friend to his grandfather.

Picture Storybooks for Teaching Point of View

Duvoisin, Roger. *See What I Am.* New York: Lothrop, Lee & Shepard, 1974.

In this concept book, each color expresses a different point of view. "I am yellow . . . I am the sun"; "I am blue . . . I am the blue sky and the blue sea"; "I am red . . . I am the sunset." They finally begin to see each other's point of view when they realize that together they can become purple and brown. Black says, "We brag too much about ourselves. None of us can do without the others."

Goble, Paul. *The Girl Who Loved Wild Horses.* New York: Bradbury Press, 1978.

A Native American girl loved horses. She understood horses, took care of them, and spoke softly to them. Once in a bad storm, she grabbed a horse's mane and rode on his back. She was carried away like the wind and was lost. A beautiful stallion told her that he was the leader of wild horses and that she was welcome to live with them. Her people searched and searched for her and finally saw her riding a beautiful horse and leading a colt. She was taken back to her family. She was glad to see them, but she missed the horses. She became ill and requested that she be allowed to go back to the wild horses. Her parents made her a beautiful dress and gave the wild horses fine things to wear when they came for the girl. The girl gave her parents the colt. Every year she returned for a visit and always brought her parents a colt. Then one year she did not return, and she was never seen again. Her people said she surely must have become one of the wild horses.

The story is told in the third person and in past tense from the narrator's point of view. The narrator tells the legend, but the girl's thoughts and feelings are also expressed. She felt sleepy, afraid, glad, and free. By concentrating on the thoughts and feelings of the central character, the writer uses a limited omniscient point of view.

Seuss, Dr. *If I Ran the Zoo*. New York: Random House, 1950.

Gerald McGrew imagines his zoological garden to contain an elephant cat, a beast called Flustard, and a bird known as Bustard. To find these animals he has to travel and search for them in strange and unusual places, like Motta-fa-Potta-fa-Pell.

If I Ran the Zoo is a zany story told in first person from the point of view of Gerald McGrew. The illustrations humorously express the point of view.

Williams, Margery. *The Velveteen Rabbit*. Illustrated by Michael Hague. New York: Holt, Rinehart and Winston, 1983 (orig. 1922).

The Velveteen Rabbit is a stuffed toy given to the boy at Christmas. The boy soon tires of playing with the toy rabbit and leaves it in the nursery. There are many toys in the nursery but the Velveteen Rabbit is lonely. The toy rabbit feels that it is not as important as the mechanical toys. The Skin Horse, a kindly old toy horse, becomes a friend of the toy rabbit. They have long conversations. The Skin Horse tells the Velveteen Rabbit what it means to be real. He explains that real happens when a child loves you. The toy rabbit asks if it hurts to be real. The Skin Horse replies that if you are real and loved you do not mind being hurt. The boy and the toy rabbit later grow very fond of each other. The Velveteen Rabbit becomes a favorite toy. When the little boy becomes ill with scarlet fever, he plays with the toy rabbit. The toy rabbit must be discarded and burned because of the contact with the disease. Because the Velveteen Rabbit is loved so much the nursery fairy turns it into a real rabbit.

The Velveteen Rabbit is told from the point of view of the toy rabbit. It is told in third person. The credibility of the story is enhanced because it is written from the Velveteen Rabbit's point of view. Children believe that the toy rabbit became real because of love.

TEACHING TIPS: THE ANIMAL GENRE AND POINT OF VIEW

Teaching the animal genre can be a delightful experience because of the great interest children and young people have in animals. Build upon this interest by introducing and expanding their knowledge with animals in literature. Help them to sharpen their perceptions, broaden their understanding of animal behavior, identify with the joys and sorrows of owning a pet, and strengthen their value system regarding human and animal relationships.

Plan the unit in advance to allow time to contact resource groups, associations, and federal agencies asking for brochures, pictures, pamphlets, speakers, exhibits, and special emphasis events. Since the focus on critical-thinking and communication skills for this unit is on research skills, a number of resources will be needed. Contact such groups as The Sierra Club, National Wildlife Federation, National Science Foundation, Smithsonian Institution, Animal Welfare Institute, Animal Protection Institute of America, Friends of Animals, American Association of Zoological Parks and Aquariums, Wildlife Management Institute, and American Society for Prevention of Cruelty to Animals (ASPCA). Addresses and additional names are listed under "Associations and Societies" in *The World Almanac and Book of Facts*. Build a resource file of information, pictures, and bibliographies to be used with student activities during this unit. Include a clipping file from current newspapers and magazines. The library media specialist is an excellent resource person to help in obtaining these materials in addition to those in the vertical file, magazines, and print and nonprint collections in the library media center.

Determine the objectives for the unit and select the book or books to be used in the teaching unit. If one title is selected for the entire class to read, be sure to check the reading level and interest level of that book and its appropriateness for the class. Selections for group assignments may be made according to special interests of the students, such as interest in horses, cats, dogs, or wildlife. More mature readers may be interested in books dealing with the love and protection of animals, such as Allan Eckert's *Incident at Hawk's Hill,* or they may be interested in books dealing with the love of hunting dogs and hunting and trapping, such as *Where the Red Fern Grows* by Wilson Rawls. These books will supply good discussion or debate material.

Begin the unit by asking the students to bring to class a stuffed animal, a ceramic or metal figure of an animal, a picture of their pet, a picture of an animal from a magazine or newspaper that would make a good pet, or a picture of an animal that they have drawn. Have a "show-and-tell" session allowing each student a sharing time. Remind students to be courteous listeners but do not become involved in discussing the presentations. Be sure to be a part of the session by personally sharing in this student activity. Tell the students that their new unit of literature study deals with animals.

Review the information from the genre introduction notes with the students. Tell the students that as they read about animals they will be focusing on the point of view of the story. Use the recommended picture storybooks or additional ones to teach the literary concept of point of view. Include the information provided in the focus on the literary element.

According to time and student interest, select several activities to include with this literature unit. Activities of many types are included as suggestions in a later section of this chapter.

FOCUS ON CRITICAL-THINKING AND COMMUNICATION SKILLS: RESEARCH AND ORGANIZATIONAL SKILLS

In this age of high tech, computers, and fax machines, it is more imperative than ever for students to know the *process* of locating, storing, retrieving, and using information in all formats. Using the whole language approach and strategies as they apply to student interest in animals and animal literature to promote research and organizational skills may help students gain success and enjoyment. These activities give students a research framework to use now and in the future.

Research skills included in the suggested activities:

1. Defining a problem or idea for research
2. Using general reference books
3. Locating topics and subtopics using an index
4. Locating specific information
5. Using information from many sources
6. Skimming to find relevant ideas
7. Drawing appropriate conclusions
8. Paraphrasing or summarizing
9. Interpreting maps, graphs, and charts
10. Preparing a bibliography
11. Observing copyright laws

Organizational skills included in the suggested activities:

1. Categorizing ideas
2. Notetaking
3. Outlining
4. Drafting
5. Writing
6. Revising
7. Evaluating

ACTIVITIES

Activities Related to Teaching the Animal Genre

1. Decorate the room with posters and illustrations of animals. Make a bulletin board for "Pets." Ask students to contribute pictures and cards containing information about their pets and to post them on the bulletin board. Make a second bulletin board with the title "Animals in

the News." Encourage students to locate and clip articles from newspapers and magazines to add to the display on the bulletin board.
2. Invite a speaker from an animal rights group to talk to the class.
3. Show a film or videotape to the class, such as *The Yearling, Flipper, Lassie Come Home, Black Beauty,* or *The Black Stallion.*
4. Plan a field trip to a natural history museum, a science center, a zoo, or a game preserve.
5. Plan a debate on the topic "resolved that animal research and experiments are beneficial to man." Allow student participants class time for research. Videotape the debate.
6. Let students produce an animated movie on the life cycle of an insect or animal.
7. Enlist the aid of the art teacher in assisting students with illustrations of animals.
8. Ask the library media specialist to assist students in making a slide/tape program on pets.
9. Let students use the computer program *Crossword Magic,* by Mindscape, to make a crossword puzzle about breeds of horses, or let them use the computer program *Wordsearch,* by Hartley Courseware, to make a wordsearch about breeds of dogs.
10. After students have completed reading the books in the animal unit, work with them on organizational skills. To teach the skill of categorizing, begin by brainstorming topics related to the theme "Animals in Literature." Write down the ideas on the chalkboard. Have a large area available for the ideas. Students probably will suggest names of animals, titles of books, breeds or types of animals, animals in fantasy books or realistic fiction, toy animals, conflicts animals face, owners of animals, geographic location of animal stories, animals as pets, characteristics of animals, wildlife, animal rights, animals that talk, animals that dress and act like humans, devotion and loyalty of animals, death of animals, animal breeding, techniques for training animals, mistreatment of animals, animals that overcome obstacles,

and wild animals as pets. According to the animal book or books that they read, they may have many other ideas or very different ideas. Whatever the ideas, use them as a basis for the lesson. After the brainstorming session ask students to categorize the ideas. This can be done as a group project using the technique of webbing, outlining, or listing. If there are a number of ideas, it may be best to make a list and duplicate it. Give it to students to work on in small groups. For instance, if one group works on the category of animals in fantasy books, they would include the categories of toy animals, animals that talk, animals that dress and act like humans, and names of animals. The same could be done for animals in realistic fiction or animals as pets. If students have not had experience in this type of activity, prepare a sample for them to follow.

11. After the students complete the categorizing activity, ask them to suggest ideas that they think would be good topics for a research project on animals. Evaluate the topics according to relevance, availability of resources, student abilities and background, too broad or too narrow a topic, and suitability for research. Suggestions for topics include: history of breeds of dogs, cats, or horses; training and care of a pet; endangered species in North America or in the world; animals and the environment; venomous animals; plight of America's wildlife; wildlife conservation; ordinances and regulations concerning wildlife as pets; U.S. Government regulations concerning the welfare of animals used in research, sporting events, and entertainment such as the circus; horse racing; animals used in research; animal rights; animals and their behavior; hunting and trapping animals; anatomy of animals; animal classification; domestic animals; extinct animals; fur-bearing animals; animal habitats; food from animals; animals that work (beasts of burden); animals who live in the zoo; animal products; animal intelligence; protective devices of animals; and sacred animals in such countries as India and Egypt. Prepare your list of topics for research. Organize the class in small groups or pairs and let students choose a

topic. Tell the students that before they begin their research, they need to review organizational skills. Review the skills of notetaking, outlining, drafting, and writing by showing them a model of these procedures. Use a nonfiction book like *Are Those Animals Real? How Museums Prepare Wildlife Exhibits*, by Judy Cutchins and Ginny Johnston, to prepare sample notes, outline, draft, and brief written report. Use a primary typewriter or computer with large print to type samples. Make transparencies of the samples and show them to the class as each point is emphasized orally. Make several copies of the notes and have them available for students to consult when they are working on their reports.

Ask the library media specialist to teach or review the research skills with the students. Request that a model using the research skills be prepared, in much the same way as the model for organizational skills. The library media specialist may choose to use an example like "Endangered Species of Birds in the Atlantic Coastal States of America." The problem for research would be to identify the endangered species, their habitat, the causes that relate to the extinction, and what is being done to remedy the problem. By showing examples of locating the needed information in general reference books, maps, charts, trade books, film and filmstrips, and magazine articles, the students gain ideas for their research. The skills of using an index, skimming, paraphrasing, observing copyright laws, and preparing a bibliography may be shown by example also. Schedule the dates for the students to use the library media center for their research projects. Ask the library media specialist to reserve those dates to be available to assist students with their research projects and bibliography. After the research is complete and the students have written their paragraphs or short papers, read, correct, and write comments on the papers. Return them to the students and ask them to revise their reports based on the comments and corrections.

12. Use a computer program like the *PFS* series or *AppleWorks* to build a database on animal classifications.

Activities Related to Teaching Point of View

1. Ask students to explain the point of view the author uses in an animal story that they read. Then ask them to retell the story from the point of view of another character in the story. Or let the students pick out a picture storybook about an animal and use it for a retelling of the point of view.
2. Use the picture storybook *Fish Is Fish*, by Leo Lionni, to demonstrate point of view as suggested by Bernice Cullinan in *Literature and the Child*, Second Edition. In this story, a minnow and a tadpole become friends. The tadpole grows into a frog and goes out to see the world. One day he returns to tell his friend, now a large fish, about the things he has seen. He describes a cow, birds, and people. The fish imagines each of these from his point of view, since he can only see things in terms of what he knows. He sees the cow as a fish-shaped animal, a bird as a large feathered fish, and people like fish who walk upright.
3. Divide the class into five groups. Give all students a copy of the following story. Ask each group to rewrite the story from the point of view of the different characters: Group I, Jinks; Group II, Jo Ann; Group III, Alan; Group IV, the mother; and Group V, the father. Tell them that this is a true story:

    Jinks, a black mixed-breed cat with white paws, disappeared around the middle of December. Jinks was a proud, haughty, but lovable pet. Jo Ann was heartbroken when Jinks did not return in a couple of days. Jinks was her special friend. He loved to climb on her bed and snuggle close. He comforted her when she was ill and rejoiced with her over a special accomplishment. When she was on an extended overseas trip, Jinks would not go inside her room until the day that she was to return. Alan loved to play with Jinks outside, take him to ride in his wagon or on a sled, or run through the fields with him. Sometimes he teased Jinks, but he was also very fond of him. They often romped through the neighbor's fields and played in the little stream. Mother had a special attachment to Jinks also. When she read the newspaper, Jinks would jump up on her lap and crunch the paper. When she used the electric can opener, Jinks came running and begging for his food. Jinks often brought her special gifts of mice he had caught, much to her horror. Jinks was jealous if anyone brought a baby to the house and did not want Mother to hold the baby. Dad also was a fan of Jinks. He marveled at Jinks's intelligence and intuition. Jinks surprised him by standing on his hind legs, clasping the doorknob in his paws, and opening the door. Jinks was eager to ride with Dad in the car except when he had an appointment with the veterinarian. Jinks would hide, run away, and greatly resist Dad's coaxing. It took the whole family to get Jinks in the car and safely in the veterinarian's office. But now Jinks was gone. The days went by and Jinks did not return. Finally on Christmas Eve, there was a banging and mewing at the front door. Jo Ann and Alan ran to the door. There stood a very thin Jinks meowing and purring as he responded to the hugs and cries of joy at his return. On close examination, one of Jinks's hind legs had a hole in it. He had been caught in someone's trap. His return home in time for Christmas brought joy and happiness to the whole family as well as to Jinks. However, the day after Christmas Jinks had to go to the veterinarian, whose treatment helped to heal Jinks's wounds.

Additional Resources

A resource of special significance to the animal genre activities is *Media Production & Computer Activities*, edited by H. Thomas Walker and Paula Montgomery. One of the suggested activities is animation. An excellent description of animation using a videotape recorder is in the article "Yes! Animation Is Possible with Your Videotape Recorder!" by Alfreda Martino and Ron Martin. Animation techniques using a super-8mm camera are provided in the informative article "Animation" by Doris Jackson. Animal topics provide many timely subjects for animation. Building a database is another suggested activity in this book. A thorough, clear, and meaningful description of using a database for instruction is presented by Sylvia Hazzard in "Around the World with a Database." There are numerous possibilities for building databases using facts about animals.

Plan an activity based on personal experiences with animals to share with the students.

For classroom reference work, order reprints of Cobblestone magazine such as "Endangered Species" (no. 186) or "Whaling" (no. 484). Using the address in the appendix, write for a list of available reprints. Back issues are ordered by number.

NONPRINT RESOURCES

Computer Programs

AppleWorks. Apple Computer.
Crossword Magic. Mindscape.
Microsoft Works. Microsoft Corporation.
PFS File. Software Publishing Corporation.
Wordsearch. Hartley Courseware.

Filmstrips

Animals. 1983 (Rev. ed.). Pied Piper Productions. Focus on *The King of the Wind* by Marguerite Henry.
The Red Pony by John Steinbeck. Society for Visual Education. Adaptation from motion picture.
Where the Red Fern Grows by Wilson Rawls. Society for Visual Education. Adaptation from motion picture.

Videotapes

The Black Stallion Returns. MGM.
Flipper. MGM.
Never Cry Wolf by Farley Mowat. Walt Disney Educational Media Company. (16mm film or video)
The Red Pony by John Steinbeck. Films for the Humanities.
The Red Pony by John Steinbeck. Phoenix/BFA and Video. (16mm film or video)
The Yearling. MGM.

References

Abrams, M. H. *A Glossary of Literary Terms.* 3d ed. New York: Holt, Rinehart and Winston, 1971.

Blount, Margaret. *Animal Land: The Creatures of Children's Fiction.* New York, William Morrow, 1974.

Cochrane, Orin, Donna Cochrane, Sharen Scalena, and Ethel Buchanan. *Reading, Writing, and Caring.* New York: Richard C. Owen Publishers, 1984.

Cullinan, Bernice. *Literature and the Child.* 2d ed. New York: Harcourt Brace Jovanovich, 1989.

Cutchins, Judy, and Ginny Johnston. *Are Those Animals Real? How Museums Prepare Wildlife Exhibits.* New York: William Morrow, 1984.

Frost, Robert. "The Pasture." In *The Viking Book of Poetry of the English-Speaking World.* Vol. 2. Edited by Richard Aldington. New York: Viking, 1958.

Lionni, Leo. *Fish Is Fish.* New York: Alfred A. Knopf, 1974.

Lukens, Rebecca. *A Critical Handbook of Children's Literature.* 3d ed. Glenville, IL: Scott, Foresman and Company, 1986.

Norton, Donna. *Through the Eyes of a Child: An Introduction to Children's Literature.* 2d ed. Columbus, OH: Merrill Publishing Company, 1987.

Purves, Alan, and Dianne Monson. *Experiencing Children's Literature.* Glenview, IL: Scott, Foresman and Company, 1984.

Sutherland, Zena, and May Hill Arbuthnot. *Children and Books.* 7th ed. Glenview, IL: Scott, Foresman and Company, 1986.

Van Vliet, Lucille. *Media Skills for Middle Schools: Strategies for Library Media Specialists and Teachers.* Littleton, CO: Libraries Unlimited, 1984.

Walker, H. Thomas, and Paula Montgomery, eds. *Media Production & Computer Activities.* Santa Barbara, CA: ABC-CLIO, 1990.

9

Adventure

"An adventure story is suspenseful. The reader alternates between fear and relief as passengers squirm out of sinking ships, heroines pull themselves up the sides of cliffs, swimmers struggle to the shore after having endured the sea for days. We want to know what happens next, and how it happens."
Karen Hubert
Teaching and Writing Popular Fiction: Horror, Adventure, Mystery and Romance in the American Classroom

INTRODUCTION

The adventure genre encompasses stories with excitement, suspense, and action. Heroes or heroines show great courage, endurance, physical stamina, fortitude, and resourcefulness meeting and overcoming obstacles. At other times they show fear, anxiety, loneliness, anger, and uncertainty. They may become entangled in a conspiracy, visit a remote country in search of a legendary treasure, risk their lives to save a friend, go to sea on a whaling vessel, or become involved in a spy case. Cliffhanging episodes and action are very important to the story.

The heroes and heroines in adventure stories for children and young people are usually likable and believable. Readers can identify with them and care about them. They try to reach a goal or get what is rightfully theirs. Readers become so involved with the protagonists that they are drawn into the plot and action. They participate vicariously in the adventures and plunge forward in anticipation of a satisfying solution.

The villain is usually a worthy opponent who uses clever, devious, and crafty means to try to overpower and undermine the protagonist. The villain can be cruel, desperate, unsure, and frightened. Or in some cases, the villain tries to tempt and lead the protagonist into traps or difficult situations while professing loyalty and friendship.

The conflict between the protagonist and an opponent is not always a conflict between people. Conflicts are often person-against-nature or person-against-society. Survival stories usually involve conflicts that are person-against-nature. Jean George's *Julie of the Wolves* portrays the survival of Julie against the forces of nature in the Arctic tundra. Conflict against society is illustrated in Joan Aiken's *Dido and Pa* when Dido and her friend become involved in a dangerous conspiracy to overthrow the king.

The basic types of adventure stories, according to Karen Hubert in *Teaching and Writing Popular Fiction: Horror, Adventure, Mystery, and Romance in the American Classroom*, are journeys involving kidnapping, returning home, discoveries, transformation, living in a primitive environment where animals reign, exploration, and man against the elements. Additional types of adventures involve survival in hostile lands, in inner cities, and in battle-torn countries.

The best adventure stories are those in which the episodes are realistic and could have happened. They are so convincing that young readers can imagine that the events are happening to them. They overcome obstacles, escape from danger, rescue someone, survive a disaster, explore new territories, find a treasure, and conquer new heights. They delight in the final victory or resolution of the conflict.

The survival story is a very prominent part of adventure stories. Elizabeth George Speare discusses the pattern for writing about survival in her article "The Survival Story" in the March/April 1988 issue of *Horn Book Magazine*. She says that basic questions must be answered regarding how the hero got into the predicament; how basic needs of food, drink, and shelter are provided; what implements, such as a knife, are available; what inner resources the hero develops and uses; how the rescue takes place; and how the lingering regret remains. She writes, "Each story is not merely a tribute to the ability of man or woman to endure and to meet extraordinary demands, but a record of spiritual growth, of the entering of the mind and heart into a new dimension and of a new appreciation of the wonder of life" (p. 172).

Adventure stories have many worthwhile themes. These include acceptance of self, developing self-reliance, identifying with people of different races, and developing good relationships. Other themes include the ability to handle problems and overcome obstacles, the importance of cooperation, the value of making sound moral judgments, and the need for support from other people.

Early adventure stories that became popular with children are Daniel Defoe's *Robinson Crusoe* and Jonathan Swift's *Gulliver's Travels*. These were later followed by Johann Wyss's *The Swiss Family Robinson* and Jules Verne's *Around the World in Eighty Days*. Howard Pyle wrote *The Merry Adventures of Robin Hood*, and Robert Louis Stevenson wrote *Treasure Island* and *Kidnapped*. These adventure stories are classics and are still enjoyed by children today.

Modern-day adventure stories that are especially popular with children and young people are Robert Peck's *Soup on Fire*, Betsy Byars's *Trouble River*, Leon Garfield's *The Confidence Man*, Jean George's *My Side of the Mountain* and *Julie of the Wolves*, Jack London's *Call of the Wild*, Gary Paulsen's *Hatchet*, Scott O'Dell's *Island of the Blue Dolphins*, and Armstrong Sperry's *Call It Courage*.

ELEMENT OF LITERATURE: FOCUS ON STYLE

Style is the highly individual way in which a particular author writes. Stan Malless and Jeff McQuain define style in *The Elements of English* as the "personality" of a piece of writing. It is the way a story is written, in contrast to what the story is about. Style is the way an author uses language, diction, grammatical patterns, and types and lengths of sentences. It is the sum of an author's talent and skill in using language to convey the meaning of the theme, the details of the plot, the sense of time and place in the setting, and the personality of the characters. C. Hugh Holman and William Harman, in *A Handbook to Literature*, define style as the author's arrangement of words to express individuality, idea, and intent. It is an "adaption of one's language to one's ideas" (p. 487).

Good style requires analytic thinking, originality, appropriate detail, and attention to lesser points. It demands accepted rules of grammar, punctuation, and grammatical structure. Good style entails attention to choice of words, transitions, and clarity of expression.

The devices of style add color, flavor, and texture to writing. Imagery appeals to the senses and helps create an emotional reaction. Connotation develops association and implication. Figurative language adds meaning beyond literal definitions by using similes, metaphors, and personification. Puns and wordplay provide humor, contrast, and a change of pace to writing.

The devices of sound can give pleasure for silent reading and for reading aloud, according to Rebecca Lukens in *A Critical Handbook of Children's Literature*. These include onomatopoeia, with words that sound like their meaning; alliteration, with its repetition of initial consonants; and cadence, or rhythm that flows through the writing.

The styles of writers vary; no two writers have styles exactly alike. Attempts to categorize styles as journalistic, scientific, literary, or poetic do not fully capture the essence of an author's style. The style of one author can vary according to a particular work, depending on the subject matter, the purpose for writing, the intended audience, and the writer's attitude toward the subject. Writers use different methods and choices of words to convey statements that are simple, emphatic, pointed, undertoned, elaborate, or eloquent. A writer's style reflects the consideration of how the language used will affect the reader.

The style of writing differs in each of the genres. In realistic fiction, word choices and language parallel contemporary usage, taking into account the age of the protagonist and the intended reader as well as regional and social differences. The characters and actions are believable and realistic as developed through the author's style. In fantasy, picturesque words and descriptions give artistic impressions to the reader. Words are chosen to depict the rich, graceful images, symbols, characterizations, and patterns of the imaginative tales. In historical fiction, language conveys the flavor of the time, portrays characters in authentic settings, reflects the customs and values of the period, and provides credible and satisfying narration. In mystery and adventure stories, language provides suspense, vigorous action, detailed settings, and crisp characterizations. It arouses emotions and a sense of danger and excitement.

The high quality of style in books for children and young people is evident in their popularity not only with children but with adults and critics as well. Robert Louis Stevenson set a standard for masterful prose style and artistic storytelling in 1883. In *Treasure Island,* he created characters with "flesh and blood" and gave them integrity and meaning. Arthea Reed, in *Comics to Classics: A Parent's Guide to Books for Teens and Preteens,* discusses what to look for in books for young adults. She states that the writing style should be tight and simple with lively language and limited descriptions. It should be "good, honest writing by an author who cares about adolescents" (p. 21). Among the many authors whose style has enriched children's literature are C. S. Lewis, E. B. White, Ursula Le Guin, Susan Cooper, Lloyd Alexander, Robin McKinley, Lewis Carroll, Katherine Paterson, Beverly Cleary, Rosemary Sutcliff, Jack London, Scott O'Dell, Madeleine L'Engle, Jean George, Helen Cresswell, Elizabeth George Speare, Jean Fritz, Gary Paulsen, Maurice Sendak, and Chris Van Allsburg.

Style in its richness, complexity, and uniqueness combines the literary aspects of a story into a meaningful whole. The classic book of style for writers is *Elements of Style* by William Strunk, Jr., and E. B. White.

Adventure stories that are written with emotional appeal, suspense, and excitement reveal the attitude of the author toward the story, and this embodies the author's style. We are given a glimpse of the author's intellect and emotions. In his *Areopagitica,* John Milton wrote, "For books are not absolutely dead things, but do contain a potency of life in them to be as active as that soul was whose progeny they are; nay, they do preserve as in a vial the purest efficacy and extraction of that living intellect that bred them" (p. 5). As Milton stated so eloquently, books do contain a part of the inner being of the writer. An involved, admiring, and sympathetic writer creates memorable adventure stories.

The following books are examples of memorable adventure stories that contain exemplary styles.

Ambrus, Victor. *Blackbeard the Pirate.* Oxford, England: Oxford University Press, 1982. RL: Grade 7. IL: Grades 6–9.

This adventure picture storybook provides an excellent example of style. It is a satirical and tongue-in-cheek story with many zany, colorful illustrations in comic-book style. Although the format is that of a picture storybook, the literary devices and allusions are above the understanding and experiences of young children. Blackbeard the Pirate steals an ancient map and sails in search of buried treasure. A young boy, Ned, joins the crew as an apprentice pirate under a government training program. To provide funds for the trip, the pirates decide to run a pleasure cruise. After adventures with Jonah and the whale, Robinson Crusoe, Japanese kamikaze flying fish, Cannibal Island, an attack by desperate unemployed film extras, a dig to find treasure that ends up in Australia, and finding the treasure chest full of dog biscuits on day "80," the crew returns to England. Ned becomes a full-fledged pirate and decides to put his training to work by becoming a solicitor. He soon is called to "the Bar."

The style of the author includes allusions to Captain Hook, Moby Dick, Jonah, the Flying Dutchman, the Ancient Mariner, and the Prince of Wales. Puns abound about the "prince of whales," "weighing the anchor," the octopus who wants "to hold your hand, hand, hand, hand," the sports of "walking the plank" and "shark-baiting," and the "Cannibal Takeaway Restaurant." The author uses personification, similes, metaphors, symbolism, and numerous hyperboles throughout the story. Dialogue is carried through comments in the cartoon illustrations. It is obvious that the author's style is comic satire.

Paulsen, Gary. *Hatchet*. New York: Bradbury Press, 1987. RL: Grade 7. IL: Grades 7–9. PB: Viking. Cornerstone.

Brian Robeson flys in a small company plane to visit his father, who is a mechanical engineer in the oil fields of Canada. His parents are recently divorced and Brian has a very difficult time accepting the divorce. His mother drives Brian to the airport where the company plane picks up drilling equipment. She gives Brian a gift to take on the trip; it is a hatchet with a steel handle, rubber grip, a stout leather case, and a belt loop. She insists that Brian wear it on his belt. Brian sits in the copilot's seat, and the pilot talks with him and shows him how the controls work. The pilot has a heart attack and dies while they are still in the air. Brian tries to remember what the pilot showed him and is able to gain some control of the plane. He tries to radio for help and to find a clearing near a lake to make a crash landing when the plane runs out of gas. He escapes serious injury in the crash when the plane lands in a lake, but he must learn to survive in the remote woods of Canada. He remembers the hatchet attached to his belt and finds it to be of the utmost importance as he prepares a shelter, looks for food, and eventually uses it to help build a fire. When he loses it in the water while searching the plane, he must dive repeatedly to locate it. Brian develops survival techniques through trial and error and persistence. After overcoming many obstacles, he makes a celebration of being alive and of hope in his new knowledge that he can take care of himself. After a tornado rips through the area and raises part of the plane, Brian finds a survival kit with a wealth of food, matches, supplies, and a radio transmitter. He tries the transmitter but is not sure that it works. A pilot picks up the signal and locates Brian. He exclaims that Brian must be the kid that they stopped looking for two months ago. Brian never loses his ability to observe and to react to happenings.

The story is told in the first person. The style of writing parallels the action. In short, crisp statements, Brian concentrates on "the divorce" and "the secret" until he is faced with the death of the pilot. His mother calls him "my little scout" when she gives him the hatchet. Staccato like expressions of "gonna die" build suspense during the crash scene, and expressions of "I'm alive!" and "Keep it simple" follow. Lilting descriptions permeate the narration, such as the faint light hitting the silver of the hatchet and flashing a brilliant light "like fire" and the "incredibly beautiful, almost unreal" scenery. When Brian finally builds a fire, he talks to it as a friend: "Hello, fire!" He keeps reminding himself to "learn from his mistakes." After the tornado he compares his situation to the "flip of some giant coin and he was the loser." When he tries to locate his hatchet from the bottom of the lake, he is "choking, heaving, gasping." The satisfying conclusion is simple, honest, and open-ended.

Ullman, James. *Banner in the Sky.* New York: J. B. Lippincott, 1954. RL: Grade 7. IL: Grades 7–9. PB: Harper.

Rudi Matt loves the mountains. He lives in Kurtal, Switzerland, in the shadow of the Citadel, one of the great mountains of the world. Rudi's father was killed while he was serving as a guide to a group trying to conquer the Citadel. Rudi's mother will not let him become a guide and insists that he learn the hotel business. Even so, Rudi climbs the peaks that have already been conquered any time he can slip away from work, school, or church. One such day, as he is climbing alone, he hears a voice call out from a crevasse. After a great struggle, Rudi rescues Captain Winter, a famous mountaineer from England. To reward him, Captain Winter buys Rudi excellent climbing gear. Old Theo, who had accompanied Rudi's father as a guide, decides to secretly give Rudi climbing lessons. No one in Kurtal will serve as guides to the "evil mountain," so Captain Winter hires a guide from another village. Hearing this, Rudi slips away from his job and joins Captain Winter. Uncle Fritz and several other guides decide to go to the mountains and bring Rudi back. However, Captain Winter persuades them to join the team and help conquer the Citadel. Rudi becomes a great asset to the team because of his small size and agile body. The climb is filled with excitement, danger, and suspense. As the team nears the summit, one of the members suffers an accident. Rudi stays to take care of the wounded man while the team reaches the summit. His father's red climbing shirt is flown from a staff at the summit as a tribute to the great Josef Matt. In this adventure story, Rudi learns a great deal about himself, including the importance of taking responsible action.

The style of *Banner in the Sky* permits the reader to participate vicariously in the adventures of climbing the seemingly unconquerable mountain. The descriptive language sets the scene. "In the heart of the Swiss Alps on the high frontier between earth and sky, stands one of the great mountains of the world." The adventure is set in motion when the reader is told that the people of the valley call the mountain "Rudisberg," or "Rudi's mountain," because long ago there lived a boy called Rudi Matt. Readers want to know why, and they race toward the exciting episodes of mountain climbing. The awesome opponent is always brought before them. The obstacles of his mother's tears, his uncle's anger, and the mountain of dirty dishes to be washed at the hotel are conveyed in short, meaningful sentences. The obstacles of the frozen surface, the steep grades, and the open crevasses are depicted in the stillness and silence of the climb: "No movement, no stirring, no sound." Rudi's heart is filled with peace and joy as he climbs. The author builds suspense and drama through imagery and connotation and conveys the theme through repetition and language patterns.

RECOMMENDED LISTS

Recommended Titles for Teaching the Adventure Genre Unit

George, Jean. *My Side of the Mountain.* New York: E. P. Dutton, 1959. RL: Grade 6. IL: Grades 5–8. PB: Dutton.

    Sam Gribley, age 13, decides to leave home and to take care of himself without the aid of "store-bought" food and clothes. He goes to property that the family owns in the Catskill Mountains and proceeds to learn the skills necessary to survive. He supplements his knowledge with information in books from a library in a nearby town. For his home, he builds a shelter in a large hollowed-out hemlock tree. He makes his own traps for obtaining meat, picks berries, digs roots, and fishes with handmade hooks. He is aided by two events. In the first event, he obtains a deer that has been killed by a poacher. He tans the hide, makes a suit for himself, and stores the meat for food. In the second event, Sam is befriended by Bando, who helps him to properly store food for the winter months. Sam is finally found by a newspaper reporter who has heard rumors of a wild boy living in the woods. Sam fights for his right to stay in the area that he loves. His family helps by establishing a new home there.

    Jean George's style is reflected through her detailed descriptions of Sam's activities of making a fire; locating, preparing, and storing food; building a shelter; training a falcon to assist in hunting; making pottery; and sewing clothes for himself. The author's choice of writing style, using diary entries for part of the story, adds realism and personal interest to Sam's accounts of many of his survival techniques.

    Also recommended for the class units are the following adventure books:

―――. *Julie of the Wolves.* New York: Harper & Row, 1972. RL: Grade 7. IL: Grades 5–9. PB: Harper. Cornerstone.

———. *The Talking Earth*. New York: Harper & Row, 1983. RL: Grade 7. IL: Grades 5–9. PB: Harper.

Paulsen, Gary. *Hatchet*. New York: Bradbury Press, 1987. RL: Grade 7. IL: Grades 7–9. PB: Viking. Cornerstone.

This book is highly recommended for reading aloud or for individual reading by all members of a class. It is a very good example of both the adventure genre and the literary element of style. See the annotation provided under Element of Literature: Focus on Style.

Speare, Elizabeth George. *The Sign of the Beaver*. Boston: Houghton Mifflin, 1983. RL: Grade 7. IL: Grades 7–9. PB: Dell. Cornerstone.

Matt, 13 years old, is left alone in the family's wilderness cabin when his father returns to Massachusetts to bring the rest of the family to their new home. The father plans to return in a couple of months, but it turns out to be six months. The setting is the Maine wilderness in the 1700s. Matt must find food and protect himself from Indians who live nearby. To complicate matters, his father's rifle is stolen. Attean, a young Penobscot Indian, and his grandfather visit Matt hoping that Matt can teach Attean to read. The boys get to know each other and become friends. Attean shows Matt how to survive by teaching him how to hunt, fish, and trap. This well-researched and engaging tale is both an excellent historical fiction and adventure story. It is included with the adventure stories because of its theme of survival, but it can be used in either genre.

Elizabeth George Speare uses her considerable writing talent to create characters that are credible, interesting, and memorable. Her vivid characterization allows the reader to experience the emotions of both boys. Her style of involving the reader is evident in the opening passages when she arouses curiosity; increases when she presents the problems that Matt has to overcome; builds when she introduces the young Indian; rises as they face obstacles together as friends; and reaches great heights as the two boys exchange gifts at the end of the story. Her attention to detail is shown through clear, concise descriptions of frontier and Indian life, different lifestyles, and the customs of Indian hunting, fishing, and trapping.

This is an excellent book to read aloud, to use in small groups, or to use for individual reading for the entire class. It is an outstanding example of survival literature and a commendable example of style.

Sperry, Armstrong. *Call It Courage*. Macmillan, 1940. RL: Grade 6. IL: Grades 5–7. PB: Macmillan.

Mafatu, the son of a Polynesian chief, grows up with a dread of the sea because his mother died in the ocean when he was three. He is rejected by his tribe because of his cowardice. Determined to conquer his fear, he sets out to sea in a canoe with his pet albatross and his dog. He survives a vicious storm and lands on a sacred island. He learns to care for himself by providing his food, shelter, and clothing. He earns the title of "Stout Heart." He returns to his island home to become an accepted and honored member.

The style of the book is in keeping with the adventures of Mafatu. With its simple sentence structure, imagery, and rhythm, the story ebbs, flows, and builds to the climax. The language is appropriate and well chosen to tell this credible and inspirational story.

This concise story is recommended as a read-aloud or as a book for individual reading by the entire class. It has been made into a movie and is available as a talking book.

Stevenson, Robert Louis. *Treasure Island*. New York: Charles Scribner's Sons, 1981 (orig. 1883). Illustrated by N. C. Wyeth. RL: Grade 6. IL: Grade 5 and up. PB: Viking.

Jim Hawkins obtains a treasure map from a sea pirate who dies in his mother's boardinghouse. He sails as a cabin boy on the *Hispaniola* in search of treasure. Villainous pirates, headed by Long John Silver, plot to get the map. A battle of violence, wit, and strategy ensues that involves Jim, the captain, doctor, squire, Long John Silver, and the pirates. Salty tales of seafaring men, buried treasure, rum, and songs combine with the action, mystery, and treachery to make this one of the classic adventure stories of all time.

The author's style is masterful in characterization and description. Long John Silver is a fascinating and memorable villain. Stevenson's intention to absorb and delight readers is expressed in vivid, clear language. Colorful patterns of language depict action and hints of events to come. Thrills and chills abound as the foes are overcome, treasure is found, and the sails are set for home.

This book is highly recommended to use with an entire class if they have not read the story or had it read to them. It is one book that is "too good to miss."

Taylor, Theodore. *The Cay*. Garden City, NY: 1969. RL: Grade 6. IL: Grades 4–8. PB: Avon.

Phillip and Timothy are cast up on a barren Caribbean island after the Germans torpedo the freighter *S.S. Hato*. Phillip and his mother had been traveling back to the United States during World War II. Timothy, a kind old black man, was a member of the freighter crew. Phillip and Timothy are the only two survivors. They share a raft, and Timothy takes care of Phillip, who has a severe head injury. When Phillip becomes blind, Timothy gets them settled on a small island. They struggle for survival, depending upon rainwater for drinking and catching fish for food. Timothy has a serious attack of malaria, and Philip nurses him back to health. Timothy helps Phillip adjust to his blindness and to survive a severe storm.

This is a good, fast-paced adventure story to share as a read-aloud for the whole class or as a book for individuals to read. Survival techniques, overcoming prejudice, and developing self-reliance can be discussed along with the author's style.

Ullman, James. *Banner in the Sky*. New York: J. B. Lippincott, 1954. RL: Grade 7. IL: Grades 7–9. PB: Harper.

This book is highly recommended for individual reading by all members of the class or by small groups who choose an adventure story about mountain climbing. An excellent example of the adventure genre, it provides opportunities for large group discussion. It was made into a movie, *Third Man on the Mountain*, by Disney Studios. See the annotation under Element of Literature: Focus on Style.

Recommended Titles for Individual or Group Study

Bawden, Nina. *Rebel on a Rock*. Philadelphia: J. B. Lippincott, 1978. RL: Grade 7. IL: Grades 7–9.

Jo is vacationing with her family in a small country ruled by a dictator. The family becomes involved in a plot to overthrow the dictator when they try to help the son of a former leader. Jo becomes concerned about her stepfather's actions and distrusts him. Her relationship within the family changes as they face a dangerous situation together.

Byars, Betsy. *Trouble River.* New York: Camelot, 1975. RL: Grade 6. IL: Grades 5–7. PB: Penguin.

In this historical adventure story, young Dewey and his feisty grandmother are forced to flee from a band of savage Indians. They fight for their lives on a homemade raft as they travel down the river, where they encounter rapids and many hardships. The style is typical of Betsy Byars who states that she writes without pattern but with hope and determination. Her characters are endowed with humor, understanding, and compassion. It is an exciting adventure story for grades 5–7.

Graham, Robin, and L. T. Gill. *Dove.* New York: Harper & Row, 1972. RL: Grade 7. IL: Grades 8–10. PB: Bantam.

Robin Graham sails alone around the world in his small 24-foot sloop. He begins his voyage at the age of 16. His adventures are exciting and sometimes dangerous. He visits many exotic places, falls in love, and almost gives up his quest. Finally he finishes the voyage, shares his adventures with *National Geographic* magazine, and writes a book. Although this is a true adventure story and not fiction like the other recommended and suggested books, it is included because of its merit and interesting journalistic style. It is especially recommended for more mature readers in grades 8 and 9.

O'Dell, Scott. *Island of the Blue Dolphins.* Boston: Houghton Mifflin, 1960. RL: Grade 6. IL: Grades 6–9. PB: Dell. Cornerstone.

Karana and her family, Ghalas-at Indians, live on an island off the coast of California. After a fierce battle when most of the men are killed, the remaining natives decide to go to another island. A ship comes for them, but Karana refuses to leave when she discovers that her little six-year-old brother is missing. Karana and her brother, Ramo, are left alone on the island. Ramo is killed the next day by a pack of wild dogs. Karana lives alone on the island for 18 years. She learns to survive by making weapons, hunting, and using her resourcefulness.

Verne, Jules. *Around the World in Eighty Days.* New York: Bantam, 1987 (orig. 1872). RL: Grade 7. IL: Grades 6–10.

Phileas Fogg, a most habitual and precise English gentleman, wagers with his gentlemen friends that he can travel around the world in 80 days. He bases this on the account in the *Daily Telegraph* that estimates one could travel by rail and steamboat from London to Suez, Bombay, Calcutta, Hong Kong, Yokohama, San Francisco, New York, and back to London in a total of 80 days. His friends say that this schedule does not take into account accidents and bad weather. Fogg declares that "the unforeseen does not exist." He proceeds to undertake the trip accompanied by his French valet, Passespartout. The two adventurers have to overcome many obstacles to keep on schedule and try to win the wager. The writing style is precise, clear, and conveys the author's belief in the characters and their exploits. It is original and contains imagery and descriptive phrases. It is a delightful book for sharing and reading aloud. The film is also excellent for sharing.

Wojchiechowska, Maia. *Shadow of a Bull.* New York: Atheneum, 1964. RL: Grade 5. IL: Grades 5–8. PB: Macmillan.

Manolo, whose father was killed in a bullring at an early age, does not want to become a bullfighter. He lacks the courage and determination to follow in his father's footsteps. He also hates the idea of killing a bull. Reluctantly, he begins his training so that he can fight his first bull around his twelfth birthday. He has his day in the bullring and finds that he has conquered his fear and has earned the right to make his own choices. The language and terminology of bullfighting and the sensitive portrayal of Manolo show the skill of the author in creating this adventurous story. It is recommended for individual selection.

Wyss, Johann. *The Swiss Family Robinson.* New York: Grosset & Dunlap, 1949 (orig. 1812). RL: Grade 6. IL: Grades 5–9. PB: Viking.

The Robinson family is shipwrecked on a deserted island. They are able to salvage some items from the sinking ship to help in building a shelter and, eventually, a marvelous tree house. They use their energy and initiative in providing food and clothing and are able to provide a comfortable lifestyle. Their ability to adapt to the natural environment and to overcome obstacles and predators makes this a classic survival story. It has been made into a movie and is part of a theme park in Disneyland. The classic writing style of Johann Wyss became a model for later writers. The book is recommended for individual reading. Note that there are a number of editions and series such as Illustrated Classic Series by Troll and Grosset & Dunlap Junior Classic Series for younger readers. The Bambi Classic Series contains the original version, has 432 pages, and is recommended for grades 9–12. Choose carefully for grade and reading level if ordering paperback editions.

Picture Storybooks for Teaching Style

Ambrus, Victor. *Blackbeard the Pirate.* Oxford, England: Oxford University Press, 1982. RL: Grade 7. IL: Grades 6–9.

This picture storybook has already been discussed as a good example of adventure stories and style.

Calhoun, Mary. *Hot Air Henry.* Illustrated by Erick Ingraham. New York: William Morrow, 1981.

Henry, a sassy Siamese cat, has an adventure in a hot-air balloon. Henry wants to fly, but "The Man" says he is not flying with that cat. It is time for The Man to solo after completing his pilot's lessons. The Man jumps out of the balloon to get his camera, and Henry leaps into the basket. Henry accidentally snags the cord that fires the burner and rises up and up. The people shout and wave, but Henry, the flying cat, keeps climbing. After his wonderful flight, Henry searches for a way to descend. He claws at a cord and as air spills from the balloon, he starts his descent. His adventures have just begun. He nearly goes into rushing water, bounces over the snow, chases after attacking birds, goes in the wrong direction, fears that an eagle will peck a hole in the balloon, meets a squadron of geese, locates the truck that tracks the balloon's flight, has to avert power lines, and uses the back of a goose to reach the cord to fire the burner for his landing. Henry is elated; he has met the challenge of the sky.

The style of *Hot Air Henry* is exciting and suspenseful. The lilting text is very suitable for the theme of the adventures of daredevil Henry. The story is enhanced by descriptive words and phrases and figurative language as in the examples given below:

"Henry grumbled and sang, 'Yow-me, Ow-me, Ow-meow-meow.'"

"His tail switched, people crunch on crusty March snow, the basket bounded, a big bird circled the fat contraption, a fearsome feline, to sizzle on the wires, and the burner boomed."

The sentence structure and patterns are straightforward and clear. The accompanying illustrations are a visual delight and communicate the style and intent of the author.

Wildsmith, Brian. *Daisy.* New York: Pantheon, 1984.

Daisy the cow was not happy grazing in her fields; she wanted some adventure in her life. She often watched television through the farmer's window and wanted to see the world. The farmer watched television and saw a tractor advertised that he would love to have. One day the farmer was so tired that he left the gate open. Daisy saw her chance and dashed through the countryside to a nearby village built on a hill. She walked from the high mountainside onto the rooftops and got close to the edge. She became frightened—very frightened. Farmer Brown came and asked the fire brigade to rescue Daisy. A television crew filmed Daisy and, a few days later, offered to buy her and make her a movie star. The farmer rented her instead and made enough money to buy a tractor. In Hollywood, Daisy acted in many movies, became the cow of the year, appeared in commercials, and ate exotic food. But Daisy became homesick. She played in one last movie, *Daisy Come Home,* flew over her pasture, and jumped out with a parachute to land in her own field. She and the farmer often watched television in the evening. Daisy often thought of her adventures, but she was happy just to be home where she belonged.

The style in *Daisy* is expressed in short, concise, straightforward language. The unique split-page illustrations add to the adventure and surprise of the text. Allusions are used to express satire, as in "she was on the cover of all the best magazines." The illustration shows a poster with the words, "Daisy, Cow of the Year." Her last movie is called *Daisy Come Home* (alluding to the famous Lassie story). The lavish lifestyle of the rich and famous is depicted in the great banquet hall. The simple message or theme of finding happiness at home, where one belongs, is stated in both text and illustration.

Additional picture storybooks that can be used as examples of adventure stories to illustrate the literary element of style are:

Provensen, Alice, and Martin Provensen. *The Glorious Flight Across the Channel with Louis Bleriot, July 25, 1909.* New York: Viking, 1983.

Stevenson, James. *Could Be Worse.* New York: Green Willow, 1977.

TEACHING TIPS: THE ADVENTURE GENRE AND STYLE

Adventure stories, with their exciting themes and daring exploits, can provide pleasure to both students and teachers as they share the many experiences of this genre.

Begin the unit by giving each student a blank 3" x 5" note card. Ask the students to write their names in the upper right-hand corner followed by the date. Next, ask them to write the word "BEFORE" in the upper left-hand corner. Then ask the students to think carefully about their definition of the word "ADVENTURE" and to write their definition on the same side of the card as their name. Collect the cards and let the students see them being stored in a file box. Tell them that the new literature unit is the adventure genre and at the conclusion of the unit they will be given their card to review their definition. They will be given an opportunity to revise their definition and to write it on the back of their card.

Obtain travel posters of exciting landscapes, an island paradise, cruise ships, airplanes, pictures of mountain climbing, skydiving, sailing, exploring caves, and other adventures through travel agencies or the travel bureaus and embassies of various countries. Ask the library media specialist, the social studies teacher, the physical education teacher, and the art teacher for their help. Write for information about survival training schools or camps such as the Outward Bound Program. Locate people who have traveled to interesting or exotic places or have firsthand information on adventures such as taking an African safari, diving for treasure, digging for artifacts, climbing the pyramids, skydiving, hiking across the country, driving in a car or motorcycle race, and hunting big game. Use the PTA, community resource file, the public library, files of the local newspapers, the historical society, newsletters, and special announcements to assist in finding these people.

Decorate the classroom with the posters and pictures of adventures. Refer to these when introducing the adventure genre. Use the notes provided and add illustrations and anecdotes from personal experiences. Be sure to let students tell about some of their travels and adventures or the adventures of friends or family members.

Plan objectives for the unit and develop a schedule. Include objectives for teaching the literary element of style and the critical-thinking and communication skills involved in vocabulary development. Also include the scheduling of resource people as mentioned. Invite them to show slides, movies, or videotapes as well as artifacts. Plan a field trip or an outdoor activity. Suggestions for activities to be used in conjunction with this unit follow. With the assistance of the library media specialist, schedule the use of media resources throughout the unit, such as videotapes, filmstrips, computer programs, audiotapes, magazines, and books.

Select the adventure book or books for class study from the recommended titles. Use the recommendations concerning books to be used as read-alouds or for the entire class to read. Obtain copies for classroom use depending upon the above criteria. Ask the library media specialist to reserve books, give a booktalk, prepare a bibliography, or give reading guidance to students if students are to make their own choice of adventure stories.

Introduce the literary element of style by using picture storybooks. Several good examples have been given. Use the notes on style and suggested activities that follow. Plan to incorporate vocabulary development skills throughout the unit in conjunction with the emphasis on style. Teach or review the use of figurative language and satire.

Plan an exciting finale to the unit that will leave a lasting impression of the adventure genre.

FOCUS ON CRITICAL-THINKING AND COMMUNICATION SKILLS: VOCABULARY DEVELOPMENT

As students read adventure stories, they often encounter words, phrases, and specialized terms out of the realm of their experience. The emphasis on vocabulary development focuses on the need for students to develop strategies for predicting and confirming pronunciation, meaning, and spelling of words associated with the unit they are studying.

Guidelines for developing these strategies are provided in each category. The student should practice the following techniques:

I. Pronunciation:
   A. Listen attentively to pronunciation of words and names by teachers, by peers, and by the narrator in films, videotapes, sound filmstrips, audiocassette tapes, and television programs.
   B. Think about the word or phrase and relate it to other known patterns of pronunciation.
   C. Learn to use the pronunciation key, syllable breaks, and phonetic respellings provided in a standard dictionary.
   D. Practice pronouncing words and phrases aloud.
   E. Confirm correct pronunciation with the teacher, peers, or the library media specialist.

II. Meaning:
   A. Use context clues to determine or predict the meaning of the word or phrase.
   B. Think about the structure and form of the word and look at its parts. Sometimes the meaning of one or more of its parts can unlock the meaning of the word.

C. Use a standard dictionary to locate the meaning. Read the explanatory notes to understand the information in each entry. Know the order of the definitions. Compare definitions in two dictionaries if the meaning provided in the first dictionary is not clear or understandable.
D. Discriminate meanings from closely related synonyms.
E. Confirm the meaning of words and phrases with the teacher, especially if they are important to the story or activity.

III. Spelling:
A. Develop respect for standard spelling.
B. Focus on the spelling process. Use known facts to predict, confirm, and relate new information to old.
C. Use writing models as guides to spelling.
D. Use a standard dictionary to predict and confirm correct spelling.
E. Use the spelling checker of a word processing computer program, if available.

Activities using many of these guidelines are incorporated into the activities related to the teaching of style in adventure stories.

ACTIVITIES

Activities Related to Teaching the Adventure Genre

These suggested activities involve planning and scheduling in advance. Take time to include some of them so that the students can have a real adventure while reading and studying about adventures.

1. Use the posters and pictures on display in the room to lead a discussion about exciting travels and adventures. Ask students to suggest adventures appropriate to the picture. For example, a picture of elephants and big game suggests hunting, a safari, or capturing wild animals via photography; a picture of a snow-covered mountain suggests mountain climbing, skiing, or

Olympic events; a picture of a balmy island paradise suggests sailing, deep-sea diving, snorkeling, or digging for treasure.

2. Carefully select one of the classic films or videotapes of an adventure story to show to the entire class, such as *The Swiss Family Robinson, Around the World in Eighty Days,* or *Treasure Island.* The selection will depend upon the choice of books being used in the teaching unit and the level of students in the class. Viewing one of these films can be an alternative to reading or can be used for comparison to the book after reading.

3. Use sound filmstrips or enhanced videos (transferred from filmstrips and electronically enhanced to suggest animation) to supplement discussion after reading an adventure story. Available titles include *Call It Courage, Hatchet, The Sign of the Beaver,* and *Julie of the Wolves.* These filmstrips also lend themselves to use by small groups or individual students.

4. Early in the unit, invite a guest speaker to share an adventure with the class. Encourage the inclusion of slides, videotapes, pictures, and artifacts. See the teaching tips for suggestions.

5. Plan an activity with the physical education class or in conjunction with an outdoor education program that includes group physical training and requires cooperation and support from other team members,.such as climbing walls or walking across a stream on a log. Discuss the need for support and cooperation as it relates to episodes in adventure stories.

6. Take a field trip to a park and conduct an "orienting" session using maps and a compass. This can be combined with a social studies class and led by a teacher familiar with the concept.

7. Select the survival theme and divide students into small groups to read one of the adventure/survival stories. For preparation, read "The Survival Story" by Elizabeth George Speare in *Horn Book Magazine* (March/April 1988, pages 163–172). This is a good explanation of the problems basic to every survival story as well as a detailed account of writing *The Sign of the Beaver.*

8. Take a field trip to a zoo. Tell students to imagine that they are stranded alone on an island, in a forest, in the mountains, or in the desert. Ask them to find animals, reptiles, and birds that they might encounter at each location and make a list of the names. As a homework assignment, ask them to think about survival needs as they look at the names, then divide the names into the categories of (1) Helpful, (2) Harmful, and (3) Both Helpful and Harmful. Remind them to use good spelling techniques and to verify the spelling. Collect the lists and discuss the answers.
9. Invite a naturalist to come to the class to discuss edible plants, roots, and herbs. An alternative would be to visit a state park and ask a ranger, naturalist, or staff member to guide a tour emphasizing edible plants and the problem of finding suitable drinking water. This trip could be combined with a science class and jointly planned with the science teacher.
10. After reading adventure stories, let the students brainstorm qualities that characters possessed to resolve the problem. Write their suggestions on the chalkboard or on a transparency. Invite the students to look for misspelled words and to assist in correcting any mistakes. Use the technique of webbing, or graphic organizers to display the suggestions. Other topics to use with graphic organizers include showing relationships in survival stories, types of adventure stories, and styles of writers.

Adding a visual dimension by using graphics with key words helps students to see and understand relationships. In the September 1990 issue of *School Library Media Activities Monthly* (Volume VII, Number I), there are two articles of special interest on the concept of using graphic organizers. They are both recommended reading. They are Daniel Barron's "Keeping Current: Graphic Organizers and the School Library Media Specialist" and Thomas Pohve's "Beyond Location: Using Graphic Organizers to Initiate Comprehension in the Library Media Program."

Activities Related to Teaching Style

While planning these activities, be sure to include vocabulary and spelling skills.

1. Put a big sign on the chalkboard that reads "STYLE." Ask the students to define the term. Have several dictionaries, including an unabridged dictionary, available. Let them check their answers by using the dictionaries. Allow them to talk about all types of styles, including dress, music, and furnishings. Ask them if they can define the popular term *lifestyle*. Let them discuss the lifestyles of the rich and famous as compared to the lifestyles of the down-and-out. Guide them in narrowing the definition to the field of literature and an author's writing style. Use background notes provided to show how an author's style in writing is an expression of the personality of the author.
2. If students are to be divided into small groups for the purpose of reading an adventure story, use an activity that reflects some of their choices of styles to assist in the grouping procedure. Give each student a copy of the following "I LIKE . . ." statements. Give them time to answer the statements as honestly and seriously as possible. Next, ask them to circulate among themselves

I LIKE . . .

My Favorites	Matching Choices: (Signature)
1. TV program _____	1. _____
2. Sport _____	2. _____
3. Type of music _____	3. _____
4. Color _____	4. _____
5. Car _____	5. _____
6. Snack food _____	6. _____
7. Season of year _____	7. _____
8. Activity _____	8. _____
9. Author _____	9. _____

and locate matching answers from students who share the same "likes." Let them trade papers and sign their names next to their matching answers. When the activity is complete, tell students to count the number of times a student's name is on their paper. Group the students together who have the most matches. Group the remaining students at random by telling them they are also special because they are individualists.

3. Another way of grouping students for activities related to their style is to let them choose their own adventure. They can be grouped in pairs or in groups of three or more according to their choice. Suggested adventure activities include treasure hunting, hot-air ballooning, big game hunting, mountain climbing, rock climbing, hiking, sailing, snorkeling, scuba diving, deep sea diving, fishing, flying, skydiving, hang gliding, motorcycle racing, automobile racing, bicycle racing, skiing, bobsledding, exploring in space, white-water rafting, and archaeological digging.

4. As students read their adventure stories, tell them to use a small notebook to make a list of all of the unfamiliar words they encounter. Tell them to title it "Adventure Dictionary." They are to include words that they do not know how to pronounce or define. They are to use a dictionary to locate and copy the pronunciation key and the definition. At selected intervals, collect and check the notebooks. Take time to privately discuss the students' progress. Make notes of words that appear in several notebooks. Discuss these words, carefully giving them the correct pronunciation. Include them in spelling quizzes. Set aside time to work on dictionary skills if it is deemed necessary.

5. Select a sample section to read to the class from such adventure stories as Gary Paulsen's *Hatchet*, Armstrong Sperry's *Call It Courage*, Elizabeth George Speare's *The Sign of the Beaver*, and Jules Verne's *Around the World in Eighty Days*. Lead a discussion about the writing styles of each author and compare and contrast these styles.

6. Review or teach types of figurative language found in adventure stories. Give examples from picture storybooks such as *Blackbeard the Pirate* by Victor G. Ambrus. Ask

students to look for examples as they read. Encourage students to use computers to make crossword puzzles or word searches using these terms.
7. Ask students to make a list of overworked words in adventure stories, such as exciting, suspenseful, survival, and anxiety, and add these to their "Adventure Dictionary." Tell them to locate and copy synonyms for these words. Let them use their dictionaries when they have an assigned writing project during the unit.
8. Demonstrate the use of a built-in computer spelling checker in such word-processing programs as *Microsoft Works*. Plug in the monitor cable to a large-screen TV monitor to facilitate viewing by the entire class.
9. Make your own list from students' writing and speaking efforts during this unit, including misused words, complex as well as simple words, wordy expressions, and faulty sentence structures. Conduct a "Style Workshop" to help students communicate through sharp, clear, simple, and direct writing. Provide a one-paragraph writing model on one of the themes in adventure stories. Assign a one-paragraph writing project to students at the end of the adventure unit, asking them to write a character sketch on one of the most memorable characters they encountered during the unit. Remind students to plan, organize, write, check spelling, check sentence structure, check content, and rewrite the paragraph using their best style.
10. Return the 3" x 5" cards given to the students at the beginning of the unit when they wrote a definition of adventure. Ask them to read their definition and turn the card over. On the back of the card, tell them to write the word "AFTER" in the upper left-hand corner and to write a revised definition of adventure based on their new knowledge and understanding of the adventure genre. Encourage students to share their "before" and "after" definitions.

Additional Activities

Many good adventure stories written from the 1950s through the 1980s are now out-of-print. However, some of these stories are available in school library media centers and public libraries. Search for these titles to share with your students. They will stimulate lively discussions.

Aiken, Joan. *Go Saddle the Sea.* New York: Doubleday, 1981. (Grades 8–10)

Baudouy, Michel–Aime. *More Than Courage.* New York: Harcourt Brace Jovanovich, 1961. (Grades 8–9)

Bosworth, J. Allan. *White Water, Still Water.* New York: Doubleday, 1966. (Grades 7–9)

Church, Richard. *Five Boys in a Cave.* New York: John Day Company, 1950. (Grades 5–8)

Forman, James. *Call Back Yesterday.* New York: Charles Scribner's Sons, 1980. (Grades 8–10)

Havrevold, Finn. *Undertow.* New York: Atheneum, 1968. (Grades 8–9)

Johnson, Annabel, and Edgar Johnson. *The Grizzly.* New York: Harper & Row, 1964. (Grades 6–8)

Norman, Lilith. *Climb a Lonely Hill.* New York: Henry Z. Walck, 1970. (Grades 6–8)

Adventure tales provide good read-aloud stories. They contain rich examples of heroic characters and intriguing episodes. Reading aloud provides language models for students and can be done in small groups as well as large groups. Remember the benefits of shared reading.

NONPRINT RESOURCES

Audiocassette

Banner in the Sky by James Ullman. Miller-Brody Productions.

Films

Banner in the Sky by James Ullman. Walt Disney Educational Media Company. (16mm film or video)

The Swiss Family Robinson by Johann Wyss. Walt Disney Educational Media Company. Excerpt from the movie *The Swiss Family Robinson*. (16mm film)

Filmstrips

Around the World in Eighty Days by Jules Verne. Eye Gate Media. (intermediate)

Around the World in Eighty Days by Jules Verne. Harvest Educational Labs. (senior high)

Call It Courage by Armstrong Sperry. Miller-Brody Productions.

Island of the Blue Dolphins by Scott O'Dell. Encyclopaedia Britannica Educational Corporation. Includes guide and related paperback.

My Side of the Mountain by Jean George. Films Inc. Edited from Paramount Film. Presents a lesson on taxonomy of plants and animals through an adaption of the novel.

The Swiss Family Robinson by Johann Wyss. Guidance Associates.

Videotapes

Hatchet by Gary Paulsen. Random House Media. (enhanced video)

Island of the Blue Dolphins by Scott O'Dell. Children's Television International.

Julie of the Wolves by Jean George. Random House Media. (enhanced video)

The Sign of the Beaver. Random House Media. (enhanced video)

References

Cochrane, Orin, Donna Cochrane, Sharen Scalena, and Ethel Buchanan. *Reading, Writing, and Caring*. New York: Richard C. Owen Publishers, 1984.

Hearne, Betsy. *Choosing Books for Children: A Commonsense Guide*. Rev. ed. New York: Delacorte Press, 1990.

Holman, C. Hugh, and William Harman. *A Handbook to Literature*. New York: Macmillan, 1986.

Hubert, Karen. *Teaching and Writing Popular Fiction: Horror, Adventure, Mystery and Romance in the American Classroom*. New York: Teachers & Writers, 1976.

Landsberg, Michele. *Reading for the Love of It: Best Books for Young Readers.* Englewood Cliffs, NJ: Prentice-Hall, 1988.

Lukens, Rebecca. *A Critical Handbook of Children's Literature.* 3d ed. Glenview, IL: Scott, Foresman and Company, 1986.

Malless, Stan, and Jeff McQuain. *The Elements of English.* New York: Madison Books, 1988.

Milton, John. *Areopagitica*, edited by George H. Sabine. New York: Appleton-Century-Crofts, 1951.

Reed, Arthea. *Comics to Classics: A Parent's Guide to Books for Teens and Preteens.* Newark, DE: International Reading Association, 1988.

Speare, Elizabeth George. "The Survival Story." *Horn Book Magazine* 64 (March/April 1988): 163–172.

Strunk, William, Jr., and E. B. White. *Elements of Style.* 3d ed. Macmillan, 1979.

Trelease, Jim. *The New Read-Aloud Handbook.* New York: Viking, 1989.

Appendix

The following is a selected list of vendors and distributors reflecting suggested print and nonprint resources to use with teaching units.

VENDORS AND DISTRIBUTORS

ABC-CLIO
130 Cremona Drive
P.O. Box 1911
Santa Barbara, CA 93116-1911

Agency for Instructional Technology
Box A
Bloomington, IN 47402

American School Publishers
A Macmillan/McGraw-Hill Company
Princeton Road
P.O. Box 408
Hightstown, NJ 08520-9377
Source for Random House Media

AppleWorks
Apple Computer, Inc.
20525 Mariani Avenue
Cupertino, CA 95014

Audio Book Contractors, Inc.
P.O. Box 40115
Washington, DC 20007

Books of the Road, Inc.
7175 SW 47th Street, Suite 202 Forest
Miami, FL 33155
Source for The Word for the World

Broderbund Software, Inc.
17 Paul Drive
San Rafael, CA 94903-2101

Caedmon Records
1995 Broadway
New York, NY 10023

Cheshire Book Companions
Department A
P. O. Box 61109
Denver, CO 80206

Children's Television International
8000 Forbes Place, Suite 210
Springfield, VA 22151

Christopher-Gordon Publishers
P.O. Box 809
Needham Heights, MA 02194-0006
Source for Book Wise Literature Curriculum Guides

Cobblestone Publishing, Inc.
Dept. 68, 20 Grove Street
Peterborough, NH 03458
Source for Back Issues of Cobblestone

Critics' Choice Video
800 Morse Avenue
Elk Grove Village, IL 60007
Source for Videotapes: FOX, MGM, Paramount, RCA

Educational Activities
Box 392
Freeport, NY 11520

Encyclopaedia Britannica Educational Corporation
310 S. Michigan Avenue
Chicago, IL 60604

Eye Gate Media
3333 Elston
Chicago, IL 60618

Films for the Humanities
P.O. Box 2053
Princeton, NJ 08540

Films Inc.
5547 N. Ravenswood Ave.
Chicago, IL 0640

Guidance Associates
Communications Park, Box 3000
Mt. Kisco, NY 10549

Harvest Educational Labs
73 Pelham
Newport, RI 02840

Library & Reference Services
Educational Services
Princeton, NJ 08541-0001
Source for BookWhiz

Listening Library, Inc.
1 Park Avenue
Old Greenwich, CT 06870

Live Oak Media
P.O. Box 34
Ancramdale, NY 12503

Mindscape, Inc.
Educational Software
Department D
1345 W. Diversey Parkway
Chicago, IL 60614
Source for Crossword Magic, Rebus Writer, Multiple Choices

National Geographic Society
17th & M Streets, N.W.
Washington, DC 20036

The Oryx Press
Suite 700
4041 North Central
Phoenix, AZ 85012
Source for BookBrain

Pellar Associates
210 Sixth Avenue
Hawthorne, NJ 07507

Pied Piper Productions
P.O. Box 320
Verdugo City, CA 91046

Random House, Inc.
400 Hahn Road
Westminster, MD 21157
Source for Miller-Brody Productions

Society for Visual Education, Inc.
1345 Diversey Parkway
Chicago, IL 60614

Software Publishing Corporation
1901 Landings Drive
Mountain View, CA 94043
Source for PFS: File

Sunburst Communications
39 Washington Avenue
Pleasantville, NY 10670-2898
Source for Magic Slate, Write a Story!

Tom Snyder Productions
90 Sherman Street
Cambridge, MA 02140

Troll Associates
320 Route 17
Mahwah, NJ 07430

Walt Disney Educational Media Company
500 S. Buena Vista Street
Burbank, CA 91521

Weston Woods Studios
389 Newton Turnpike
Weston, CT 06883

Index

Abilities, teaching based on, 4
Ability level, 5
Abstract reasoning, 61
Across Five Aprils, 154, 163–164, 171
Action
    adventure genre and, 209–236
    characters developed through, 128
    mystery genre and, 46, 49
    plot and, 48
    realistic fiction and, 118
Action verbs, 178
Activities, 4, 5
    adventure genre and, 228–234
    animal genre and, 201–207
    characterization and, 146–149
    critical-reading skills and, 63–65
    fantasy genre and, 88–90
    historical fiction genre and, 172–180
    humor genre and, 40–43
    listening skills and, 40
    mystery genre and, 61, 62
    oral communication skills and, 146
    point of view and, 205–206
    realistic fiction and, 144–150
    science fiction genre and, 111–114
    setting and, 175–177
    teaching style and, 231–233
    teaching visual communications and, 89–90
Activity periods, scheduling, 12
Adams, Richard, 183, 193
Administrative support, 11
Adventure genre, 209–236
    activities and, 228–234
    audiocassettes and, 234
    displays and, 226, 228–229
    films/videotapes and, 219, 226, 229, 234–235
    group discussion and, 220
    individual or group study and, 220–223
    introduction to, 209–211
    nonprint resources and, 234–235
    picture storybooks and, 213–214, 223–225
    reading aloud and, 219–220, 222, 234
    realistic fiction and, 210
    recommended lists, 217–225
    setting, 46, 155
    style and, 213, 217–225
    teaching resources, 217–220
    teaching tips and, 225–227
    themes, 97, 211
    vocabulary development and, 226, 227–228
Advertising, 38

Affection, tone of, 27
Against Time! 22, 154
Aiken, Joan, 48, 50–51, 210
Alexander, Lloyd, 67, 81
Alexander, Martha, 107
Alexander and the Terrible, Horrible, No Good, Very Bad Day, 36–37
Alice's Adventures in Wonderland, 67, 73
All I See, 71
Alliteration, 24
All-knowing point of view, 187
Aloneness, science fiction genre and, 105
Alternate Worlds, 93, 94, 95
Ambrus, Victor, 213–214, 223, 232
Amelia-Bedelia, 20, 24, 36
The American Girls Collection, 171
Amis, Kingsley, 95
Analysis/analyzing skills, 5
  mystery genre and, 63–64
  reading for, 110–111
Anastasia Krupnik, 23–24, 31, 155
And Maggie Makes Three, 130, 149
Anderson, Celia, 19–20
Anderson, Douglas, 73
Animal genre, 183–208
  activities and, 201–207
  fantasy and, 193
  films/videotapes and, 207
  introduction to, 183–186
  nonprint resources and, 207
  organizational skills and, 200–201, 202–203
  point of view and, 186–188, 197–199
  realistic fiction and, 189, 191–192
  recommended lists, 188–199
  recommended titles for teaching, 188–195
  research skills and, 199–200
  setting and, 155
  teaching tips and, 199–200
  themes and, 97
  titles for individual or group study, 195–197
  types of, 184

Animals
  behaving as people, 184, 185
  fantasy genre and, 185, 186
  realistic fiction genre and, 184–185, 186
Animation, 73, 206
Anno, Mitsumasa, 71, 90
Anno's Flea Market, 71, 90
Annotated bibliography, science fiction genre and, 114
The Annotated Hobbit, 73–74
Anthropomorphism, 185
Apseloff, Marilyn, 19–20
Arbuthnot, May Hill, 3, 96
Are You There God? It's Me, Margaret, 97
Around the World in Eighty Days, 211, 222, 232
Art teachers, 71, 202
Asimov, Isaac, 93, 94, 109–110
At the Back of the North Wind, 83
Audiocassettes, 38
  adventure genre and, 234
  fantasy genre and, 85–86, 90
  historical fiction and, 180
  humor genre and, 41, 43
  mystery genre and, 62, 65
  realistic fiction and, 145, 150
  science fiction and, 112, 114
Authors
  atmosphere created by, 22
  attitude toward a work, 21
  biographical information about, 62
  illustrations and, 71, 73–74
  learning about, 25
  point of view and, 187
  style and, 211–212, 231
  tone and, 21
Avi, 24, 25–26, 38, 47, 51

Babbitt, Natalie, 13, 73, 75
Backdrop, 155
Bagthorpes Abroad, 24, 28
Banks, Lynne, 81
Banner in the Sky, 215–217, 220
Barnet, Sylvan, 96
Barron, Daniel, 11
Barton, Harriett, 78

Basal readers, 11
Bauer, Caroline Feller, 13, 19, 135–136, 142
Baum, L. Frank, 67
Bawden, Nina, 220–221
The Bear, 183
A Bear Called Paddington, 183
Beauty: A Retelling of the Story of Beauty and the Beast, 77–78
Behn, Harry, 154
Belden, Wilanne, 97
Bellairs, John, 51–52, 56–57
Bennett, Jill, 58
Bibliographies, 8, 65, 114
Big Red, 185
Biracial family, 33
Black family, 30
Blackbeard the Pirate, 213–214, 223, 232
Bloom, Lloyd, 176
Bloom's Taxonomy, 13
Blos, Joan, 136–138, 142, 154, 175
Blount, Margaret, 185
Blubber, 155
Blume, Judy, 20, 32, 97, 119, 155
Bodart, Joni, 13
Bond, Michael, 183, 185
Bonnell, Jo Anne, 80
The Book of Merlin, 83
Book of Nonsense, 20, 40
Book talks, 8
The Borrowers, 24
The Borrowers Afloat, 82
Boston, Lucy, 184
Brainstorming
    adventure genre and, 230
    animal genre and, 202–203
    characterizations and, 149
    oral communication skills and, 144
    science fiction genre and, 112
A Bridge to Terabithia, 155
Brittain, Bill, 52–53
The Bronze Bow, 166
Brooks, Bruce, 125
Building Blocks, 74, 80
Bulletin boards, mystery genre and, 65

Bunting, Eve, 24, 26, 47, 62, 119, 138–139, 148
Burch, Robert, 118, 119
Burnett, Frances Hodgson, 145
Burnford, Sheila, 183, 188–189
Burton, Hester, 153
But Martin!, 107–108, 109
Byars, Betsy, 119, 145, 211, 221

Calhoun, Mary, 223–224
Call It Courage, 211, 219, 229, 232
The Call of the Wild, 196
Card catalog, mystery stories and, 61
Caring tone, 27
Carroll, Lewis, 37, 67, 73
Carter, Candy, 38–39, 110
Cartoons, 89–90
Cassie Binegar, 134
Castle of Llyr, 81
The Cat Ate My Gymsuit, 28–29, 155
Cat in the Hat, 20
Cause-and-effect relationships, 61
The Cay, 220
Censorship, 129
The Change Masters, 5
Characterization
    activities and, 146–149
    historical fiction setting and, 175
    picture storybooks and, 135–140, 142, 150
    realistic fiction and, 119–125, 126, 127, 128, 129, 132, 146–149
    science fiction and, 95
    teaching tips and, 140–143
Characters
    authors' opinions expressed through, 24
    background, 122, 131
    secondary, 122, 124
Charlotte's Web, 67, 97, 183, 187
The Child Garden, 98
Child of the Owl, 135
Chorao, Kay, 59
Christopher, John, 98, 99–100, 105–106, 110, 154
Chronicles of Narnia, 74
Citizen of the Galaxy, 102–104, 113

The City of Gold and Lead, 105
Clapp, Patricia, 160, 165, 172
Clarke, Arthur, 109–110
Class time, for reading, 4
Cleary, Beverly, 20, 23, 27, 28, 40, 119, 188, 190
Cleaver, Bill, 140
Cleaver, Vera, 140
Cober, Alan E., 75
Collier, Christopher, 13
Collier, Sam, 13
Come Sing, Jimmy Jo, 134
Comedians, 21
Comedy sketches, 19
Comic books, 89–90
Comic satire, 213–214
Communication, listening skills and, 38–40
Communication skills, 11–12
  emphasizing, 11–12
  reading critically, 61–62
  vocabulary development, 227–228
  writing skills and, 172
Community resources, 15
Compact Disc–Read Only Memory (CD-ROM), 4
Companionship theme, science fiction genre and, 105
Comprehension, 24, 61, 110
Computer-Assisted Instruction (CAI), 4
Computer-Based Instruction (CBI), 4
Computer programs, 4–5
  animal genre and, 202, 204, 206–207
  characterization and, 148
  figurative language and, 232–233
  historical fiction and, 169, 179–180
  humor genre and, 43
  mystery genre and, 61, 65
  reading levels and, 9–10
  realistic fiction and, 149–151
  resources for, 14
  science fiction and, 113, 114
  spelling checker, 228

Concern, tone of, 30
Conclusions, 62
Condescension, 22
The Confidence Man, 211
Conflict
  adventure stories and, 210
  animal genre and, 184
  good plot and, 48
  mystery genre and, 45
  opposing forces and, 49
Conford, Ellen, 33
Connotation, style and, 212
Constance: A Story of Early Plymouth, 165, 172
Contemporary world, realistic fiction and, 117, 118
Context clues, science fiction genre and, 113
Conventional behavior, poking fun at, 31
Cooper, Susan, 75–76, 90
Cooperative teaching, 11, 12
Could Be Worse, 225
Counsel, June, 107–108, 109
Craven, Margaret, 133
Crazy Vanilla, 132–133
Cresswell, Helen, 24, 28
The Cricket in Times Square, 82
Crime stories, 45
Critical analysis, mystery genre and, 63
Critical-thinking skills, 12
  listening skills and, 38–40
  oral communications, 143–144
  reading critically, 61–62
  reading for detail and analysis, 110–111
  visual communications, 87–88
  vocabulary development, 227–228
Cry of the Crow, 97, 183, 184
Cullinan, Bernice, 13, 186
Curriculum, expansion of, 9–10
Curriculum connection, teaching literature and, 10–11
Curriculum guides, 13
Cutchins, Judy, 204

Dahl, Roald, 20
Daisy, 224–225
Danger, mystery genre and, 45
Danza!, 187
Danziger, Paula, 28–29, 33, 106, 119, 155
The Dark is Rising, 75–76
A Day No Pigs Would Die, 196–197
Daydreaming, 39
de Paola, Tomie, 35
Dear Lovey Hart, I Am Desperate, 33
Dear Mr. Henshaw, 27, 40
The Death of Grass, 98
Death of the Iron Horse, 170
Defoe, Daniel, 211
Deitch, Gene, 73
The Delikon, 106
Demonic forces, mystery genre and, 52
Description
   historical fiction and, 154
   humor and, 24
Descriptive language, 42
Design/illustration, 86
   jacket cover art and, 74
   point of view and, 72
   fantasy genre and, 69–74
   meaning and, 70
   picture storybooks for teaching, 83–85
   teaching tips and, 85–87
Destiny, taking control of one's, 100
Detail
   author's attention to, 218
   reading for, 110–111
Detective stories, 45, 53–54
Developmental stages, 9
Devil's Race, 48, 51
Dialogue
   characters developed through, 128
   humor and, 24, 26
   realistic fiction and, 120
Diary, 146–147, 187
Dicey's Song, 134–135
Dictionaries, 227, 228, 231, 232
Didacticism, 23

Dido and Pa, 210
Diggs, Lucy, 195
Dillon, Diane, 3
Dillon, Leo, 3
Discussion groups
   fantasy genre and, 89
   mystery genre and, 62
   science fiction and, 109
Discussion periods, 4
Displays, 4, 5, 111
   adventure genre and, 226, 228–229
   animal genre and, 201
   fantasy genre and, 88
   historical fiction and, 169–170, 178
   humor genre and, 41–42
   mystery genre and, 65
Do Bananas Chew Gum?, 22, 23, 29–30
Dr. Dolittle in the Moon, 98
Donelson, Kenneth, 22, 95
Door in the Hedge, 89
Dove, 221
Dragon Dance, 99–100
Dragon's Blood, 80–81
Dragonwings, 167–168
Dramatic plot, 49
Drawing conclusions, mystery genre and, 63–64
Dreams, 50–51
Driving Me Crazy: Fun on Wheels Jokes, 37
Du Bois, William Pene, 98
Duvoisin, Roger, 188, 197
Dygard, Thomas, 133

The Eagle of the Ninth, 166
Eccentric characters, 28
Eckert, Allan, 184, 190–191, 200
Eight Days of Lukeby, 154
Electronic age, 4–5
Elements of Illustration and Story, 73
Empathy, tone of, 27, 30
Enchantress from the Stars, 99, 101
Encyclopedia Brown, (series) 58, 63

Engdahl, Sylvia, 99, 101
Entertainment tools, 4
Episodes, arrangement of, 48
Episodic plot, 49
Ernest and Celestine's Picnic, 183
Escher, M. C., 90
Espionage stories, 45
E. T., 109
Evaluation, author's tone and, 24
Everyday Friends, 195
Evil, science fiction genre and, 97. See also Good versus evil
Exaggeration, humor and, 24, 30–31, 35

Fairy tales, 68, 72
Family members, science fiction genre and, 108–109
Famous people, historical fiction and, 158, 159, 162
Fantasy for Children, 68, 69
Fantasy genre, 67–92
  activities related to teaching, 88–89
  animals and, 185, 186, 193
  audiocassettes and, 90
  author's desire and, 68–69
  book design and, 74
  cartoon format, 89–90
  defined, 67–68
  design/illustration, 69–74
  elements of, 88–89
  films and, 90–91
  good over evil and, 68
  humor and, 68
  nonprint resources and, 90–91
  oral tradition, 68
  picture storybooks and, 90
  purpose of, 68
  recommended lists, 74–85
  science fiction versus, 69
  setting in, 155
  style of writing and, 212
  teaching tips and, 85–87
  titles for individual or group study, 81–83
  titles for teaching, 74–81
  universal truths and, 68
  visual communications and, 69–74
Fantasy Literature: A Core Collection and Reference, 86
The Far Side of Evil, 99
Farrar, John, 67
Fat Men from Space, 107
Faulkner, William, 183
Field trips, 8, 12
  adventure genre and, 229
  animal genre and, 202
  fantasy genre and, 90
Figurative language, 227
  adventure stories and, 224
  humor and, 24
  style and, 212
Films/videotapes, 4–5
  adventure genre and, 219, 222, 223, 226, 229, 234–235
  animal genre and, 202, 207
  design/illustration and, 73
  fantasy genre and, 85–86, 89, 90–91
  historical fiction and, 172–173, 178, 179, 180–181
  humor and, 21, 40, 42, 43
  mystery genre and, 60, 65–66
  realistic fiction and, 142, 145, 151
  science fiction and, 109, 111, 114–115
  setting and, 170
A Fine White Dust, 23, 119, 121–123, 131
Fire Ball, 110
First-person narrator, 187–188, 194
Fish is Fish, 205
Fisher, Margery, 141
Fitzgerald, John, 63
Five Weeks in a Balloon, 93
Flashbacks, 48, 51, 64, 187
Flender, Molly, 13
Fodgers, Mary, 34

Foley, June, 34
Folk tales
  animals and, 185
  fantasy and, 68
  humorous, 42
  mystery and, 58
Follow the Drinking Gourd, 168–169
Following the Mystery Man, 48, 53–54
Forbes, Esther, 161–162, 171
Formal operational stages, 9
Fox, Paula, 13, 126–127, 154, 162
Freaky Friday, 34
Free Fall, 85, 86
Freedom, science fiction genre and, 100, 103–104, 105–106
Friendship
  animal genre and, 195
  interracial, 107–108
  science fiction and, 102, 105, 108
Fritz, Jean, 162–163, 171
Frog and Toad Are Friends, 183
From Star Wars to Jedi: The Making of a Saga, 111
From the Mixed-Up Files of Mrs. Basil E. Frankweiler, 149
Frost, Robert, 183
Fry, Edward, 9, 10
Fry's Readability Formula, 9–10
Future theme, science fiction genre and, 105

Gammel, Stephen, 83–84
Garfield, Leon, 57, 211
Garner, Alan, 76
Garraty, Gail, 77
A Gathering of Days, 154, 175
Geisel, Theodor, 20
Generalizations, 61, 63–64
Genre approaches to literature
  adventure, 209–236
  animal, 183–208
  communication skills and, 11–12
  fantasy, 67–92
  gathering resources, 13–15
  historical fiction, 153–181
  humor, 19–44
  literary elements and, 11–12
  mapping the way, 9–10
  mystery, 45–66
  planning and, 7–9
  realistic fiction, 117–152
  science fiction, 93–115
  theme and, 97
Gentle Ben, 184, 196
Gentlehands, 133
George, Jean, 13, 97, 155, 183, 184, 210, 211, 217
George, John, 184
Georgiou, Constantine, 67, 118, 154
Gernsback, Hugo, 93, 94
Gerstein, Mordicai, 35
The Ghost Belonged to Me, 57
Ghost stories, 45, 46, 52–53, 57
Gibson, Flo, 145
The Gift of the Sacred Dog, 185
Gilbert, Christine, 14
Gill, L. T., 221
Gillespie, John, 14
Gilson, Jamie, 22, 24, 29–30
The Girl Who Loved Wild Horses, 197–198
Glass, Andrew, 108–109
The Glorious Flight Across the Channel with Louis Bleriot, July 25, 1909, 225
Goble, Paul, 170, 185, 187, 197–198
Godfrey, Martyn, 102, 113
The Gold Cadillac, 154
Good versus evil, 45
  science fiction and, 98–99, 100–101, 104–106
  fantasy literature and, 68, 75–76, 97
Graham, Kenneth, 185
Graham, Robin, 221
The Grandpa Days, 136–138, 142

Graphics, adventure genre and, 230
The Great Gilly Hopkins, 21, 97
Green, Bernard, 169–170
Greene, Bette, 30, 119
Greenfeld, Howard, 70
Greenlaw, M. Jean, 7
Greenstein, Mina, 71
Group activities, 4, 10
    adventure genre and, 220–223
    animal genre and, 195–197
    fantasy genre and, 81–83
    historical fiction and, 165–168
    humor genre and, 32–34, 42
    mystery genre and, 64–65
    realistic fiction and, 133–135
    science fiction and, 105–107
Group discussions
    adventure genre and, 220
    animal genre and, 200
    characterization and, 142, 147–148
    historical fiction and, 174, 175
    mystery genre and, 63
    realistic fiction and, 145–146
    science fiction and, 100, 112, 113–114
    style and, 232
Guest speakers, See Speakers
Gulliver's Travels, 211
Gunn, James, 93, 94–95
Gunning Fog Readability Index, 9

Hague, Michael, 198
Hahn, Mary Downing, 48, 53–54
Halfback Tough, 133
Hall, Lynn, 187, 195
Hall, Susan, 12
Hamilton, Virginia, 57, 119
Hardy Boys books, 47, 63
Harman, William, 211
Hatchet, 97, 155, 214–215, 218, 232
Hazzard, Sylvia, 206–207
Hearing impaired, 42
Hearne, Betsy, 14, 19, 47, 73
Heart's Blood, 74
Heinlein, Robert, 93, 94, 102–103, 113

Heir of Sea and Fire, 81–82
Henry, Marguerite, 183, 186, 191–192, 195–196
Heroes/heroines
    adventure genre and, 209–236
    realistic fiction and, 120, 146
Himler, Ronald, 138
Hinton, S. E., 119, 147–148
Historical fiction genre, 153–181, 221
    activities and, 172–180
    computer programs and, 179–180
    filmstrips and, 180
    introduction to, 153–154
    nonprint resources and, 180–181
    recommended lists, 160–169
    setting and, 154–160
    style of writing and, 212
    teaching tips and, 169–172
    themes and, 97
    titles for individual or group study, 165–168
    titles for teaching, 160–165
Hitchcock, Alfred, 60
The Hobbit, 67, 73, 97
Hoke, Helen, 60
Holman, C. Hugh, 211
Homecoming, 97
Homesick: My Own Story, 162–163
Hoover, H. M., 106
Horror stories, 45
Hot Air Henry, 223–224
The House of Dies Drear, 57
The House on Maple Street, 154
House with a Clock in Its Walls, 56–57
How To Eat Fried Worms, 32
Howe, James, 53–55
Howliday Inn, 54–55
Hubert, Karen, 209, 210
Huens, Jean-Louis, 80
Human intelligence, superiority of, 102
Humor, 22
    animal stories and, 185
    exaggerated, 28
    fantasy genre and, 68
    folk literature and, 20

science fiction genre and, 108–109
setting and, 155
sources of, 23
therapeutic value, 21
Humor genre, 19–44
activities, 40–43
introduction to, 19–21
listening skills and, 39–40, 41
nonprint resources, 43
recommended lists, 25–37
teaching tips, 37–38
titles for teaching, 25–32
tone and, 23–25, 37–38
Hunt, Irene, 154, 163–164, 171
Hurry Home, Candy, 188
Hyperbole, 24

I Heard the Owl Call My Name, 133
I Spent My Summer Vacation Kidnapped into Space, 102, 113
If I Ran the Zoo, 198
Illustration. *See* Design/illustration
I'm Deborah Sampson: A Soldier in the War of the Revolution, 160–161
Imagery, 42, 212
Incident at Hawk's Hill, 184, 190–191, 200
The Incredible Journey, 183, 184, 188–189
The Indian in the Cupboard, 81
Individual study
adventure genre and, 220–223
animal genre and, 195–197
fantasy genre and, 81–83
historical fiction and, 165–168
humor genre, 32–34
realistic fiction and, 133–135
science fiction and, 105–107
Inference, 61
author's tone and, 24
mystery genre and, 63–64
Ingraham, Erick, 223–224
Interactive Video Disc (IVD), 4
Interdisciplinary organization, 8
Interpreting skills, 5
Interviews, oral communication skills and, 144

The Invisible Man, 93
Irony, 24, 28, 36
Island of the Blue Dolphins, 186, 221–222
It's an Aardvark-Eat-Turtle-World, 33
It's No Crush, I'm in Love, 34
It's Raining Cats and Dogs, 20

Jacket design, 70–71, 74, 75, 76
Jackson, Doris, 206
James and the Giant Peach, 20
Jeffries, Roderic, 22, 154
Johnny Tremain, 161–162, 171
Johnston, Ginny, 204
Johnston, Tony, 176
Jokes, 19, 37. *See also* Humor genre
Journalistic story, 221
Journey to the Center of the Earth, 98
Journeys, adventure genre and, 210
Joy, tone of, 27
Julie of the Wolves, 97, 155, 210, 211, 217, 229
Juster, Norton, 67, 76–77
Justice theme, science fiction genre and, 103–104

Kanter, Rosabeth, 5
Keats, Ezra Jack, 139–140, 142
Keller, Charles, 20, 37
Kellogg, Steven, 58–59
Kerr, M. E., 133–134, 140
Kidd, Ronald, 55–56
Kidnapped, 211
King, Stephen, 46
King of the Wind, 183, 186, 195–196
Kjelgaard, Jim, 185
Knight's Fee, 21–22, 156–158
Knobler, Nathan, 70
Konigsburg, E. L., 119, 127, 149
Kruise, Carol Sue, 13
Kulleseid, Eleanor, 11

Lacy, Lyn Ellen, 70, 85, 87
Landes, Sonia, 13
Landesberg, Michele, 14

252 • Index

Language
  historical fiction and, 158, 160, 163
  tone and, 22
Language arts teachers, 8
The Language of the Night, 95–96, 99
Larrick, Nancy, 46
The Last Battle, 78–79
Lawson, Robert, 188, 192–193
Le Guin, Ursula K., 69, 74, 77, 90, 95–96, 97, 99
Lear, Edward, 20, 40
Learning styles, 4
Legends, 68
L'Engle, Madeleine, 96, 97, 104, 106, 110
Lenski, Lois, 119
Lewis, C. S., 74, 78–79, 98
Library media specialist, 5
  adventure genre and, 226
  animal genre and, 199, 202, 204
  fantasy genre and, 89
  historical fiction and, 169, 171, 178
  planning with, 8
  scheduling with, 12
  science fiction and, 111, 112
Lifestyles, 231
Lima, Carolyn, 109
Lima, John, 109
Limericks, absurd, 20
Lindgren, Astrid, 20, 24, 30–31, 67
Liquid-Crystal Imaging Device (LCID), 4
Listening rates, 39
Listening skills, 38–40
Literary elements, 11–12, 109–110
Literature, tone of, 21–25
Literature-based instruction, 10, 11
Little House in the Big Woods, 167
The Little Prince, 79–80
Lobel, Arnold, 183
Locale, mood and, 22
Locating skills, 5
Lofting, Hugh, 98
London, Jack, 196, 211

Lord of the Rings, 86
Love, gently poking fun at, 26
Love and hate theme, science fiction genre, 104
Lowry, Lois, 23–24, 31, 119, 120, 127–128, 145, 154, 155
Lukens, Rebecca, 14, 21, 22, 23, 95, 96, 120, 186, 212
Lynn, Ruth, 68, 69, 86

McCully, Emily Arnold, 136, 142
MacDonald, George, 83
MacDonald, Margaret, 60
McIntosh, Margaret, 7
McKeating, Eileen, 80
McKillip, Patricia, 81
McKinley, Robin, 77, 89
MacLachlan, Patricia, 13, 134
McQuain, Jeff, 14, 96
Madlee, Dorothy, 104–105
Magic, 52, 57, 101
Magical theme, fantasy genre and, 67
Malless, Stan, 14, 96
Manhood, growing toward, 100
Manson, Cynthia, 64
Martin, Rafe, 83–84, 86
Martin, Ron, 206
Martino, Alfreda, 206
Marty McGee's Space Lab, No Girls Allowed, 107
Mary Poppins, 34
Mase, Thomas, 20, 36
The Master Puppeteer, 164–165
Maudie and Me and the Dirty Book, 128–129
Media production, 113, 206–207
Melville, Herman, 186
Memories, mystery genre and, 52
Meph, the Pet Skunk, 184
The Merry Adventures of Robin Hood, 211
Message, content of, 39
Metaphors, 28, 99
Miles, Betty, 128–129
Milton, John, 213
Mind control, 100

Mind-Call, 97
Misty of Chincoteague, 191–192
Moby Dick, 186
Monson, Dianne, 184
Montgomery, Paula, 206–207
Mood, 22
    illustrations and, 71
    setting and, 155
Morey, Walt, 184, 196
The Moves Make the Man, 125
Movies. *See* Films/videotapes
Mowat, Farley, 183, 184
Mrs. Frisby and the Rats of NIMH, 183
Music, 38
    historical fiction and, 172–173, 179
    science fiction and, 113
My Brother Sam is Dead, 13
My Brother Tries To Make Me Laugh, 108–109
My Mama Says There Aren't Any Zombies, Ghosts, Vampires, Creatures, Demons, Monsters, Fiends, Goblins, or Things, 59–60
My Mom Travels a Lot, 135–136, 142
My Side of the Mountain, 211, 217
Mysterious Disappearance of Leon (I Mean Noel), 58
Mystery genre, 45–66
    introduction to, 45–48
    picture storybooks and, 58–60
    plot and, 45–46
    reading critically and, 61–62
    recommended lists, 49–60
    setting and, 155
    style of writing, 212
    titles for individual or group study, 56–58
    titles for teaching, 49–56
    well- versus poorly written, 47
The Mystery of the Stolen Blue Paint, 58–59
Myths, 68
    animals and, 185
    fantasy and, 94

Nancy Drew books, 47, 63
Narrative presentation, 143
Natural text, 10
Nature, conflict against, 210
Negative elements, tone and, 22
Never Cry Wolf, 183
Nichols, Peter, 94, 98
Nichols, Ralph, 39
Night Fall, 48, 50–51
Nightmares, 50
Nilsen, Alleen, 22, 95
Nixon, Joan Lowry, 130, 149
Nonprint resources, 8
    adventure genre and, 234–235
    animal genre and, 207
    fantasy genre and, 90–91
    historical fiction and, 180–181
    humor genre and, 43
    mystery genre and, 65–66
    realistic fiction and, 150–151
    science fiction and, 114–115
    vendors and distributors, 14
Nonsense literature, 19–20
North, Sterling, 184, 185, 196
Norton, Andre, 98, 104–105
Norton, Donna, 9, 46, 68, 96
Norton, Mary, 24, 82

Objectives, planning, 7
O'Brien, Robert, 183
O'Dell, Scott, 158–160, 164, 186, 211, 221–222
Omniscient point of view, 187, 189, 191, 192
The Once and Future King, 83
One-Eyed Cat, 13, 126–127
Onomatopoeia, 212
Oral communication skills, 143–144, 146
Oral performances, 39, 40, 42
Ordinary Jack, 33
Organizational skills, animal genre and, 200–201, 202–203
Otherworldliness, fantasy genre and, 67
Out of the Silent Planet, 98

Outerworlds, future life in, 102
The Outsiders, 147–148
The Owl Service, 76
Owls in the Family, 184

Paddington Bear stories, 185
Palladini, David, 78
Papadopoulos, Gus, 74
Paragraph, steps in writing a good, 177–178
Parish, Peggy, 20, 24, 36
Parker, Nancy Winslow, 135, 142
Park's Quest, 123–125, 130, 148–149
Paterson, Katherine, 3, 21, 97, 117, 119, 123, 130, 134, 148–149, 155, 164–165, 172
Paulin, Mary Ann, 95, 150
Paulsen, Gary, 97, 155, 214–215, 218
Peck, Richard, 57, 119, 127, 130–131, 149
Peck, Robert, 119, 196–197
Pet owners, 183–184
The Phantom Tollbooth, 67, 76–77
Philip Hall Likes Me, I Reckon Maybe, 30
Picture storybooks, 12, 70, 73
    adventure genre and, 213–214, 223–225
    characterization and, 135–140, 142, 150
    fantasy genre and, 86, 90
    illustrations and, 70
    mystery genre and, 58–60
    plot and, 58–60
    point of view and, 197–199, 205
    realistic fiction and, 135–140
    science fiction, 109–110
    setting and, 168–169
    style and, 223–225, 226–227
    teaching design/illustration and, 83–85
    teaching theme and, 107–109
    teaching tone and, 35–37
Pinkwater, Daniel M., 107
Pippi Longstocking, 20, 24, 30–31, 67

Planning, teaching literature and, 7–9
Pleasure, tone of, 30
Plot
    defined, 48
    dramatic, 49
    episodic, 49
    historical fiction setting and, 175
    multilayered, 125
    mystery genre and, 45–46, 48–49
    science fiction and, 95
    teaching tips and, 60–61
    theme and, 96
Plotting structures, 61, 64
Poe, Edgar Allan, 62, 93
Poems, humorous, 37, 42
Point of view
    activities and, 205–206
    animal stories and, 186–188, 197–199
    author and, 187
    design/illustration and, 72
    historical fiction setting and, 175
    picture storybooks and, 197–199, 205
    teaching tips and, 199–200
The Pool of Fire, 105–106
Potter, Beatrix, 183, 185
Power, consequences of, 101
Preiss, Leah Palmer, 78
Problem novels, 117, 118, 145–146
Professional resources, 13–15
Pronunciation, 227
Protagonist, struggles of, 49
Provensen, Alice, 225
Provensen, Martin, 225
Pryor, Bonnie, 154
Psychic powers, conscious control over, 101
Puns, 20, 36, 37
Puppetry, characterization and, 150
The Purloined Letter, 62
Purves, Alan, 184
Pyle, Howard, 211

Questions, listening skills and, 39

Rabbit Hill, 188, 192–193
Rabble Starkey, 120, 127–128, 145
Race, science fiction genre and, 107–108
Radio, 38
Ramona and Her Father, 23, 28
Ramona Quimby, Age 8, 28
Rascal, 184, 185, 196
Rashkis, Zora, 38–39, 110
Raskin, Ellen, 22, 48, 56, 58, 63
Rawling, Marjorie Kinnan, 97, 184
Rawls, Wilson, 187, 193–194, 200
Reading
  class time for, 4
  critically, 61–62
  curriculum connection and, 10
  for detail and analysis, 110–111
  establishing purpose for, 4
  gateways to, 3–5
  for pleasure, 11
  silently, 4, 10, 46
  vocabulary development and, 110
Reading aloud, 4, 8, 10, 109
  adventure genre and, 219–220, 222, 234
  historical fiction and, 169
  mystery genre and, 60, 62, 64
  realistic fiction and, 140
  science fiction and, 109, 113
Reading levels, 9, 38, 50, 60
Reading skills, 4, 110
Reading specialists, 8
Reading-interest levels, 9
Realistic fiction genre, 117–152
  activities and, 144–150
  adventure stories and, 210
  animals and, 184–185, 186, 189, 191–192
  audiocassettes and, 150
  characterization and, 119–125, 126, 127, 128, 129, 132, 146–149
  computer programs and, 149–151
  criteria for, 118–119
  films/videotapes and, 142, 151
  humorous elements, 20

  nonprint resources and, 150–151
  picture storybooks for teaching, 135–140
  plot and, 117
  real-life situations and, 117–119
  recommended lists, 125–140
  setting and, 117, 155
  style of writing, 212
  subject types, 117–118
  teaching tips and, 140–143
  themes, 97
  titles for individual or group study, 133–135
  titles for teaching, 125–133
Reality, fantasy genre and, 68
Rebel on a Rock, 220–221
The Red Pony, 197
Reed, Arthea J. S., 4, 9, 213
Reiss, Johanna, 97, 154, 166, 172
Reminiscence, 187, 194
Representing Super Doll, 130–131
Research
  animal genre and, 199–200, 203–204
  fantasy genre and, 88
  historical fiction and, 173
  science fiction and, 112
Resource file, animal genre and, 199
Resources, 13–15
Return of the Jedi, 111
Riddles, 19, 20, 37, 42–43
Ride a Wild Dream, 195
Righting wrongs theme, science fiction genre and, 105
Robertson, Keith, 119
Robinson Crusoe, 211
Rockwell, Thomas, 32
Roll of Thunder, Hear My Cry, 167
Roll Over!, 35
A Romance of the Year 2660, 93
Romeo and Juliet—Together (and Alive) at Last, 24, 25–26, 38
Rootabaga Stories, 20, 24, 40
Rosenbloom, Joseph, 20, 37
Rudman, Marcia, 13
Rule of thirds, 71

256 • Index

Rylant, Cynthia, 23, 71, 119, 121–123, 131
Ryman, George, 98

Saint-Exupery, Antoine, 79–80
San Souci, Daniel, 78
Sandburg, Carl, 20, 24, 40
Sanderson, Ruth, 72
Sarah Bishop, 158–160, 164
Satire, 19, 227
Sayers, Frances Clark, 3
Scary books, controversy of, 46–47, 62
Scary, Scary, Halloween, 47, 62
Scheduling, time for, 7
School, organizational pattern of, 7–8
School-based management, 10–11
The Science Fiction Encyclopedia, 98
Science fiction genre, 93–115
    activities related to teaching, 111–114
    discussion groups of, 109–110
    fantasy versus, 69
    field trip and, 114
    film/video and, 111
    influence of, 94–95
    media, 109
    picture storybooks and, 109–110
    plot and, 95
    reading for detailed analysis, 110–111
    recommended lists, 99–109
    research activity, 112
    setting in, 155
    teaching tips and, 109–110
    theme and, 96–99
    titles for individual or group study, 105–107
    titles for teaching, 99–105
    visual and supplementary material, 111–114
Science fiction magazines, 93–94
The Secret Garden, 145
Secrets of the Shopping Mall, 127, 149
See What I Am, 188, 197
Selden, George, 82
Sendak, Maurice, 62, 84–85

Setting, 22, 154–160, 168–172, 175–177, 178, 179
Seuss, Dr., 20, 198
Sexes, battle of, 107
Shadow of a Bull, 222
Shepard, Ernest, 83
The Shining Company, 167
Short stories, mystery genre and, 64
"Show-and-tell"
    animal genre and, 200
    historical fiction and, 175
The Sign of the Beaver, 13, 97, 218–219, 229–230, 232
The Sign of the Chrysanthemum, 172
Silverstein, Shel, 37
Sixth-Grade Sleepover, 24, 26
Sizzle and Splat, 55–56
Skills lessons, 8
Skits
    characterization and, 147
    realistic fiction and, 140, 141
Slapstick, 19
The Slave Dancer, 154, 162
Sleeping Beauty, 72
SMOG Readability Formula, 9
The Snowy Day, 139–140, 142
Sobol, Donald, 58, 62, 63
Socks, 188, 190
The Son of Someone Famous, 133–134
Sound, devices of, 212
Sound filmstrips, adventure genre and, 229
Space Station Seventh Grade, 34, 97
Space travel, 102
Speakers
    adventure genre and, 226, 229, 230
    animal genre and, 202
    scheduling, 12
Speaking rates, 39
Speare, Elizabeth George, 13, 97, 166, 172, 210–211, 218–219, 229–230
Speech patterns, ethnic and regional, 39, 42
The Spell of the Sorcerer's Skull, 51–52
Spelling, 228, 230, 232, 233

Sperry, Armstrong, 211, 219
Spinelli, Jerry, 22, 34, 97
Stahlschmidt, Agnes, 11
Star Wars, 109, 113
Starring Sally J. Freedman as Herself, 32
Steinbeck, John, 197
Stetler, Susan
Stevens, Leonard, 39
Stevenson, James, 225
Stevenson, Robert Louis, 211, 213, 219–220
Stewart, Mary, 140
Storyboards, historical fiction and, 178
Storytelling, realistic fiction and, 140
Stranger at Green Knowe, 184
Strega Nona, 35
Strickland, Dorothy, 11
Sturgeon, Theodore, 93
Style, 211–217
  activities related to teaching, 231–233
  adventure genre and, 212, 213, 217–225
  devices of, 212
  humor and, 24, 31
  picture storybooks and, 223–225, 226–227
  teaching tips and, 225–227
Subplots, 49, 50–51
Superfudge 20
Supernatural characters, 45, 46, 67
Survival stories, 210–211, 218–219, 229–230
Suspense
  mystery genre and, 45, 49
  science fiction and, 106
  See also Adventure genre
Sutcliff, Rosemary, 21, 156–158, 166–167, 171–172
Sutherland, Zena, 3, 96
Swift, Jonathan, 211
Swiss Family Robinson, 211, 223
Switcharound, 154
The Sword in the Stone, 83
Synonyms, 233

The Tale of Peter Rabbit, 183
Tales of a Fourth Grade Nothing, 20
The Talking Earth, 218
Tall tales, 19
Tapes. *See* Audiocassettes; Films/videotapes
Taylor, Mildred, 119, 154, 167
Taylor, Theodore, 184, 220
Teacher evaluation, 11
Teaching literature
  communication skills and, 11–12
  curriculum connection and, 10–11
  gathering resources, 13–15
  mapping the way, 9–10
  planning and, 7–9
Teaching resources
  adventure genre, 217–220
  animal genre, 188
  fantasy genre, 74–81
  historical fiction, 160–169
  humor genre, 25–32
  mystery genre, 49–56
  realistic fiction genre, 125–140
  recommended lists, 99–109
  science fiction genre, 99–109
  tone and, 35–37
  vendors and distributors, 237
Teaching tips
  adventure genre and, 225–227
  animal genre and, 199–200
  characterization and, 140–143
  design/illustration and, 85–87
  fantasy genre and, 85–87
  historical fiction genre and, 169–172
  humor genre and, 37–38
  mystery genre and, 60–61
  point of view and, 199–200
  reading levels, 110
  realistic fiction genre and, 140–143
  science fiction genre and, 109–110
  setting and, 169–172
  style and, 225–227
  theme and, 109–110
  tone, 37–38

Technology
  science fiction and, 94–95
  teaching and, 4
Technology on Microfiche (TOM), 4
Teeny Tiny, 58
Television, 4–5
  humor and, 21
  listening skills and, 38
  mystery genre and, 62
Tell Me If Lovers Are Losers, 135
Tenniel, John, 73
Tension, good plot and, 48
Text, design/illustration and, 71–72
Theme
  activities related to teaching, 113–114
  adventure stories, 211
  authors' narrative, 113
  definition of, 96–97
  explicit statements of, 97, 113
  fantasy genre and, 68
  genre approach and, 97
  historical fiction and, 175
  illustrations and, 71
  implicit statements of, 97, 113
  literary element of, 109–110
  picture storybooks for teaching, 107–109
  plot versus, 96
  science fiction genre and, 96–99
  teaching tips and, 109–110
  universal, 98
Thinking speed, 39
Third-person point of view, 187, 189, 190, 191, 193, 198
This Place Has No Atmosphere, 106
Through the Eyes of a Child, 9, 46, 68
Through the Looking Glass, 37, 73
Time and place settings, 112, 154–160
The Time Machine, 93
Tolkien, J. R. R., 67, 73, 86, 97
The Tombs of Atuan, 69, 74, 77, 97
Tone, 21–25
  humorous picture books and, 35–37
  negative elements and, 22
  teaching tips, 37–38

Tongue-in-cheek, 31, 32, 36
Tongue twisters, 20
Topic sentence, 178
Touch Magic, 68
Transportation, historical fiction and, 158, 159, 161
Travers, P. L., 34
Treasure Island, 211, 213, 219–220
Trouble River, 211, 221
The Trouble with Tuck, 184
True adventure story, 221
Trust theme, science fiction and, 105
Truth, tone of, 29
Truths, universal, fantasy genre and, 68
Tuck Everlasting, 75
The TV Kid, 145
Twenty-One Balloons, 98
Twist These on Your Tongue, 20, 37
Two-Minute Mysteries, 62
Tymn, Marshall B., 86

Ullman, James, 215–217, 220
Understanding, tone of, 26
Understanding of self, realistic fiction and, 118
Unexpected situations, humor and, 24, 26–27
Unhappy endings, realistic fiction and, 118
The Upstairs Room, 97, 154, 166, 172

Van Vogt, A. E., 93
Vaudeville, 19
The Velveteen Rabbit, 198–199
Verbal humor, 24, 28
Verne, Jules, 93, 98, 109–110, 211, 222
Videotapes. See Films/videotapes
Villains, adventure stories and, 210
Vincent, Gabrielle, 183
Violence, comic books and, 89–90
Viorst, Judith, 36–37, 59–60
Visual
  communications, 85–88
  dialogue and meaning, 70, 87

literacy, 69–70, 88
propaganda, 88
reports, fantasy genre and, 90
Vocabulary
adventure genre and, 226, 227–228
historical fiction and, 175
science fiction and, 110, 113
Voigt, Cynthia, 74, 80, 97, 135

Walker, H. Thomas, 206–207
The Wall, 138–139, 148
The War of the Worlds, 93, 98, 112
Watership Down, 183, 193
We Interrupt This Semester for a Very Important Bulletin, 33
Welles, Orson, 112
Wells, H. G., 93, 98, 109–110, 112
Wells, Rosemary, 140
Wersba, Barbara, 132–133
The Westing Game, 22, 48, 56
What's Gnu? Riddles from the Zoo, 20, 36
Where the Red Fern Grows, 187, 194, 200
Where the Sidewalk Ends, 37
Where the Wild Things Are, 62, 84–85, 86
White, E. B., 6, 97, 183, 187
White, T. H., 83
The White Mountains, 99, 100, 105–106, 110, 154

Who Knew There'd Be Ghosts?, 52–53
Whole language learning, 10, 200–201
Wiesner, David, 85, 86
Wilder, Laura Ingalls, 167
Wildsmith, Brian, 224–225
Williams, Margery, 198–199
Will's Mammoth, 83–84, 86
Wind in the Door, 106
The Wind in the Willows, 185
Winter, Jeanette, 168–169
The Witch of Blackbird Pond, 166, 172
"Witch World Series," 98
Wojchiechowska, Maia, 222
Wonderful Wizard of Oz, 67
Word play, 36
A Wrinkle in Time, 97, 104
Writing, 172
historical fiction setting and, 176
humor genre and, 40, 41
mystery genre and, 63
steps in good paragraph and, 177–178
style and, 232–233
Wyss, Johann, 211, 223

The Yearling, 97, 184
Yearly plan-book, 12
Yep, Lawrence, 135, 167–168
Yolen, Jane, 68, 72, 74, 80
Yonder, 176
Young love, 26, 30

www.ingramcontent.com/pod-product-compliance
Lightning Source LLC
Chambersburg PA
CBHW051805230426
43672CB00012B/2641